Linguistic-Culture

A Russian Picture of the World

Valentina Maslova

www.Russian-Academic-Translations.com

Linguistic-Culture: A Russian Picture of the World

Contents

From the Author

Linguistics in the twenty-first century is steadily moving towards the view that language is a national cultural code rather than merely a tool for communication and knowledge. The fundamental basis for this approach is grounded in the work of Wilhelm von Humboldt, Alexander Potebnja and others. For example, Wilhelm von Humboldt argues that "the borders of the language of my nation mark the borders of my world views."

According to this view, language not only reflects reality, it interprets it, creating in the process a special reality inhabited by man. It is precisely for this reason that, for almost one thousand years, philosophy has developed through the use of language. Martin Heidegger, the great thinker of our times, called language the "house of being." Accordingly, **linguistics**, the science of language, **occupies a prime position in the methodology of any humanist system of knowledge,** and the study of culture is impossible without it.

In this work, language is viewed as an instrument that can be used to understand the contemporary mindset of a nation, as well as the views of ancient peoples, modern society, and ourselves. Echoes of bygone eras are preserved in proverbs, sayings, phraseology, metaphors, symbols, culture, etc., and reverberate through the centuries towards us.

Man only becomes man when, as a child, he assimilates the language and culture of his people. All the fine print of a nation's culture is reflected in its language, which is idiosyncratic and unique, since the details of the world and its people are reflected differently. For example, it is impossible to translate into Czech, a language closely related to Russian, the title of the famous book by Boris Pasternak *My Sister— Life*, since in the Czech language "life" is masculine, whereas in Russian it is feminine.

Much of the information a person receives about the world comes through linguistic channels. We do not just live in a world of concrete objects and things. Primarily, we live in a world of concepts created for intellectual, spiritual, and social purposes. Philosophers say that it is enough to know the name of an object or phenomenon to be able to master the material world. A large portion of information comes to us through words. Social success depends on how well one commands words beyond the level of cultural speech and on one's ability to penetrate the mysteries of language.

This book is dedicated linguistic-culturology, the study of the interaction between language and culture. Through the use of language, linguistic-culturology tries to reveal the mentality of a people and their culture.

Why specifically study phraseology, metaphors, and symbols? Because they are valuable sources of information about the culture and mentality of a nation. They somehow unite a nation's myths, legends, and customs. The well know Russian linguist Boris Larin[1] wrote, "Phraseology directly reflects the views of nations, social classes, ideologies and eras. Reflected like the morning sunlight is reflected in a drop of dew." And, the same is true for metaphors and symbols.

This book emphasizes what we believe is the crucial idea of this field; the mystery of language is the most important mystery of humanity. If one can solve this mystery, one can uncover much of the knowledge that has been hidden or lost throughout the centuries. Our goal is to identify the cultural background that stands behind every unit of language, allowing us to correlate the superficial structure of language with its deeper essence.

This textbook primarily studies Slavic cultures and languages. The Russian and Belorussian languages are used most frequently, since the study of closely related languages allows for the observation of nuanced meanings between language units. When the need for a different cultural-linguistic phenomenon arises, data from non-Slavic languages is used, the Kyrgyz language being one example.

---

[1] 17 January 1893–26 March 1964. Soviet linguist, member of the Academy of Sciences of the Ukrainian SSR. Worked on the history of the Russian language, Lithuanian language, sociolinguistics, and Sanskrit. (Footnotes are the translator's unless otherwise indicated).

CHAPTER 1
Language - Culture - Man – Ethnos
A paradigm shift in linguistics. The role of linguistics in a new paradigm of knowledge

The idea that **language is anthropocentric** is considered a generally accepted view, and in many language constructs, the concept of man acts as a natural starting point.

This scientific paradigm, which developed at the turn of the millennium, has set new challenges for the study of language and requires new methods for describing and approaching the analysis of elements, categories, and rules.

The concept of the paradigm as a model for posing problems and solutions gained traction after the 1962 publication of the well-known book *The Structure of Scientific Revolutions* by Thomas Kuhn (translated into Russian in 1977). Kuhn conceives of a paradigm as a scientific community guided in its research by a defined body of knowledge and approach to the object of study (in our case language). It is well known that in linguistics (and in the humanities in general) paradigms do not replace one another but are superimposed on each other and coexist at the same time while ignoring each other.

Traditionally, there are three scientific paradigms: comparative historical, systemic- structural, and anthropocentric.

The **comparative historical paradigm** was the first scientific paradigm in linguistics because the comparative historical method was the first method of language research. The entire 19th century fell under the aegis of this paradigm.

Under the **system-structural paradigm**, attention is focused on the object, thing, or name, making the word the center of inquiry. Even in the third millennium, it is possible to explore language through the system-structural paradigm, as it is still prevalent in linguistics today. This approach still has many followers, and textbooks, grammars, and reference books continue to be written under this paradigm. Basic research conducted within this framework is a valuable source of information not only for today's researchers, but also for future generations of linguists who may be working within other paradigms.

In the **anthropocentric paradigm**, interest shifts from the object of knowledge to the subject. In other words, this approach analyzes the person in the language and the language in the person, holding to Jan Baudouin de Courtenay's view that "language exists only in individual brains, only in souls, only in the psyche of individuals or peculiarities that make up this linguistic community."

The idea that language is anthropocentric is key to modern linguistics. In our time, the purpose of linguistic analysis cannot simply be to identify the different characteristics of a linguistic system.

Language is a complex phenomenon. Several decades ago, Émile Benveniste claimed, "The properties of language are so peculiar that one could say language has not one but several structures, each of which could serve as a basis for the emergence of a comprehensive linguistics." Language is a multi-dimensional phenomenon that emerged in human society: it is a system and an anti-system, an activity and the product of this activity, spirit and matter, a spontaneously evolving object and an orderly, self-regulating phenomenon, both voluntary and produced, etc. By describing language in all its complexity, from opposite sides, we expose its very essence.

To describe the highly complicated nature of language, Yuri Stepanov[2] presented it in the form of multiple images, none of which by itself can fully describe all aspects of language. The images are as follows: 1) language of the individual; 2) language as part of a family of languages; 3)

---

[2] July 1930 — January 2012 — Russian scientist, philologist, semiotician. Member of the Russian Academy of Sciences. Author of, *Constant of World Culture. Alphabets and Alphabetical Texts in the Age of Dual Belief*, Moscow, 1993 (in collaboration with S. G. Proskurin). "Constants. Dictionary of Russian Culture". Moscow, 1997. "Language and Method. Towards a Modern Philosophy of Language", Moscow, 1998. "Proteus: Essays on Chaotic Evolution, Moscow, 2004. "Concepts. A Thin Film of Civilization", Moscow, 2007. "Imaginary literature", Moscow, 2010.

language as structure; 4) language as system; 5) the character and type of language; 6) language as a computer; 7) language as a space for thought and as the "dwelling place of the soul" (Heidegger), i.e. language as the result of the complex cognitive activities of man. According to the seventh image: first, language is the result of human activities; second, it is the result of the creative activities of the individual and the result of language normalization activities (the state institutions that produce rules and regulations).

At the end of the twentieth century, another image was added: language as a product of culture, as an important component and condition of existence, a factor in the formation of cultural codes.

According to the anthropocentric paradigm, a person understands the world through self-awareness and through his/her theoretical and substantive work in the world. There is abundant linguistic evidence that we see the world through the prism of human metaphors— for example: the blizzard broke out, the blizzard blanketed the town, snowflakes dance, sound asleep, birch earrings, mother winter, the years go by, shadows fall, engulfed in sorrow. Especially impressive are bright poetic images: "the world awakened, roused itself, lazily breathing in the noonday, the azure skies laugh, the heavenly firmament staring listlessly" (Fyodor Tyutchev).

No abstract theory can tell us why we think about feelings in terms of heat and fire, using terms like "the flame of love", "fire in the heart", "the warmth of friendship", etc. Awareness of oneself is the measure of all things, giving a person the right to create in his mind an anthropocentric order of things that cannot be examined at the level of daily life but only at a scientific level. This order, which exists in the mind, in the consciousness of the individual, determines one's spiritual essence, the motives behind one's actions, and the hierarchy of one's values. All of this can be understood by examining a person's speech, the expressions used most frequently and displaying the highest level of empathy.

In the process of forming this new scientific paradigm, a thesis was declared: "The world is the totality of facts, not of things" (Ludwig Wittgenstein). Language was gradually

10

refocused on facts and events; the center of attention became the personality of the speaker of the language (Linguistic Personality, Yuri Karaulov[3]). The new paradigm offers new methods and goals for the study of language, as well as new key concepts. In the anthropocentric paradigm, the means of constructing the object of linguistic research have been changed; the very approach to the selection of general principles and the methods of research have been changed. There are now several competing meta-language descriptions (Rebekah M. Frumkin[4]).

The advent of the anthropocentric paradigm led to a shift in linguistics towards man and his place in culture, as the heart of culture and tradition is rooted in linguistic identity in all its diversity: the physical I, the social I, the intellectual I, the emotional I, the speech-thinking I. These "I" hypostases may take various forms. For example, the emotional I can manifest itself in different social and psychological roles. The phrase, *today the sun shines brightly*, contains the following thoughts: the physical I will experience the beneficial effects of sun light; this is known by the intellectual I, which sends this information to third parties (via the social I), indicating the feelings of the emotional I by means of the speech-thinking I. The characteristics of any of these I hypostases may affect the personality aspects of the listener. Thus, linguistic individuality becomes part of communication in a multi-faceted manner and correlates the strategies and tactics of verbal communication with the social and psychological roles of the communicator; the cultural meaning of the information is included in the communication. Man perceives the surrounding world only after having temporarily taken himself out of that world; he seems to contrast the "I" with all that is "non-I." This is apparently the very structure of our thought and language: any act of speech-thinking always

---

[3] August 1935–May 2016. Soviet and Russian linguist specializing in general and Russian linguistics, lexicology and lexicography, and applied linguistics. Member of the Russian Academy of Sciences. Author of *The Russian Language and Linguistic Identity.*

[4] Russian linguist, psychologist, essayist. Member of the Department of Linguistics of the Russian Academy of Science.

assumes a priori recognition of the existence of the world when reporting a reflection of the subject's world.

Given the above, one should keep in mind that the anthropocentric paradigm in linguistics is something that may not be ignored, even if the researcher is working within a traditional systemic-structural paradigm.

Thus, the anthropocentric paradigm puts man at the forefront, with language his fundamental characteristic and most important component. The human intellect, like man himself, is unthinkable without linguistic abilities such as the generation and perception of speech. If language did not penetrate all thought processes, if it were not able to create new mental spaces, then man could not move beyond the immediately observable. The text produced by man reflects the movements of human thought and builds new possible worlds. Language captures trends of thought and ways of representing the world.

The main trends in modern linguistics, formed under this paradigm, are cognitive linguistics and linguistic-culturology, which "focus on the cultural factors in language and the language factors in man" (Veronica Teliya[5]). Accordingly, linguistic-culturology is the result of an anthropological paradigm in linguistics that has formed in the last decades.

Key concepts of cognitive linguistics include: information and its processing by the human mind, knowledge structures and their representation in the human mind, and language forms. Cognitive linguistics, cognitive psychology, and cognitive sociology all try to answer the questions of how the human mind is organized in principle, how man learns about the world, what information about the world becomes knowledge, and how the mental universe is created. The focus of linguistic-culturology, however, is entirely on the individual in culture and in language. It deals with questions such as: how a person sees the world, what is the role of metaphor and symbol in culture, what is the role of centuries-old

---

[5]1930–2012. Prominent scientist in the field of language theory, semantics, and the pragmatics of language units. Published more than 100 scientific papers.

phraseology as a representation of culture, why are these is so necessary for people?

Linguistic-culturology studies language as a cultural phenomenon.

It provides a specific vision of the world through the prism of the national language, where language acts as an expression of the national mindset.

All of linguistics has been permeated by cultural and historical content because its subject is language, which is both the foundation and product of culture.

Among the linguistic disciplines that are more "culturally bearing" are the historical linguistic disciplines: social dialects, ethnolinguistics, stylistics, vocabulary, phraseology, semantics, theory of translation, and others.

The Status of Linguistic-Culturology Among Other Linguistic Disciplines.

Questions about the relationships and interconnections between language, culture, and ethnos are interdisciplinary, so solutions are possible only through the combined efforts of several sciences, from philosophy and sociology to ethno-linguistics and linguistic-culturology. For example, issues concerning ethnic language thinking are a prerogative of linguistic philosophy, while psycholinguistics studies the specifics of ethnic, social, or other language relationships, etc.

Language is tightly bound with culture. It grows, develops, and expresses itself within it.

Linguistic-culturology is a new science. It formed in the 1990's and can be viewed as an independent branch of linguistics. The term "linguistic-culturology" appeared in the last decade in connection with the phraseological school headed by Veronica Teliya and comprising the works of Yuri Stepanov, Nina Ariutunova[6], Vladimir Vorobyov[7], Victor Shaklenin[8], Valentina Maslova, and other researchers. If

---

[6] Member of the Russian Academy of Sciences at the Department of History and Philology.

[7] October 1929 — May 2003, Russian geographer, director of the Institute of Geography at the Russian Academy of Sciences.

cultural studies focus on a person's self-awareness in relation to nature, society, history, art, and other spheres of social and cultural life, and if philology focuses on worldviews reflected and fixed in language as mental models of the language picture of the world[9], then linguistic-culturology focuses on language, culture, and their mutually influenced dialogue.

The traditional ways of examining interactions between language and culture through language use several representations of culture. Our approach, on the other hand, examines the ways that language units embody, store, and transmit that culture.

Thus, linguistic-culturology occupies the juncture between linguistics, cultural studies, and the cultural expressions of the people as manifested in language. Ethno-linguistics and sociolinguistics are closely related—so much so that Veronica Teliya viewed linguistic-culturology as a branch of ethnolinguistics. Nevertheless, linguistic-culturology is essentially an independent science. It is important to remember that ethnolinguistics has its roots in Wilhelm von Humboldt and in Americans Franz Boas, Edward Sapir, and Benjamin Whorf. In Russia, the works of Dmitry Konstantinovich Zelenin, Yefim Karsky, Alexey Shahmatov, Alexander Potebnja, Alexander Afanasyev, Alexey Sobolewski[10], and others played a significant role in its development.

The practitioner of ethno-linguistics Vladimir Zvegintsev[11] characterized his field as a study of the interactions between language and culture, national customs, socio-cultural relations, or nations. **Ethnicity** comprises the

---

[8] Chief editor of the Friendship University Journal *Russian and Foreign Languages and Methods of Teaching Them*.

[9] The picture theory of language, also known as the picture theory of meaning, was introduced by Ludwig Wittgenstein in the Tractatus Logico-Philosophicus. The term is based on Wilhem von Humboldt's ideas about the internal structure of language and on the Sapir-Whorf hypothesis of linguistic relativity.

[10] December 1856–May 1929. Russian and Soviet linguist, historian of literature. A member of the Imperial Academy of Sciences.

[11] October 1910–April 1988. Soviet linguist. One of the organizers of the Department of Theoretical and Applied Linguistics at Moscow State University and the first director of this department.

language and cultural traditions of a community of people who share a common understanding of their origins and historical fate, a common language, cultural and psychic idiosyncrasies, and who recognize themselves as a distinct cultural unit. Ethnic self-awareness is the recognition by members of an ethnos that they form a group-unit that is different from analogous formations.

At the center of contemporary ethno-linguistics are those elements of a language's lexical system that correspond to specific material and cultural-historical systems. For example, ethno-linguists have put together an entire inventory of various types of cultures, rites, and ceremonies based on material from Belorussian and Ukrainian Polesia, a "pivotal" region for the systematic study of Slavic antiquity (Nikita Tolstoy[12] and Svetlana Tolstoy[13]).

Within the framework of ethno-linguistics, it is possible to discern two independent branches based on two important issues: 1) the reconstruction of ethnic territory around language (which can be found in the works of Ruth

Ageva[14], Samuil Bernstein, Vyacheslav Ivanov, Tamaz Gamkrelidze, and others); and 2) the reconstruction of the material and spiritual culture of ethnic groups based on language (which can be found in the works of Vyacheslav Ivanov, Vladimir Toporov, Tatiana Tsivyan[15], Tamara Sudnik[16], and Nikita Tolstoy and his school).

---

[12] April 1923–June 1996. Slavic, philologist and folklorist. Great-grandson of Leo Tostoy.

[13] Russian linguist, professor, and head of the Department of Ethnolinguistics and Folklore at the Institute of Slavic Studies of the RAS. Wife of Nikita Tolstoy, mother of journalist Anna Tolstoy.

[14] Editor of the scientific journal *Academia*. Published several works including: "Etymology of the Names of Rivers and Lakes" (1985), "Hydronyms of the Russian North-West as a Source of Cultural and Historical Information" (2004), "Countries and Peoples: Origin of Names" (2002), "What Kind of Tribe are We? Peoples of Russia: Names and Fates. Dictionary" (2000).

[15] Professor in the Linguistics Department of Moscow State University and the Slavic Studies Department of the Russian Academy of Sciences.

[16] Member of the Slavic Department of the Russian Academy of Sciences.

Vyacheslav Ivanov and Tamaz Gamkrelidze relate linguistic systems to specific archaeological cultures. Semantic analysis of reconstructed words and their correlation with denotation (objects of extra-linguistic reality that refer to the speaker uttering the given speech segment) allow one to establish the cultural, ecological, historical, and geographic characteristics of these denotations. The reconstruction of Slavic culture, like any other culture in its most ancient form, is based on the interactions of linguistics, ethnography, folklore, archeology, and cultural studies.

In the second half of the twentieth century, several scientific movements arose in the USSR, headed by the great scientists Vladimir Toporov, Vyacheslav Ivanov, Nikita Tolstoy and his school of ethno-linguistics, Yuri Sorokin[17] and his ethno-psycholinguistics, Natalia Ufimtseva[18] and others. Their studies treat language as a natural substratum of culture, penetrating all aspects of it, as well as an instrument for ordering the world and a method for fixing ethnic perspectives.

The term ethnicity (from the Greek *ethnos,* meaning "tribe" or "people") has been in widespread use since the 1970's. It is defined as a group phenomenon, a kind of social organization of cultural differences. According to Sergey Cheshko[19], "Ethnic identity is not chosen but inherited." Human culture represents a totality of diverse ethnic cultures, as different nations meet similar needs in different ways. Ethnic identity is manifest in everything: in the way people work, rest, eat, and speak in various circumstances. For example, collectivism (sobornost) is thought to be the most important feature of the Russian people. This is because they

---

[17] May 1936–October 2009. Russian scientist, linguist, and writer. Published several works on psycholinguistics, including: *Translation Studies, The Status of the Translator and Psycho-hermeneutics; Russians and Russianness, a Linguistic-Culturalogical Study.*

[18] Head of the A.A. Leonteva Scientific Educational Center for Intercultural Research. Published over 200 scientific works. Coauthored *The Slavic Associative Dictionary: Russian, Belarusian, Bulgarian, Ukrainian.*

[19] Deputy Director of the Department of Ethnology and Anthropology at the Russian Academy of Sciences. Author of *The Ideology of Disintegration* (1993), *The Collapse of the Soviet Union* and other scientific works.

are distinguished by a sense of belonging to a specific society, a feeling of warmth and emotion associated with interaction. These characteristics are reflected in the Russian language. According to Anna Wierzbicka, "Russian language pays much more attention to emotions (in comparison to the English language) and has a much richer repertoire of lexical and grammatical expressions for their differentiation."

Building an edifice based on Slavic spiritual culture, the ethnolinguistic school led by Nikita Tostoy achieved the most fame. In essence, the school postulates unity between culture and language, applying the principles and methods of contemporary linguistics to the study of culture.

According to Nikita Tolstoy, the purpose of ethno-linguistics is to provide historical perspective, i.e. to identify national stereotypes and reveal a nation's folkloric picture of the world. Sociolinguistics, on the other hand, is only one aspect of the relationship between language and society (language and culture, language and history, language and ethnicity, language and the church, and so forth). Essentially, sociolinguistics studies the features of the languages of various social and age groups (Nina Mechkovskaya[20]).

Thus, ethno-linguistic and sociolinguistic studies are fundamentally different than linguistic-culturology. Ethno-linguistics relies predominantly on historically significant data and tries to find historically significant facts in modern materials about one or another ethnic group; sociolinguistics focuses exclusively on contemporary materials. However, linguistic-culturology *studies both historical and contemporary linguistic facts through the prism of spiritual culture.* To be fair, it should be said that there are other opinions on this issue. Veronica Teliya, for example, believes that linguistic-culturology examines only the synchronous interaction of language and culture. It explores the living communication processes as they relate to the expressions of the speaker and the current mindset of the nation.

---

[20] Professor at the Department of Theoretic and Slavic Languages at the Belarusian State University.

Language is a means of accumulating and storing culturally meaningful information. For the native speaker, the meaning of certain word units is implicit. Hidden differences can only be indirectly extracted. But the differences are there. They "work" on a subconscious level (for example, the word-stimulus SUN provides clues that come from the semantics of myth: the moon, the sky, the eye, God, head, and others). The cultural linguist should apply special techniques for extracting cultural information embedded in linguistic symbols.

My concept of linguistic-culturology is different. Veronica Teliya believes that the object of study is cultural information that is not purely national, but common to humanity—for example, that which is encoded in the Bible or universally present in all cultures. I am interested only in the cultural information that is inherent in a particular people or a group of closely related peoples, such as Orthodox Slavs.

Regional linguistic-geography and linguistic-culturology differ in that regional linguistic-geography studies existing national realities, as found in language. The focus is on linguistic units that have no equivalents to other languages (according to Yevgeny Vereshchagin[21] and Vitally Kostomarov[22]); meaning is specific to a particular cultural phenomenon.

Ethno-psycholinguistics is very similar to linguistic-culturology. Ethno-psycholinguistics establishes how elements of **behavior related to specific traditions** are reflected in speech activity, analyzing the differences in verbal and non-verbal behaviors of those who are native speakers of different languages; it studies the speech etiquette and the

---

[21] Director of the V.V. Vinogradov Russian Language Institute of the Russian Academy of Sciences. Together with Vitally Kostomarov, he wrote *Linguistic Problems in Area Studies for Teaching Russian Language to Foreigners* (1971) and "Language and Culture: Linguistic and Cultural Studies for Teaching Russian as a Foreign Language" (1973).

[22] Director of the Lomonosov Moscow State University Russian Language Center, founder of the Alexander Pushkin State Institute of Russian Language (1973), president of the A.S. Pushkin Vinogradov Russian Language Institute. Former president of the International Association of Teachers of Russian Language and Literature. Chief editor of the magazine *Russian Speech*.

"color picture of the world," the lacunae in the text of intercultural communication, and it studies bilingualism and multilingualism as a feature of the speech behavior of different people, etc. The basic research method in ethno-psycholinguistics is the use of associative experiments. On the other hand, linguistic-culturology uses a variety of linguistic methods, including psycholinguistic methods. This, then, is their primary difference.

Culture: Approaches and purpose of cultural studies.

An understanding of culture is fundamental for the study of linguistic-culturology. Therefore, I believe it is necessary to closely examine its ontology, semiotic character, and other factors relevant to our approach.

The word "culture" derives from the Latin *colere*, which originally meant *cultivation, education, development, reverence, worship*. In the eighteenth century, culture began to include everything stemming from the activities of man and his purposeful reflections. These meanings are preserved in the later uses of the word *culture*. However, the word originally focused on the impact of man on nature, changing nature for the benefit of man, that is, the cultivation of the earth (i.e. agriculture).

Anthropology was one of the first sciences to deal with man and culture. It studied human behavior and the establishment of norms, prohibitions, and taboos associated with the inclusion of an individual within a system of social and cultural relations, as well as the influence of culture on gender distinctions, love as a cultural phenomenon, mythology as a cultural phenomenon, and other issues. It first appeared in English-speaking countries in the nineteenth century and was divided into several branches. For our purposes, the most interesting branch may be **cognitive anthropology**.

The basis of cognitive anthropology is the concept of culture as a system of symbols—a uniquely human way of knowing, organizing, and mentally structuring the world. Language, according to the supporters of cognitive anthropology, includes all the cognitive categories that form the basis of human thought and serve as the essence of culture. These categories are not inherent in people; they are formed in the process of familiarizing man with culture.

In our country, cultural studies formed as an independent science in the 1960s. It arose at the crossroads of philosophy, history, anthropology, sociology, psychology, ethnology, ethnography, linguistics, art, semiotics, and informatics, synthesizing data from these sciences into a single vision.

Culture is one of the fundamental concepts of social and humanistic perception. The word came to be used as a scientific term in the second half of the eighteenth century, the "Age of Enlightenment." The original definition of culture in the literature is attributable to Edward Tylor, who understood culture as a complex that includes knowledge, belief, art, law, morals, habits, and other abilities and customs acquired by man as a member of society. According to Pavel Gurevich[23], the definitions of culture have now reached quadruple digits. This may be proof of widespread interest in the phenomenon; however, it is also proof of the many methodological difficulties of contemporary culturology. Up to now, there is no single definition of culture or general consensus on how to study culture in a way that could overcome this methodological inconsistency.

Currently, culturology has many approaches for understanding and defining culture. These are a few of them.

1. Descriptive—this approach simply lists individual elements and expressions of culture, such as customs, activities, values, ideals, etc. Under this approach, culture is defined as the totality of achievements and institutions that separate our lives from those of our animal-like ancestors. Culture serves two purposes: protecting humans from nature and structuring relations between individuals (as Sigmund Freud believed). The disadvantage of this approach is that the list of cultural expressions is obviously incomplete.

---

[23] Member of the Russian Academy of Natural Sciences and the Academy of Pedagogical and Social Sciences. President of the Moscow Interregional Psychoanalytic Association.

2. Values—according to this approach, culture is interpreted as a set of spiritual and material values created by people. For an object to have value, an individual must recognize the presence of such a property in the object. The ability to endow an object with value is associated with the formation of value concepts in the mind of the individual. However, imagination is also important, as it allows one to create a complete image or ideal with which to compare the real existence of an object. This is how Martin Heidegger understands culture: a realization of the highest values by cultivating the highest human virtues. This is also how Max Weber, Georgi Frantsov[24], Nicholai Chavchavadze[25], and others view it.

The values approach to culturology is insufficient due to its narrow view of culture; it fails to consider the diversity of human activity beyond values, focusing humanity's highest achievements and ignoring its ignoble failures.

3. Activity—according to this approach, culture is understood as a unique means by which people satisfy their needs, a special type of activity. This approach owes its existence to Bronisław Malinowski, who uses a Marxist theory of culture as a form of human activity (Edward Markayan[26], Yuri Sorokin, Evgeny Tarasov[27]).

4. Functional—culture is characterized by the function that it fulfills in society, whether informational, adaptive, communicative, regulatory, legal, evaluative,

---

[24] (1903-1969)—Soviet scientist specializing in the history of religion and atheism, philosophy, and sociology. In 1959, he published "The Origins of Religion and Free Thought" about the origins of religion and atheism. In 1965, he published "the Historical Path of Social Thought," in which he highlighted some of the problems of religious ideology.

[25] Georgian philologist who wrote "Culture and Values."

[26] Russian-Armenian sociologist. Author of over 150 scientific works, including: *On the Concept of Local Civilizations* (1962); *Essays on Cultural Theory* (1969); *The Systematic Study of Society* (1972), *On the Genesis of Human Activity and Culture* (1973); *Integrative Tendencies in the Social and Natural Sciences* (1977); *Theory of Culture and Modern Science* (1983); *The Culture of Life and Ethnicity* (1983); Cultural Studies in the Armenian SSR (1984), etc.

[27] Soviet and Russian linguist specializing in psycholinguistics, linguistic consciousness, and ethno-cultural specificity. Chief editor of the magazine *Issues of Psycholinguistics* (2006).

integrative, social, or other. The flaw in this approach is its undeveloped theory of function and the absence of non-conflicting classifications.

5. Hermeneutics treats culture as a collection of texts or, more precisely, a mechanism that creates an accumulation of texts (Yuri Lotman). Texts are the blood and sweat of culture and can be viewed as stores of information to be retrieved. However, the unique, strikingly original personality of the author's work also possesses its own value. The disadvantage of this approach is that it is impossible to understand a text unambiguously.

6. Regulatory—this approach views culture as a set of regulations and laws governing our lives, a kind of lifestyle code (Valery Sagatovsky[28]). This method was further developed by Yuri Lotman and Boris Uspensky, who understood culture as an inherited collective memory that gets manifested in specific systems of prohibitions and prescriptions.

7. Spiritual. Proponents of this approach define culture as the spiritual life of society, as the flow of ideas and other products of spiritual creativity. The objective spiritual reality of society is culture (Lev Kertman[29]). This approach is limited by a narrow understanding of culture that fails to recognize the existence of material culture.

8. Dialogical—according to this school, culture is a "dialogue" (Vladimir Bibler[30]), a form of communication between its subjects (Vladimir Bibler, Sergey Averintsev[31], and Boris Uspensky). This approach emphasizes the ethnic and national cultures created by different peoples and groups. National cultures are further divided into subcultures

---

[28] (1933–2014)—Soviet and Russian philosopher. Worked on theories of anthropo-cosmism and the noosphere.

[29] (1917–1987)—Soviet historian at the University of Perm.

[30] (1918–2000)—Soviet and Russian philosopher and cultural historian. Creator of the doctrine of the dialogue of cultures and author of works on the history of European thought, the logic of cultural development, and the theory of scientific knowledge.

[31] (1937–2004)—Philologist, member of the Union of Soviet Writers, President of the Bible Society. Member of the International Mandelstam Society. Wrote religious poetry.

associated with different social strata and groups (youth subcultures, criminal subcultures, etc.). There is also meta-culture, such as the Christian culture, which unites separate nations and brings cultures together in dialogue. The more developed a national culture is, the more it tends to engage in dialogue with other cultures. It becomes richer from these contacts, absorbing the achievements of its interlocutors, while at the same time becoming unified and standardized.

9. Informational—this approach presents culture as a system for creating, storing, using, and transferring information. Society uses this system of symbols to encode social information. In other words, people provide culture with content, significance, and meaning (Yuri Lotman). Here, one can draw an analogy with computers, or more precisely, with their information functions: machine language, memory, and information processing programs. Culture also has language, social memory, and a program of human behavior. Hence, culture is an information program that manipulates social information stored within a society by means of a system of symbols.

10. The symbolic approach focuses on the use of symbols in culture. In this view, culture is a "symbolic universe" (Lotman). Some of its elements acquire a particular ethnic sense and become symbols of the nation: the white birch, cabbage soup, kasha, the samovar, bast shoes, and the sarafan for Russian culture; oatmeal and legends about ghosts in castles for the English; spaghetti for Italians; beer and sausage for Germans, etc.

11. Typological (Merab Mamardashvili, Sergey Averintsev). When meeting members of other nations, people tend to perceive the behavior of foreigners from the standpoint of their own culture; in other words, they "measure using their own yardstick." For example, Europeans who encounter Japanese people are struck by the fact that the Japanese smile when they talk about the death of loved ones, which Europeans see as a sign of callousness and cruelty. However, from the standpoint of Japanese culture, this behavior demonstrates refined politeness—a reluctance to burden their interlocutor with personal problems. Similarly, what one nation considers to be a manifestation of intelligence and prudence, another might see as cunning and greed.

There are other approaches to the problem of culture. The modern researcher Eric Wolf questions the very notion of culture, arguing that no culture is an independent monad and that all cultures are interrelated and constantly flowing into one another, with some cultures undergoing substantial change and some ceasing to exist altogether.

All these approaches have their rational elements and each one points to some essential features of the concept of "culture." But which of these features is more essential? It all depends on the researcher's own position and how that individual understands culture.

For example, I believe that the most essential cultural features are those inherent in collective memory and expressed in specific systems of prescriptions and prohibitions, as well as those that view culture via a dialogue of cultures. Culture consists of labor methods and techniques, customs, rituals, communication features, and ways of viewing, understanding, and transforming the world. For example, a maple leaf hanging on a tree is part of nature, but the same leaf preserved in a herbarium is now part of culture; a stone lying on the side of the road is not culture, but the same stone laid on the grave of an ancestor is culture. Thus, culture is made up of the typical lifestyles and activities of a given people of the world. Culture is also the relationship between people (customs, rituals, communication traits, etc.) and ways of seeing, understanding, and transforming the world.

What makes culture so difficult to define and understand? The most important feature of culture, the thing that makes the creation of a unified and consistent definition almost impossible, is not just its complexity and multidimensionality. It is its **antinomy**. In our view, antinomy is the unity of two opposite but equally well-grounded propositions. For example, the introduction of culture into a group promotes socialization while at the same time creating the preconditions for individualization. In other words, it contributes to the revelation and acceptance of the uniqueness of personality. To a certain extent, culture does not depend on society; however, it does not exist outside of society and is created entirely within society. Culture ennobles man—it has a positive impact on society as a whole; however, it can also produce negative effects, such as subjecting man to certain powerful influences like mass culture. Culture exists as a process for preserving traditions, but it continuously shatters norms and customs, drawing its vital force from innovation. It has the remarkable ability to continuously renew and regenerate itself.

The analysis of culture is complicated not only by a multitude of definitions, but by the fact that many researchers (cultural experts, anthropologists, philosophers, ethnographers and other scholars) frequently return to reexamine the concept, not only because their conception has been refined, but because their views have changed outright. For example, in addition to the definition listed above, Yuri Lotman offers the following evolving definitions of culture: "...a complex semiotic system; its purpose is memory; its main feature is accumulation" [32] (1971); and "culture is something general for any collective or group of people living in a common time and connected by specific social organizations... Culture is a form of communication between people"[33] (1994).

A similar picture emerges from other authors. Moses Kagan[34] relates cultural theory to a philosophical analysis about the nature of man and an aesthetic essence of art (the most complex areas of the human spirit): "Dealing with the results of the study of culture leads to the conclusion that it is similar to the theoretical study of man and art. This is because if art models or recreates an illusion integral to human beings, then culture turns it into reality, a precisely human and fully historical development of human qualities and abilities. In other words, **everything that is human, as it appears in culture, is just as versatile, rich, contradictory, and similar**

[32] Lotman, Yuri. *Two Models of Communication in the System of Culture*//Semiotics. Tartu, 1971. № 6. S. 228. (Author's footnote).
[33] Lotman, Yuri. *Talks on Russian Culture: The Life and Traditions of Russian Nobility*. Saint Petersburg, 1994. (Author's footnote).
[34] May 1921–February 2006. Soviet and Russian philosopher and anthropologist specializing in the history of culture and values.

as humans themselves, who are the creators of culture and their main creations."[35]

When we study culture from various points of view, we find different results every time: the psychological-activity approach provides one result, the sociological approach yields a different result, and so forth. It is only by looking at all aspects of culture that we come close to a holistic representation of the phenomenon.

In view of the many pre-existing definitions of culture, I will propose the following working definition. Culture is an aggregate of all forms of the subject's activity in the world, based on a system of directives and instructions, values and norms, patterns and ideals, and an inherited collective memory that "lives" only in dialogue with other cultures. So, by culture we mean a **set of "rules of the game" for collective existence, a series of methods of social practice that is stored in the collective social memory and worked out by individuals for social, practical, and intellectual purposes.**

The purpose of cultural studies, philosophy, and cultural theory, it seems to me, is to understand culture in its entirety and in its different forms, structures, functions, and developments. They also answer questions about the source of the vitality of a culture, about the specific national characters of different cultures, and about how a cultural personality interacts with that of other cultures, etc.

Culture and Man. Culture and Civilization.

I shall try to outline the general features of culture according to the various perspectives that will be further developed in this textbook. As noted earlier, it seems as if the most promising perspectives are the activity-centered, regulatory, dialogical, and comparative approaches to culture, which we will examine in more detail in what follows.

Culture does not exist outside of human activity and social communities because it is precisely human activity that

---

[35] Kagan, M.S. *Philosophy of Culture*. Saint Petersburg, 1996. S.19-20. (Author's footnote).

gives rise to it; culture, according to Moses Kagan, is a new "extra-natural" habitat, a fourth form of existence. To refresh your memory, the first three forms of existence are nature, society, and man. Culture, then, is a world of human activity, that is, a world of artifacts (from the Latin *arte*, meaning "artificial", and *factus*, meaning "made"). It is the transformation of nature by man under the laws of a society. This artificial environment is sometimes called a "second nature" (by Aron Gurevich and other researchers).

The great 20th-century philosopher Martin Heidegger wrote ". . . human activity is conceived and consummated as culture. Thus, culture is the realization of the highest values, through the nurture and cultivation of the highest goods of man. It lies in the essence of culture, as such nurturing, to nurture itself in its turn and thus to become the politics of culture."[36]

But culture is not just a collection of artifacts, i.e. a physical world created by human hands; it is a world of meanings that people insert into the products of their activities and into the activities themselves. The creation of new meanings itself becomes a meaning of activity in spiritual culture, that is, in art, religion, and science.

The world of meanings is a product of human thought, existing in the realm of human reason, limitless and immense. Therefore, culture, which is shaped by human activity, encompasses the individual both as the subject and the means of activity. It includes a variety of items (material and spiritual) that objectify the activity and its product, but de-objectify the source of that culture. Since culture is derived from human activity, its composition must be determined by the structure that generates this activity.

Any culture is both an agent and a product of change—a way of adapting to an environment. It follows from this that cultural differences are not due to the different contemplative assimilation of the world; it is not even due to methods of environmental adaptation. **Rather, cultures differ by the**

---

[36] Martin Heidegger, *The Age of the World Picture, The New Technocratic Wave in the West*. - M. , - S. 93. (Author's footnote).

types of material and spiritual appropriations, i.e., activities, active behavioral responses to the world. The subject's activity in the world is based on the norms and guidelines derived from culture. Furthermore, culture is not just a way of appropriation; it is also the selection of the object for appropriation and interpretation.

In any act of appropriation, we can identify external (expansive) and internal (intensive) aspects. The former describes the extent of the act's impact. Over time, the impact expands as an individual incorporates new material resources during the process of appropriation. The latter reflects the manner of assimilation. In our view, changes in the sphere of assimilation are global and international in character, but **the manner of assimilation always has a specific national flavor that reflects the behavioral tendencies of a people.** Different cultures, then, are distinguishable by several factors: what they assimilate (the object of assimilation), what we get from the assimilation (the product), the way in which this assimilation occurs, and the selection and interpretation of items assimilated. National culture is characterized by the same principles of formation. Its foundations include components common to all people, such as the biological and psychological nature of man and the unchanging properties of human societies. However, the selection of objects and the methods of appropriation and interpretation used have their own national characteristics.

Although humanity is a single biological species, it is not a unified social group. Different communities of people live in different natural and historical conditions, which has allowed them to develop specific ways of living that act upon each other whenever the communities themselves interact. Where does Russian culture come from? Russian icon painting comes to us from the Byzantine Empire and the Greeks. Where does Russian ballet come from? From France. Where is the great Russian novel from? From England and Dickens. Pushkin wrote Russian imperfectly, but he wrote French flawlessly despite being the most Russian of poets! Where is Russian theater from? Russian music? From the West. In its essence, Russian culture is a combination of two cultures. One

28

is folk culture—a natural, pagan Russian culture that has rejected everything foreign and closed itself off, almost immutably frozen. The second has assimilated the fruits of European science, art, and philosophy—the culture of the secular nobility. Together they form one of the richest national cultures of the world.

Thus, culture "in general" does not exist, as each culture embodies a specific set of social practices for a specific community or nation. For example, Russian culture has remained Russian for many centuries (despite the expansion of industrial activity of the Russian people during this period); it did not become Georgian in the Caucasus or Uzbek in Central Asia. Over time, Russian culture has nurtured ancient traditions of pan-sacredness, peeling away distinctions between Heaven and Earth, divine and human, sacred and profane, holy and ordinary (consider the concept of the God-man in Russian religious philosophy).

A disdain for human affairs and a contempt for the individual distinguish East Slavic culture in a significant way. Herzen said that no European would dream of giving Spinoza a thrashing or drafting Pascal into the army. For Russia, these are commonplace occurrences: Taras Shevchenko endured decades of military service and Pyotr Chaadaev was declared insane.

Any given national culture is always in dialogue with others, a process that brings to light things that might not have been noticed in one's local culture alone. Of this, Mikhail Bakhtin commented, "We pose questions to a foreign culture that it has not asked itself; we look for answers to our questions and the foreign culture answers them, revealing to us new depths of meaning."[37] This is the pattern of cross-cultural communication, the study of which is of particular interest to us.

As noted by Émile Benveniste, the entire history of modern thought and the main achievements of spiritual culture

---

[37] M. M. Bakhtin. *The Aesthetics of Verbal Creativity*. - Moscow, 1979. - S. 335. 20. (Author's footnote).

in the Western world are connected to how people produce and grapple with a few dozen basic words. Two such words, in our view, are the words "culture" and "civilization."

The term **civilization** (Latin *civilis*, meaning "civil", "social") appeared in the seventeenth century. At that time, civilization was understood as simply the opposite of barbarism and was practically synonymous with culture. German scientific literature began to distinguish these two terms at the end of the nineteenth century. Certain thinkers began to see civilization as the totality of material and social benefits acquired by society through the process of social production. Culture, on the other hand, was recognized as the spiritual content of civilization. Issues concerning the relationship between these two concepts were studied by Oswald Spengler, Arnold Toynbee, Nikolai Berdyaev, Pitirim Sorokin, and others.

In *Decline of the West* (published in 1918 and translated into Russian in 1993) German philosopher Oswald Spengler wrote that every culture has its own civilization, which is in fact the death of culture. He summarizes the relationship as follows: "Culture and Civilization are the living body of a soul, and its mummy." Culture produces diversity, but it also creates inequality and unique individual of personalities; civilization, on the other hand, strives for equality, unification, and standards. Culture is elitist and aristocratic; civilization is democratic. Culture rises above the practical needs of the people, occupying itself with spiritual ideals; civilization is utilitarian. Culture is national; civilization is international. Culture is associated with the cult, the religious, the mythical; civilization is atheistic.

Spengler speaks of European civilization as the final phase of European evolution. For him, civilization is the last stage in the development of any sociocultural community; it is the era of its decline.

The Anglo-American tradition offers a different conception of civilization. The great twentieth-century historian Arnold Toynbee labels many different societies "civilizations", meaning that practically any individual sociocultural community could be considered a civilization.

The contemporary American scholar Samuel Huntington defines civilization as a cultural community of the highest order, the highest level of cultural identity a people can reach. He identifies eight major civilizations: Western, Confucian, Japanese, Islamic, Hindu, Slavic-Orthodox, Latin American, and African.

In the Russian language, the word "civilization" appeared relatively late compared to French and English, in which the term arose in 1767 and 1777, respectively. But the issue in question does not concern the appearance of the word, but the concept attached to it.

Like Oswald Spengler, Gustav Shpet viewed civilization as the degeneration of culture. He argued that civilization is both the end and outcome of culture. Berdyaev held a similar position. According to him, culture has a soul, while civilization only has ordinary tools and techniques.

Other scholars use different criteria to distinguish culture from civilization. For example, Andrei Bely in his *Crisis of Culture* wrote: "The crisis of modern culture is due to the blending of civilization and culture; civilization is manufactured from what nature has given us. What had once grown hard and cold becomes a consumer product for civilization." Culture is "the act of preserving and growing the life forces of the individual and the race, developing these forces in a creative transformation of reality; therefore, culture is initially rooted in the development of the individual, its sequel. Individual growth is the sum of personality."[38]

According to Merab Mamardashvili, culture is something that can only be attained through one's own spiritual efforts, while civilization is something that can be extracted and used. Culture creates the new; civilization merely replicates the known.

Dimitry Likhachev believed that culture contains only eternal unchanging values—a striving towards the ideal. By contrast, in addition to its positive features, civilization has dead-ends, twists, turns, and blind alleys, with its ultimate

---

[38] Andrei Bely At the Crossroad. A Crisis in Culture. — M., 1910. — C. 72. 22 (Author's footnote).

objective being a more convenient way of life. Culture, on the other hand, is not merely utilitarian and is free from the need to ensure the survival and preservation of the species. Civilization, however, is pragmatic. "A screw off" has real culture, according to Likhachev.

In sum, one should note that culture has developed along two paths. One involves the satisfaction of human material needs, a path that evolved into civilization. The second involves the satisfaction of spiritual needs, i.e. one's culture, which has symbolic characteristics. The second branch should not be thought of as an extension of the first but rather as an important independent branch.

Cultural historians are well aware that the most primitive tribes, even those verging on extinction, can have very complex and extensive systems of spiritual culture involving myths, rites, rituals, beliefs, etc. The primary motivations of these tribes, however strange it may seem to us, are not to improve their biological chances of survival, but rather to ensure the continuation of their spiritual progress. This behavior has been observed in many societies, so it cannot be attribute to mere coincidence or error. Spiritual culture, then, cannot be considered as secondary to the material sphere (see Marx's theory that "being determines consciousness").

Thus, culture creates the means and methods of the spiritual principle in man while civilization furnishes his livelihood, aiming to meet his practical needs. Culture ennobles and elevates the soul of man while civilization provides comfort for the body.

The civilization/culture antinomy has serious theoretical underpinnings, although these are expressed in different ways. Aron Brudny[39], for example, described it as the two hands of mankind—can the right really not know what the left is doing? This is self-deception; the right simply does not want to know what the left is doing. Self-deception,

---

[39] (1932 - 2011) - Soviet and Kyrgyz psychologist and anthropologist. His major publications include: The Science of Understanding, Psychological Hermeneutics. Space of Possibilities, Personetics.

however, is typical of mankind—perhaps even one of its necessary conditions—and takes various forms, all of which are part of culture.

Making distinctions between culture and civilization provides answers to questions like: How does man relate to humanity? Through culture and sexual selection. How does man relate to society? Through civilization.

In linguistic-culturology, culture is of greater interest than civilization because culture is symbolic, while civilization comprises the material realm. Linguistic-culturology primarily studies myths, customs, habits, rites, rituals, cultural symbols, etc. These phenomena are part of culture because they are forms of domestic behavior and language. Data derived from observing such phenomena serve as the material basis for this field of study.

The above can be summarized by Alvin Toffler who claims that culture is not set in stone—it is something we recreate daily. Although this process may not occur as rapidly as Toffler proposes, it is clear that culture does change and evolve. As we have seen, it develops in two branches— material and spiritual culture. It is "split" into two entities— culture and civilization.

At the start of the 20th century we began to see culture as a specific system of values and ideas. Culture in this sense is the totality of absolute values created by man – human relations expressed through objects, actions, and words. This system of values is one of the most important elements of culture and the most important components of this axiology include norms, standards and ideals. This value system is considered to be the core of spiritual culture and is evidenced in concepts such as faith, heaven, hell, sin, conscience, law, order, happiness, home, etc. However, subtle value differences can be found in societies the world over, from desert-dwellers to mountain folk, as well as in the Christian worldview.

The theory of "cultural determinism" holds that the religion and culture of a country or nation (if a country is a multinational) ultimately determine the extent of its economic development. According to Nikolai Berdyaev, the Russian soul blends both a Christian and a pagan-mythological view of the world: "There have always been two components to the Russian people, a primitive natural paganism and the Byzantine Orthodox Church, an austere yearning for the other world."[40]

Thus, the mentality of the nation as a whole is based on religion, although important roles are reserved for history, climate, and a shared space, i.e. "the topography of the Russian terrain" (according to Nikolai Berdiaev), and the particulars of the language.

The famous Russian cultural scholar Valery Sagatovsky highlights the following features of the Russian character: unpredictability (the most important feature), spirituality (or religiosity, the desire to search for a higher meaning), soulfulness, the concentration of power (which often turns into relaxation), desire to contemplate, smoke too much, pour their souls out, maximalism, a weakness of character, all of which generate Oblomovism.[41] The contradictory properties of the Russian character have been noted by numerous commentators, including Alexey Tolstoy, who described the sweep of the Russian soul thusly:

Kohl loves, without reason, Kohl threatens, it's not a joke . . .
Kohl asks, with all his heart, Kohl feasts, so feast lavishly!

Nature can be thought of as having one dimension: the material, since it consists of matter in its various forms (physical, chemical, biological). Society seems just as one dimensional: a legal and economic system of relations. However, culture is not so unidimensional. It is divided into the material and the spiritual, the external and the internal, the individual and the national. Other dimensions of culture include the sectoral, legal, artistic, moral, and communicative.

---

[40] Berdyaev Nikolai. *The Philosophy of Inequality* // Russian Abroad. — Moscow, 1991. — pg. 8. (Author's footnote).

[41] The term is based on the name of the hero in the novel of Ivan Goncharov *Oblomov*. The word refers to personal stagnation, routine and apathy. Aleksandrovich Dobrolyubov wrote an article "What is oblomovism?", about the origins of oblomovism. In his opinion, it lies in the traditional feudal way of life in Russia before the reforms of Alexander II.

Culture is realized and differentiated in a particular space and time within a specific society or nation: for example, that of ancient Greece or Egypt. Every national culture is multi-layered and includes components like peasant culture or the culture of the "new Russian."

Thus, culture is a complex and multifaceted phenomenon of communicative value and symbolic nature. It establishes an individual's place in the system of social production, distribution, and consumption. It is a unified whole with individual characteristics and a common idea, a unique approach to the struggle between life and death, the spiritual and the material.

The early Slavic culture fixed onto language, the material used in this text, was a mythological culture. However, this language has not disappeared without a trace.

The material used in this manual is taken from the language of early Slavic culture (a mythological culture). However, this language has not disappeared without a trace. Having transformed itself, often beyond recognition, it lives on in metaphors, phraseology, proverbs, sayings, folk songs, etc. This is why it is said that the **origins of Slavic culture were based on a mythological archetype.**

Each new native speaker forms a vision of the world. But this world vision is not based on independent thought and experience; it is based on a framework of ancestral experiences as enshrined in language, myth and archetypes. When assimilating these experiences, we merely use and slightly refine them. New meaning is created in the process of this conceptualization of the world and becomes part of the linguistic heritage of the culture. Language is a means of discovering what was previously unknown (see Humboldt's *On the Diversity of Human Language*). Language does not just name the things within a culture; it does not just express culture; language creates culture, developing within it and then sprouting from it.

It is precisely this interaction between language and culture that linguistic-culturology studies.

Questions and tasks

1. What paradigm in linguistic-culturology preceded the new anthropological paradigm?

2. What unites linguistic-culturology and ethno-linguistics, linguistic-culturology and sociolinguistics, linguistic-culturology and regional linguistic geography? What distinguishes them?

3. Give a working definition of culture. What approaches to the understanding of culture can be identified by the turn of the millennium? Explain the advantages of the values approach.

4. Culture and civilization. How are they different?

CHAPTER 2
History and Theoretical Foundation of Linguistic-Culturology

Linguistics is saturated with cultural-historical content. After all, its primary subject matter is language—the condition, foundation, and product of culture. At the end of the twentieth century, Rebecca Frumkina wrote that in words "there arose a kind of impasse—it turned out that the science of man left no place for the primary creation of man and his intellect: culture."[42]

We do not actually deal with the world itself; rather, we experience representations of it—cognitive pictures and models. Thus, the world is presented through a cultural and linguistic prism of the particular group of people observing it. Perhaps this is why Yuri Stepanov held that language unconsciously guides the thought of philosophers and scholars. Indeed, some of the most important philosophers of the twentieth century—Pavel Florensky, Ludwig Wittgenstein, Niels Bohr, and others—have given language a central place in their work. The great Hans-Georg Gadamer asserted that "language is the only hope for freedom," and Martin Heidegger thought it was language, not nature or the surrounding environment, that was man's primal "house of being," as language not only reflects, but also creates, the reality in which man lives. In this context, linguistics is of strategic importance for the methodology of the social sciences.

Language, in its own way, guides the mind through its analysis and evaluation of the world. Vladimir Dal offers the following parable on this topic: A Greek man was sitting on the beach quietly singing a song to himself before suddenly bursting into tears. A Russian man who had overheard him wanted to know what provoked such a reaction and asked him to translate the song. The Greek man obliged him and said, "A

---

[42] R. M. Frumkin Linguistics in search of epistemology // Linguistics at the end of the XX century: Results and Prospects: Proceedings of the International Conference. - M., 1995 -T. II. C. 104. (Author's footnote).

bird was sitting—I don't know how to say it in Russian—it was sitting on a hill and sat for a long time and then it flapped its wings and flew far, far away, through the woods, flew away." Then he said, "It doesn't make any sense in Russian, but in Greek it's so sad!"

In the same vein, Grigori Vinokur[43] noted that any linguist who studies a given culture's language becomes a researcher of that culture and of the achievements of the chosen language.

Issues of interrelationships between language, culture and ethnicity are not new. As early at the beginning of the nineteenth century, German scientists Brothers Grimm tried to solve this problem; their ideas found expression in Russia in the 60-70's of the nineteenth century in the works of Fyodor Buslaev, Alexander Afanasyev and Alexander Potebnja.

The ideas of Wilhelm von Humboldt gained widespread traction around the world. According to Humboldt, language is the "national spirit" and the "very existence" of a nation. Culture manifests itself primarily in language. It is the true reality of a culture and serves to introduce the individual to culture. Language encapsulates a culture's firmly-established views about the universe and about the culture itself. The cliché about the "power of language" (or the Sapir—Whorf hypothesis) is being increasingly discussed in the humanities, although it is interpreted in different ways: early on, Mikhail Bakhtin understood it as the "shackles" of another's words, while Lev Vygotsky thought of it as personal sense in relation to meaning, etc.

At the beginning of the 20th century, the Austrian Wörter und Sachen school ("words and things" in English) studied the "language and culture" issue by carrying out concrete analyses of constituent elements, the "building blocks" of language and culture. This demonstrated the importance of the culturological approach to various branches

---

[43] November 1896 — May 1947. Soviet linguist and literary critic. Specialist on Russian literature, history of the Russian language, theory, theory of word formation.

of linguistics and, above all, to the study of vocabulary and etymology.

The neo-Humboldtian movement and its well-known offshoot, the Sapir—Whorf school, were based on the idea of the continuity and unity of language and culture and postulated the dependence of thought on language. Leo Weisgerber, a neo-Humboldtian, argued that language is an "intermediary world" between thought and reality.

Another academic working on these issues was Claude Levi-Strauss, who noted that language is a product of culture, an important component of it, and the condition for its existence. Moreover, language is the specific way in which culture exists and a factor in the formation of cultural codes.

Vladimir Vernadsky contributed to the dialogue by claiming that the critical importance of language was in the creation of a new form of biochemical energy that he called "the energy of human culture."

Culture shapes and organizes ideas about linguistic identity, forming both linguistic categories and concepts. The study of culture through language is an idea that "has been in the air" in recent years. This approach holds that linguistic material consists of robust, often self-contained information about the world and the individual within it.

Thus, we can see that the study of culture through language is not new. Thinkers such as Aleksander Brückner, Vyacheslav Ivanov, Vladimir Toporov, Nikita Tolstoy and others have all written about it. At the cusp of the third millennium, Polish anthropologist Jerzy Bartmiński also made great contributions to resolving these questions. He sees culture not only as contiguous to language, but as a phenomenon whose deep analysis is essential to understand the mysteries of man, language, and text.

At the end of the 20th century, the work of the scholars discussed above allows for the following linguistic hypothesis: language is not only connected to culture; it grows out of it and expresses it. Language is at once an instrument for the creation, development, and storage (in the form of texts) of culture, and it is also a part of it, because it allows for the creation of real, objectively existing works of material and spiritual culture. At the turn of a new millennium, a new science has emerged based on this idea: linguistic-culturology.

Linguistic-culturology emerged at the juncture of linguistics and culturology and deals with the cultural expressions of groups of people as they are reflected and entrenched in language. However, one should not think of this new science merely in terms of its position at the border between two existing fields. It is not a simple compounding of two adjacent sciences; rather, it is a new scientific field that seeks to overcome the limitations of a narrowly departmentalized field of study, thereby providing new perspectives and accounts.

Thus, linguistic-culturology is not a temporary union of linguistics and culturology, but an interdisciplinary science with its own independent aims, objectives, methods, and objects of study.

Linguistic-culturology emerged as a special branch of science in the 1990's. Nevertheless, any attempt to provide a clear and consistent chronology of its formation is unlikely to succeed. First of all, too little time has passed since its inception. Secondly, placing the establishment of a science within a certain time frame cannot be done objectively because it is bound to reflect the subjective opinions of a particular researcher working in a specific scientific field, as Rebecca Frumkina correctly noted.

That being said, it seems reasonable to distinguish two periods in the development of linguistic-culturology. The first period includes all of the prerequisites necessary for the development of the science—the works of Wilhelm von Humboldt, Alexander Potebnja, Edward Sapir, and others. The second period involves the formation of linguistic-culturology as an independent field of research. The historical dynamic of scientific development suggests a third, future period that we are currently at the threshold of: the emergence of Linguistic-culturology as a fundamental, interdisciplinary science. Our research is dedicated to the formation of this very science.

Several schools of linguistic-culturology have now formed.

1. One approach engages in the linguistic-culturological study of a particular social or ethnic group in a specific culturally significant period. This focuses on a concrete linguistic-culturological context.

2. Diachronic linguistic-culturology studies changes in the linguistic culturological state of an ethnic group over a specified period of time.

3. Comparative linguistic-culturology focuses on the linguistic-culturological manifestations of different but interconnected ethnic groups.

4. Contrastive linguistic-culturology is still in its infancy. To date, it is represented by only a few works, the most interesting of which is a work by Maria Golovanivskaya[44] titled *The French Mentality From the Point of View of a Speaker of the Russian Language*, in which the particularities of the French mentality are studied from the perspective of Russian language and culture. In this work, Golovanivskaya analyzed abstract nouns in both Russian and French including fate, danger, luck, soul, mind, conscience, thought, idea, and others.

5. Linguistic-culturological dictionaries compile linguistic-geographical lexicons (see: *Americana*. English-Russian Linguistic and Geographic Dictionary, edited by Heli Chernov - Smolensk, 1996; Great Britain: Linguistic and Geographic Dictionary, Adrian Rum - 1999; Germany: Country and Language: Linguistic and Geographic Dictionary, Dina Maltseva - 1998; Austria: Linguistic and Geographic Dictionary, Natalya Viktorovna Muravlyova - 1997; Greece: Linguistic and Geographic Dictionary, Natalya Nikolay - 1995; Countries of the United Kingdom: Linguistic and Geographic Reference / Comp. Genady Tomahin - 1999; USA: Linguistic and Geographic Dictionary, Genady Tomahin, 1999; France: Linguistic and Geographic Dictionary / Edited by Ludmila Vedenin. Moscow, 1997; and others).

---

[44] Russian writer, translator, professor at the Department of Area Studies of Moscow State University.

As we can see, this last school is developing particularly rapidly. Let us briefly examine one of these linguistic-geographic dictionaries. That of Dina Maltseva contains 25 themed linguistic units that reflect different geographical realities of Germany: climatic features, flora and fauna, history, folk customs, belief systems, traditions, superstitions, legends, numerological symbolisms, color symbolisms, weddings, funerals, holidays, religious beliefs, monetary systems, systems of measurement for length, weight, volume, and area, industrial development, trade, science, technology, medicine, delivery of mail, and the history of architecture and urban planning. Other topics found in the dictionary include: language, typography, writing, students and student life, school, national dress, traditional cuisine, games, folk dances, traditional greetings and well-wishing, etiquette, gestures, first names and surnames, linguistic units of literary origin, aphorisms, songs, and the national character. By using such dictionaries, the study of the interaction between language and culture becomes quite productive. At the very end of the 20th century, four schools of linguistic-culturology arose in Moscow.

1. The linguistic-culturological school of Yuri Stepanov, which is similar in methodology to that of Émile Benveniste. It aims to describe the diachronic aspects of cultural constants. Verification of their content is carried out using texts from different epochs, as if from the perspective of an external observer rather than a native speaker.

2. The linguistic-culturological school of Nina Ariutunova explores universal cultural terms as derived from the texts of different times and peoples. These cultural terms are also constructed from the perspective of an external observer and not a native speaker.

3. The linguistic-culturological school of Veronica Teliya, known in Russia and abroad as the Moscow School of Linguistic-Culturological Analysis of Phraseology (MSLCFraz). Veronica Teliya and her student studied linguistic entities from the perspective of a native speaker of a living language. It views the command of cultural semantics directly through the subject of language and culture. This

approach is similar to one used by Anna Wierzbicka (lingua mentalis, or mental linguistics) and involves a simulation of the speech-act mental states of the speaker.

4. The linguistic-culurological school of the Peoples' Friendship University of Russia established by Vladimir Vorobyov, Victor Shaklein [45] et al. The concept was further developed by Evgeny Vereshchagin and Vitaly Kostomarov·

Thus, linguistic-culturology is a branch of the humanities that studies material and spiritual culture as it is embodied in a living national language and its linguistic processes (Elena Oparina[46]). It establishes and explains that one of language's fundamental functions is to act as an instrument for the creation, development, storage, and transmission of culture. Its objective is to study the ways in which language embodies, stores, and transmits culture.

Goals and Objectives of Linguistic-Culturology

Despite the differences between the various linguistic-culurological schools mentioned above, contemporary linguistic-culturology is unified by the fact that all schools study the cultural semantics of linguistic symbols. Such symbols are formed upon the interaction of two different codes—linguistic and cultural—as every linguistic identity is at the same time a cultural personality. Therefore, linguistic symbols can function as the "language" of culture, as evidenced by the ability of a language to represent the cultural-national mentality of its speakers. This also explains the existence of "cultural barriers," which can occur even when all linguistic rules are complied with. One example of this is offered by Anna Wierzbicka, who relates an incident in which an English conductor was invited to lead a German orchestra. The collaboration was not going well, and the conductor concluded that the reason for the difficulty was that

---

[45] Head of the Department of Russian Language and Teaching Methodology at the philological faculty of the People's Friendship University of Russia.

[46] Researcher in the Department of Linguistics of the Institute Social Sciences at the Russian Academy of Sciences; Specializing in field of stylistics and phraseology of the English language.

he spoke English, so the musicians couldn't accept him as "one of their own." To rectify this, he decided to learn German, and the first thing he asked his teacher was how to say the following sentence: "It seems to me like it might be better if we perhaps played like this." The teacher thought for a moment and said, "Of course, it's possible to construct a sentence like that, but it's better to just say: 'play it like this.'" This anecdote shows us that cultural barriers occur when there are differences in the norms of verbal behavior, as well as when conversation participants attach different meanings to the same words due to insufficient background knowledge, etc.

The place and weight of culturological arguments in the modern science of language began to change around the turn of the century, above all in cognitive semantics. The analysis of linguistic units within a cultural context led to the formulation of a range of new problems in linguistics. My work distinguishes those cases in which one can use linguistic data to understand something about a culture from those in which we examine cultural realia to learn facts about a language. Linguistic-culturology, as an independent branch of knowledge, should solve the problems specific to it; it should answer a number of questions which, in their most general form, can be stated as follows:
1) What role does culture play in the formation of linguistic concepts?
2) To what part of a linguistic symbol is "cultural meaning" attached?
3) Are the speaker and listener aware of these meanings and how they affect speech strategies?
4) Is there in fact the cultural-linguistic competency of a native speaker that would allow for cultural meaning to be embodied in text and understood by native speakers? The following is a working definition of cultural-linguistic competency: a linguistic personality's natural command of speech creation and perception and, most importantly, of cultural norms. To support this, we need a new method of linguistic-culturological analysis of linguistic units.

5) What are the conceptosphere (the set of fundamental concepts for a given culture) and cultural discourse that represent the native speaker of a particular culture and of multiple cultures (universal); what are the cultural semantics of given linguistic symbols, as formed by the interaction of two different subject areas - language and culture;

6) How to systematize the fundamental concepts of the given science, i.e. to create a conceptual apparatus that not only allows us to examine the interaction between language and culture, but that also ensures mutual understanding within a given scientific paradigm, whether anthropological or anthropocentric.

This list, however, is not conclusive. In answering one set of questions, we only arrive at new ones.

These are the overarching, general epistemological questions that Rebecca Frumkina considers common to all sciences. However, there are specific questions associated with translation, language education, and dictionary compilation in which cultural information must be considered. These questions can only be resolved after answering—or at least making some progress on—the general epistemological questions.

In answering these questions, there is one very important factor that must be considered due to the additional difficulties it raises for the field: the cultural information contained within linguistic symbols is predominantly implicit and is seemingly hidden behind linguistic meanings.

For example, the Russian idiom "выносить сор из избы" (literally "taking the trash out of the hut," similar to the English expression "airing your dirty laundry") has the following dictionary definition: "to disclose information about any unpleasantness involving a narrow circle of people" (Dictionary of Figurative Expressions of the Russian Language). There is rich cultural information hidden deep within this expression. In fact, it reflects a Slavic archetype: one mustn't take the trash out of the hut because in so doing we weaken "our own" space, rendering it vulnerable and opening our family members to possible harm, and a person should not weaken those close to him. Therefore, an indication of disapproval is the marker of cultural information in this idiom, and it is included in most modern phraseological dictionaries.

Another example is the idiom "ни кола, ни двора" (literally "neither stake nor yard"[47]) meaning not having your own yard or farm. It has become a cultural indicator expressing the following cultural more: it is inappropriate for a person not to have his own home and property.

Veronica Teliya suggests another way of interpreting the national and cultural meanings of linguistic units—from the perspective of an observer *within* the language. For example, when interpreting the collocation "sick conscience" from a linguistic-culturological perspective, it is not only the value factor that is important (as if one's conscience were suffering from a disease), but also the fact that it creates a psychological discomfort, since the moral flaw draws the disapproval and condemnation of society. Furthermore, the phrase is used in informal settings by interlocutors of particular sociocultural statuses and positions.

Our theory incorporates Teliya's internal method of analyzing linguistic facts but adds the approach of adopting the perspective of an external observer.

It is no longer possible to work in linguistics without acknowledging the existence of linguistic-culturology. Ignoring it violates the ethos of the scientific community, where one of the basic premises is the requirement of constancy (even if it includes a reasoned denial). One can't help but see that many aspects of the character and behavior of a nation can be explained by cultural factors. For example, in Russian one must use the patronymic as a way to show honor and respect to fellow tribesmen. As the Russian saying goes, "a name is for addressing, but a patronymic is for praising."

Methods and Methodology of Linguistic-Culturology

---

[47] Refers to someone's extreme poverty, having no place to live. Perhaps, not a pot to piss in or a window to throw it out from.

Philosophy defines methodology as **a system of principles and methods for organizing theoretical and practical activity, as well as this system's doctrine** (Philosophical Encyclopedic Dictionary. - M., 1983 - p. 365). It is a collection of the most essential elements of the theory that undergirds the development of the science itself. Methodology, unlike theory, does not contribute new knowledge and, unlike a concept, does not serve as a basis for practice. Rather, it provides a ground for these elements, which in turn make the further development of the science possible. Methodology is a concept for scientific development and concept is a methodology for transitioning from theory to practice.

Method is closely related to methodology. Method is a specific approach to the phenomenon being investigated, a set of techniques that allows us to study the given phenomenon. Therefore, method is always a system. Its nature is determined by the object and purpose of the research. Any method is directly or indirectly dependent on philosophical theories.

The methodology of any science (including linguistic-culturology) has three levels: the philosophical, the general scientific, and the specific methodology (a set of principles about scientific research methods themselves).

The philosophical is the highest level. Its basic laws, principles and categories of dialectics were formulated by Heraclitus, Plato, Kant, Fichte, Schelling, and others. It includes the law of attraction and repulsion of opposites, the law of transformation of quantitative into qualitative, the law of a negation of a negation, the categories of the general, the individual and the separate, necessity and chance, etc.

The scientific methodology includes the general methods and principles various sciences use to study a phenomenon. This method includes observation, experiment, modeling and interpretation. General scientific methodology changes with the progress of science, resulting in the emergence of new methods and significant modifications of the old ones.

Individual methodology is a method for a particular science, in our case, linguistic-culturology.
However, in relation to theory, method is secondary. Vladimir Zvegintsev rightly points out that, in and of itself, a method can only be a means of perceiving an object, and only to the extent permitted by the theory it serves. A method "supplies" the facts needed to verify or correct a proposed hypothesis. Therefore, the distinguishing features of a method are determined by the

theoretical views about the object under investigation and by the method's objective.

Methods of linguistic-culturology include the complex of analytical techniques, processes, and procedures used in analyzing the interrelationship between language and culture. Since Linguistic-culturology is an integrative field of knowledge, it incorporates research from cultural studies, linguistics, ethno-linguistics and cultural anthropology – a set of cognitive methods and operations are grouped around the semantic center of "language and culture." The methods from both cultural studies and linguistics are used in the process of linguistic-cultural analysis.

Any given method of scientific research has its own scope of application; the idea that every method has limitations is an axiom of modern science. The interactions between language and culture are so multifaceted that it is impossible to know their nature, function and genesis by using a single method alone. This explains the wide array of methods used to examine such relationships.

Linguistic-culturology can use linguistic, cultural and sociological methods. For example, it can use techniques of content analysis, framing analysis and narrative analysis that go back to Vladimir Propp or it can use the methods of field ethnography (descriptive, classification, leftover methods and others). It can use open interviews such as those used in psychology and sociology or methods of linguistic reconstruction of culture such as those used by the school of Nikita Tolstoy. It is possible to research the material using the traditional methods of ethnography as well as through experimental methods of cognitive linguistics, where the most important source of material is the native speaker (informants). These methods are mutually complementary, having specific conjugations of varying cognitive principles and methods of analysis, thus allowing linguistic-culturology to explore its complex subject matter - the interaction of language and culture.

One such method that can be employed by linguistic-culturology is the system of metaphor analysis proposed by George Lakoff. This approach wields substantial explanatory power and goes a long way towards solving many problems related to language and culture. For example, his cognitive theory of metaphors explains why some foreign idioms can be easily understood and even borrowed, while others cannot. It also establishes a cognitive foundation for any discrepancies found between two languages. Such differences are not coincidental and testify to the unique ways in which different groups of people perceive fragments of the world.

Veronica Teliya proposed using a macro-component model of knowledge to describe linguistic-cultural values. The seven-dimensions of this model include such blocks of information as data about presuppositions, denotation, rational assessments, the motivational basis of the symbol, emotional and emotive evaluations and evaluations of the symbol usage. Each block is used by the cognitive operator and indicates the procedure for processing the corresponding mental structures.

In addition to the macro-component model, we suggest actively using psycho-social experiments as part of linguistic-culturological research and using greater amounts and varieties of prepared texts. This is because the cultural information embedded in linguistic units is, for the most part, hidden behind its own linguistic nature. For example, the idiom "neither stake, nor a yard, nor chicken feather" means "to have nothing at all." The cultural information is conveyed by the cultural connotations of the proverb, "the unworthy man has nothing." Accordingly, it includes the dictionary annotation, "scorn."

A special area of research is linguistic-cultural analysis of texts, true and precise custodians of culture. The union of man and culture takes place through the assimilation of the texts of "others." Being an insignificantly small part of the world, the text (book) is absorbed into the world and becomes the real world of the reader, in lieu of the entire world. Therefore, it is important to analyze texts within this hermeneutic paradigm (hermeneutics being the science of understanding). We use a variety of research methods and techniques - from interpretive to psycholinguistic.

Object and Subject Matter of Research in Linguistic-Culturology

I distinguish between the object and the subject of research, understanding an object of research to be a domain of reality having a set of interrelated processes and phenomena. The subject matter of research on, the other hand, is a specific part of the object, having its own specific characteristics, processes and parameters. For example, the general object of research for the humanities is the person, but the subject matter for each branch of the humanities is a specific aspect of the person and his activities.

The object of study for linguistic-culturology is the interaction between language (the transmitter of cultural information), culture (norms and preferences) and man (who created this culture through language). This object is viewed from the "crossroads" of several basic sciences – linguistics, cultural studies, ethnography and psycholinguistics.

The subject matter of linguistic-culturology are the language units that have acquired symbolic, figurative and metaphorical significance in culture. They encapsulate the fruits of human consciousness, the archetypal and prototypical elements recorded in myths, legends, rituals, rites, folklore, religious discourse, poetry, prose, idioms, metaphors, symbols and proverbs (adages and sayings), etc.

Furthermore, a single linguistic-cultural unit can simultaneously belong to several semiotic systems: the stereotype of a ritual can become a saying, and then turn into a phraseological unit. For example, there was a time in the ancient world when "one ate an oath." It meant that someone swearing an oath would actually eat the ground. This symbolized an intertwining with the land, as if sacrificing one's self in doing so. The custom attached itself onto the phraseological unit, "eating the ground."[48] Another example is the song "Poor Lazarus", sung by the poor and the downtrodden. The term is semantically strengthened by the name of Lazarus himself "God has helped" and is reinforced by the biblical legend of Lazarus, who was rewarded in the next world for his suffering (Gospel of Luke). This was transformed into the idiom, "the song of Lazarus" meaning "to move with pity or to elicit sympathy."

Sometimes, the same linguistic-cultural unit is embodied in a myth, a saying and a phraseology: "wolf" contains a concept for the ancient Slavs about robbers, murderer, massacres, i.e. the mythologem of the "wolf-thief", which influences the metaphor of a "killer wolf." The wolf's unchanging predatory nature is reflected in the saying "every year the wolf sheds its coat, but never sheds its habits", and then fixed itself onto the phraseological unit "wolf's grip" among others.

Within the broader object of investigation, it is possible to distinguish several linguistic-culturological subjects, each of which consists of individual linguistic-culturological units. I have highlighted many of these subjects, but there are more. Primarily, they include the following: 1) the subject of regional linguistic geography, lexica having no equivalents or lacuna. And since regional linguistic geography is an integral part of linguistic-

---

[48] In Russian "землю буду есть" is literally to eat the land. It was an oath not to leave your ground and is currently used in jailhouse jargon.

culturology, it too is an object of study; 2) language units of mythology: archetypes and mythologems, rites and beliefs, rituals and customs fixed in language; 3) the paremiological stock of the language; 4) The phrases of the language; 5) models, stereotypes and symbols; 6) metaphors and linguistic images; 7) stylistic norms of the language; 8) verbal behavior; 9) speech etiquette. These main points seem to form a heterogenous mix rather than an organized homogeneous set. Nevertheless, they are the most "culturally bearing" and should therefore be investigated first.

Let us examine each of the subjects mentioned above.

1. The subject of investigation for linguistic-culturology should be the **words and expressions that serve as the subject being described in regional linguistic geography** (i.e. the regional linguistic geography of Eugene Vereschagin and Vitaly Kostomarov). These are words and expressions such as *baklusha*[49] (dawdle time away), shchi (cabbage soup), porridge, sauna (give a bath)[50], disappear like a Swede at Poltava, etc.

The sphere of area studies emphasizes sources quoting Russian classics (with popular catchwords) – "a man in a case"[51], "a Khlestakov"[52], "fathers and sons"[53] as well as slogans and political discourse – "the train of history", "labor guard"[54], "road to life"[55], "the struggle for the harvest"[56], "pass the torch and so on. These are essentially national expressions, but their presence in phraseologies, metaphors or national realities are not always indicative of a cultural connotation that could affect the thinking of the people (Veronica Teliya).

Linguistic units having no equivalents (according to Eugene Vereschagin and Vitaly Kostomarov, 1980), indicate phenomena specific to a given culture (accordion, to brow beat[57], and others). They are the product of the cumulative (accumulated, reinforced experience of native speakers) functions of language and

---

[49] Баклуша – Baklusha. A stump of wood (usually aspen or birch), processed to produce various hollowed wooden products (spoons and other utensils).

[50] задавать баню - literally, to give a bath; meaning, to beat severely.

[51] Meaning lonely man who is closed off from the world, creating a shell around himself. From "The Man in a Box", by Anton Chekhov.

[52] Main character in "The Inspector" by N. Gogol.

[53] Referring to a generation gap.

[54] Intensive continuous work.

[55] The first Soviet movie with sound, 1931.

[56] Poem by Demyan Bedny.

[57] In Russian, it means to humble one's self, to go cap in hand.

can be thought of as repositories of a speaker's background knowledge, i.e. knowledge available in the consciousness of the speakers. Differences between languages are due to differences in cultures and are most clearly visible in lexical units and phraseologies, since the nominative material of language is most directly related to extra-linguistic reality.

The distinct national or cultural character imparted by nominative units is evident not only by the existence of non-equivalent units in a language, but also by the absence of certain words and expressions in other languages. These absences are known as lacunae, or blank spots on a language's semantic map (according to Yuri Sorokin and Irina Markovina). Often the existence of such lacunae in a language is explained not by the lack of corresponding denotata, but by the fact that the culture in question does not find it necessary to make such a distinction.

In these language units, reality itself is national and, accordingly, the word naming it contains a national-cultural component. However, we can attribute a wider range of linguistic phenomena to the subject of linguistic-culturology. National-cultural "appropriation" of the world occurs under the influence of the native language, since we can only think about the world through language units and their conceptual network, i.e. remaining in the circle circumscribed to us by language (Wilhelm von Humboldt). Accordingly, different nations have different tools for conceptual formation, forming different pictures of the world, which are in fact the basis of national cultures (Leo Weisgerber).
We should note here that linguistic-culturology is not concerned with all of the linguistic differences between languages, as not all such differences are culturally significant. This idea can be found in the work of Anna Wierzbicka.

Thus, it is necessary to distinguish the instances where linguistic units themselves play the role of cultural stereotypes from instances where they merely name the cultural objects. They are both fundamentally different aspects of culture as reflected in language and therefore, they are both subjects of linguistic-culturology. However, we are primarily interested in instances of the first type, while instances of the second type are the domain of regional linguistic geography.

2. Another subject of linguistic-culturology is the **mythologized language unit: the archetypes and mythologems, rites and beliefs, rituals and practices embodied in the language.**

A phraseme reflects a particular mythologem rather than a myth in its entirety. A mythologem is a character or situation that plays an important role in a myth—a kind of essential element that can be repeated from myth to myth. The core of a myth is the archetype, an image that arises within an individual consciousness and spreads throughout the rest of the culture (Savely Senderovich). This concept was introduced by Carl Jung in his 1919 article "Instinct and the Unconscious." Jung believed that we all have an innate ability to subconsciously generate common symbols— archetypes that manifest themselves in dreams, myths, fairy tales, and legends. Archetypes, on this view, express the "collective unconscious," i.e. that part of the unconscious that is formed not by personal experience but that is inherited from one's ancestors. The archetype is described as a "psychic organ" that grows in the human soul "like a flower." Modern science, in fact, has confirmed that the archetype is a deeper level of the unconscious.

According to Carl Jung's theory of "genetic memory," the archetype is central to mythology, which can be thought of as a repository of archetypes. The proto-image serves as the foundation of an archetype and is always collective—it is held in common by unconnected groups of people across time and space. Thus, the most important mythological motifs are also shared by a variety of peoples spanning a range of historical eras. In fact, humans do not appreciate the profound influence of archetypes on their lives, and even contemporary people would be surprised at the extent to which their behavior is governed by the irrational.

Take, for example, these phrasemes based on the "bread": "to eat someone else's bread,"[58] "to live off someone else's bread," "to earn one's bread," "no need to give bread."[59] In these examples, the archetypal image of bread symbolizes life, prosperity and material wealth. Thus, bread should be "yours" and earned through your own labor (reminiscent of the Biblical reprimand directed at the first couple, Adam and Eve: "In the sweat of thy face shalt thou eat bread." Furthermore, eating someone else's bread is frowned upon in society, especially given the Biblical command that bread be produced through one's own labor. Furthermore, bread (as an archetype) has historically been viewed as a ritual object with power over various aspects of human life through its association with various rites of spring, divination, fortune telling, and incantations. Bread is also a symbol of the sun god, making it not only a gift from

---

[58] To sponge of someone.
[59] To do something gladly.

God but a divine entity in and of itself. Thus, archetypes are an important component of a culture's phenomenology. In ancient times, it was believed that if a person eats "your" bread it could harm you. There is also an exact opposite point of view: "if a stranger tastes our salted bread, he can no longer feed us hostile feelings and becomes a person related to us." Many sources illustrate the sanctity of bread for the Slavs. For example, it was a Slovak custom to place a piece of bread into a newborn's swaddling clothes to prevent the baby from being cursed. Czechs and Ukrainians also believed that bread could protect them against evil spirits, which is the origin of the Russian proverb "bread and salt keeps evil way." In fact, bread and salt are left for 40 days after one's death as a kind of guardian amulet. Even today, these archetypal ideas about bread remain common among Slavs. For example, in Ukraine they sprinkle grain on the four corners of a plot of land they plan to build a house on. If the location is good, the grain will remain in place over the course of three days. In Russia they place bread beneath huts being built. In Belarus, karavai, a type of ceremonial bread, is widely used as an offering to the sun.

Rites. Alexander Veselovsky, in his *Historical Poetics*, noted the leading role of ritual in the development of culture, but saw no connection between ritual and myth. However, most modern scholars accept the view that myth and ritual form a semantic unity, which serves as the theoretical and practical aspects of the same phenomenon.

An action can become a rite when it loses practical utility and adopts a purely symbolic meaning. Rites are closely linked with myths and rituals. Some scholars even trace the origin of myth to the rites and rituals of bygone eras (e.g. Levi Strauss, Yeleazar Meletinsky). Compared to ritual, a rite is more complex in structure, involving multiple stages and is a longer duration. It is usually accompanied by special songs, dramatic arts, khorovods (a type of folk song and dance activity, plays, fortune telling, etc. Myth may serve to explain the origin of certain rites.

In essence, every rite symbolizes and reproduces a creative work. Rites reinforce the basic world-ordering principles of a particular tradition. They are conventional, symbolic actions that evolved from customs and habits and that have been consecrated by centuries of tradition. They maintain a stable relationship between humans, nature, and other humans, helping people communicate, compile and transmit social knowledge, alleviate human suffering, and generally feel like a member of a community of likeminded people. Examples of rites include birth rites, christenings, matchmaking, weddings, burials, and funerals. For example, the Belarusian phraseological unit пасадзіць на] means "to prepare a place for the bride and groom to sit in the corner of honor at a wedding" or "to give away in marriage." Thus, this phraseme incorporated into its semantics the rite of seating a young woman in a place of honor at a wedding, particularly on a type of large vessel covered with a sheepskin (Alexander Sergputousky[60]).

Ritual is a system of acts performed in a strictly defined order according to tradition and during specific times. It is a form of "transformation of consciousness" (Werner Sombart), the main mechanism of collective memory which, to a large extent, even today determines the life of man.

Ritual can also be found among other animal species that live in large social groups. According to Konrad Lorenz, rituals emerged in humans from nature, meaning that both human and animal ritual share a common source. Lorenz identifies three functions of ritual: 1) reducing aggression, 2) identifying members of one's own group, 3) rejecting those who are foreign. In fact, ritual is so important to humanity that some have hypothesized that language itself originated in ritual.

According to Victor Witter Turner, ritual is an important means of maintaining the common norms and values of a people, because the complex system of ritual is connected to symbols, imitations and perceptions, i.e. it is based on fundamental elements of human psychology. Therefore, **an act becomes a ritual when it loses practical utility and becomes wholly symbolic.**

Victor Turner wrote: "…ritual and its symbolism are not merely epiphenomena or disguises of deeper social and psychological processes, but have ontological value… Deciphering ritual forms and discovering what generates symbolic actions may be more germane to our cultural growth than we have supposed.[61] At the dawn of human history, rituals were non-verbal cultural texts, and knowledge of these rituals was itself a marker of an individual's mastery of the group's culture and social practices. The imitative character of ritual behavior required each individual to follow a pre-determined model, thereby rejecting individual creativity. In this

---

[60] June 1864 – March 1940. Belarusian ethnographer and folklorist.
[61] Victor Turner, Revelation and Divination in Ndembu Ritual (Ithaca: Cornell University Press, 1975), p.31."

way, individual identity was weakened and almost completely subsumed under the collective identity.

Ritual cannot be reduced to theatrical performance and should not be thought of merely as myth enacted. Myth permeates all forms of human activity. The oral translation of myth, like ritual activity, ensured a commonness of worldly views for all members of the community; it united everybody who was "inside" and separated them from those "outside." We can assume that the semantics of the symbols of human language, which appears based on ritual, must primarily reflect the structure of prototypical situations.

Ritual cannot be reduced to theatrical performance and should not be thought of merely as myth enacted. Myth permeates all forms of human activity, not just ritual. The oral transmission of myths, like ritual activity, ensures that all members of the community share a unified worldview, uniting those inside the group and setting off those outside of it. The semantics of human language, whose symbols arose from rituals, primarily reflects the structure of certain prototypical situations.

Ritual magically connected people with the living forces of nature, with personified mythical creatures and gods. Ancient rituals were rites protecting practitioners from harm. For example, the evil eye was a specific type of harm inflicted by visual means. Hence, to protect oneself from the evil eye, one must not catch or look into someone's eye. The evil eye is thus part of the archetypal world. The eye in general is thought of as a window into the netherworld. Windows themselves are dangerous, as they are the means by which the netherworld enters into one's home. Vampires and monsters, for example, sneak into your house through the window

Laugher, or more precisely ritual laughter, offers protection from evil.

Even in the earliest stages of cultural development, alongside more serious cultic traditions, there were those that laughed at, scoffed at, and ridiculed the gods. They sought to access the true vital principles underlying the "moribund" divinities. The laughter that accompanied these cults was ritual laughter, and it helped free ancient and medieval people from religious dogmatism, mysticism, and veneration. Ritual laughter created a second and parallel world where people lived. It was necessary because official celebrations did not completely correspond with human nature, distorting it by being absolutely serious.   ';

Laughter is semantically ambivalent. In pagan society it possessed a sacred symbolism and was considered a special kind of magical act. In Christian culture, laughter is heard around evil spirits like death and the devil, giving rise to the phraseme "diabolical laughter." Some believe that we are all born with both an angel to protect us and a devil to tempt us. While the angel rejoices when his charge does good deeds, the devil grins and laughs when he sees evil. It is worth noting that Christ and his apostles and saints never laugh, they merely smile and rejoice.

Forbidden laughter also finds its expression in Slavic folklore, in those Russian fairytales where the living enter the world of the dead. In the fairy-tale of Baba Yaga, the hero is warned, "when you go inside the hut, do not laugh!" The absence of laughter is a sign of being in the realm of the dead, for the dead do not laugh. When they do laugh, it is because they are trying to trick us into believing that they are still alive. This is also why the mermaid laughs in Valery Bryusov's poem: "Even more tender and even more insidious, \ she laughed and swayed with the reeds." According to Slavic superstition, there is a forest spirit who uses laughter to lure people into his trap. In his poem "Fern," Bryusov writes: "apparitions from every affiliation, \ laughing in the bushes all around."

Closely related to the prohibition on laughter is the phraseme "sardonic laughter" (like the laughter of the dead). This phraseme originates in a custom found among the ancient people of Sardinia, where they would kill the elderly while laughing loudly.

Laughter was frowned upon by the ancient Slavs, which gave rise to expressions such as "fools are known by their laughter" (дурня па смеху пазнаеш); tightwads are known by their patches and a dumb people are known by their laughter (па латках пазнаеш скупого, а па смеху -- дурного) (Belorussian). Russian idioms and sayings equate ridiculous laughter with negative connotations. Laughter without reason is a sign a fool, etc. The expression "Homeric laughter" also has negative connotations—it is the kind of thunderous laughter heard at Olympian feasts in *The Iliad*.

Behavioral phrases may include phraseological units using "laughter" as a component: laugh to tears (и смех и грех), to make a laughing stock of someone, (поднимать на смех) Russian; to make a laughing stock of someone (памграць ад смеху), not in jest, (не на смех), to burst your belly with laughter, (надрываць жываты ад смеху), to the point of laughter (паехаць ад смеху) Belorussian, and others, which encode a ban on laughter in their semantics.

But there is another side to laughter. Alexander Potebnja sees a connection between laughter and light or life. Many cultures share myths about being swallowed by fish, and in these stories, laughter is the key to salvation. According to Ukrainian lore, ravens can kidnap children and take them to the netherworld. If a mother manages to make her child laugh in time, the child can remain with her, but if she fails, the raven takes it away. Traces of these associations can be found in phrasems like to breakup with laughter (смех разбирает), to have a case of the giggles (смешинка в рот попала), and others.

This ancient, ambivalent semantics of laughter has shaped the contemporary attitude of eastern Slavs towards it. Thus, laughter is not only an expression of joy, but the source of such words as "to mock" and "mocking bird" (which, in ancient mythology, is the source of echoes).

Spells. According to Tatyana Tsivyan, an injury is semantically similar to an incantation in that an injury can be brought about through words. To escape the harmful effects of these phenomena, a spell is needed. Spells and incantations have their origins deep in antiquity. First mention of them among the Eastern Slavs can be found in tenth century chronicles and eleventh century contracts between Russians and Greeks. Later, spells made their way into Old Russian artefacts and in the sixteenth and seventeenth centuries they are mentioned

Theories about the origins of spells and incantations vary widely. For example, Fyodor Buslaev and Alexander Afanasyev insist that they are related to myths (Fyodor Buslaev "Historical Reviews on Russian Folk Literature and Art", Saint-Petersburg, 1861, Volume 1; Alexander Afanasyev "Poetic Views on the Nature of Slavs", Moscow, 1866, Volume 1).

Alexander Potebnja saw spells as storehouses of ancient poetic thought. He characterized them as "verbal expressions of wishes through comparison" (Alexander Potebnja "On Some Symbols in the Slavic Folk Poetry", Kharkov, 1914, page 147).

There are different opinions about the origins of spells: based on Byzantine Apocrypha (Alexander Veselovsky), based on the Chaldean books (Vsevolod Miller), based on black magic[62].

3. Proverbs are an object of research in linguistic-culturology since most proverbs are stereotypes of people's consciousness and thus provide ample selection. Traditionally, proverbs and sayings were studied in folklore as a genre of literature. Their study in linguistics has just begun. From a pragmatic point of view, the purpose of proverbs is not clear. One and the same proverb can be a reproach, a comforting statement, a moral admonition, a piece of advice, a threat, etc. For example: old age is no fun (Старость – не радость).

Linguistic-culturology also studies a language's paremiological content, since most proverbs contain stereotypes originating in the popular consciousness and thus provide a sufficiently broad selection of study material. Traditionally, proverbs and sayings were studied as text of folkloric genre, but linguistics is only just beginning to take notice of them. From a pragmatic point of view, the purpose of proverbs is unclear. The same proverb can at the same time serve as a reproach, a reassurance, a moral teaching, a piece of advice, a threat, etc. For example, the Russian idiom *old age is no fun* (Старость не радость).

Not all proverbs, however, are the subject of linguistic-culturology. For example, the biblical proverb, "one swallow doesn't make it summer," has become part of Slavic culture, as well as for French, Italian and other cultures. Although it reflects knowledge of a general experience passed from generation to generation, it is not intrinsic to any particular culture or ethnic group. It cannot therefore be considered a subject of study for linguistic-culturology. According to our conception of it, the field should focus on only those proverbs and sayings whose origins and functions are inextricably linked with the history, culture, way of life, and moral system of a particular ethnic group or nation. For example, not every sneeze needs a "be healthy."[63] This proverb is based on the Slavic custom of wishing good health to those who

---

[62] The following volumes of spells are the best known: Zamovy / Compiled by Galina Bartashevich, Minsk, 1992; Russian Hexes / Compiled by Nina Savushkina, Moscow, 1993; Spells and Incantations of the Vitebsk Region / Compiled by Valentina. Poklonskaya, Vitebsk, 1996. (Author's footnote).
[63] In English we say, "God bless you" after someone sneezes.

sneeze. For example, not everyone wishes health after a sneeze. At the heart of this proverb is the Slavic custom to wish good health in response to a sneeze.

4. **The phraseological reserves of a language** are a valuable source of information about the culture and mindset of the people, as they reveal people's beliefs about myths, customs, rites, rituals, habits, morals, behaviors, etc. Accordingly, Boris Larin notes that idioms always indirectly reflect a nation's prevailing views, the social structure and ideology of its era. These phenomena are reflected in phrasemes in the same way that the morning light is reflected in a drop of water (see the paragraph on phraseology).

5. **Etalons, stereotypes, symbols.** Here we will deal only with those etalons, stereotypes and symbols discussed in Chapter 4.

Examples of **etalons** include these expressions: "as healthy as an ox", "beautiful cow eyes" (standard of beauty among the Kirghiz), "fat as a barrel." These etalons reflect not only how a nation views the world but how it understands the world, since the models are a result of national and typological regulation of world phenomena. **Etalons measure the world figuratively.** Most often, etalons exist in language as a form of stable comparisons: "stupid as a valenok" (felt boot), "as cheerful as a bird", "as angry as a wolf/dog." Generally, however, an etalon can be any representation comparing the world to human beings: "stuffed to the gills" and "head over heels in love," for example.

In analyzing the semantics of the phraseme "to tremble over every kopek", Veronica Teliya notes that the important thing is not the kopek as a coin but knowing that a kopek is the smallest unit of currency. This conception of the figurative nature of phrasemes and etalon words highlights the value of phrasemes in cultural language. In this way, according to Alexander Potebnja, a symbol becomes an image (etalon) that exerts a powerful influence on the listener.

Thus, an **etalon is an entity that measures the properties and qualities of objects, occurrences and phenomena**. A model, at the social and psychological level, acts as a manifestation of normative ideas about phenomena of nature, society, human beings, about their qualities and properties. A model contains instructions in hidden form; it affects selectivity and evaluation.

A **stereotype,** unlike an etalon, measures things like activities and behavior. Behavioral stereotypes, the most important kinds of stereotypes, can sometimes transform into rituals. The difference is that when acting out a stereotype, a person may not be aware of the reasons behind his or her behavior, while ritual always implies introspection about the meaning of its performance. Ritual is arbitrary and conventional, a means of resolving social issues.

6. **Metaphors and images** are also subjects of linguistic-culturology. These topics will be examined in more detail in their section in Chapter 4.

The image is one of the most important linguistic sources of information about the connections between words and culture. Traditionally, imagery refers to the ability of language units to create visual-sensory representations of objects and phenomena of reality.

Describing imagery as a linguistic category, Sergey Mezenin notes that any form of imagery, whether verbal or linguistic, has a logical structure of three components. 1) a referent, which correlates to the epistemological concept of the object that is represented; 2) the agent, or the object in its represented form; 3) the foundation, or the common properties of the object and its representations, which follows from the principle of similarity. The simile is the form of imagery in which these three components are manifested linguistically. Imagery is a real property of linguistic units that allows them to evoke "pictures" in our minds. The image evoked by a metaphor or phraseme is "grasped" not from a dictionary interpretation or from their decoded meaning, but from their internal form (IF). The internal form, according to Joseph Brodsky, is the trace or what remains when you glance at something.

The concept of the internal form (IF) was introduced to Russian linguistics by Alexander Potebnja in 1892, and further developed in the late 20s and 30s in the works of Boris Larin[64] and Gregory Vinokur who dealt with the problems of poetic speech.

The internal form (IF) of a word is the literal meaning, derived from the morphemes that make up a word (i.e. from the meanings of its root, prefix and suffix). For example, the words

---

[64] January 1893 — 26 March 1964. — Soviet linguist, a member of the Academy of Sciences of the Ukrainian SSR (1945), Academy of Sciences of the Lithuanian SSR 1949. Author of *The Esthetics Words and Language of a Writer, The History of Russian Literary Language, The History of the Russian language and General linguistics.* Was also a literary translator of Lithuanian.

"horseman", "equestrian" and "rider" have the same meaning – a man on horseback - but the IF is different.

The internal form (IF) contributes to the meaning of a word. However, its influence is not total. For example, the IF of the Russian word "snowdrop" (подснежник) "or something found under the snow" could denote not only a flower, but also to any other object under the snow in the winter: galoshes, caps, stumps, etc. Alexander Potebnja called the IF "the closest etymological meaning." The closest meaning is created by the active word-forming bonds of the derived word (for example, the Russian word "windowsill" (подоконник} can also mean "something under a window.") "The further etymological meaning" is the earliest reconstruction motivations of the root word; as a rule, for the layperson it is limited in time: the window from the eye (окно из око), i.e. the further meaning is "an eye into the world" (око в мир), in the English and Icelandic languages it is the "eye of the storm" (глаз ветра).

Thus, the internal form (IF) is a method of expression in words established by the speaker; it is represented differently in different languages: the Russian word for "currant" (смород) is connected to the expression "to have a strong odor, смород"; the Belorussian word for currant is "парэчи" originating from the place where it grows – along the river.

Alexander Potebnja considered a word's internal form to be its image. He believed that a word is as much a human creation as a saying, riddle or proverb. Accordingly, he associated the IF with things like the direct (literal) meaning of a metaphor. This is why the IF is of such interest to culturologists studying the formation of national world-views.

Semantic development of a words means that the IF may fade, be forgotten or conflict with the lexical meaning of the word. For example, ink (чернила, in Russian the word has the same root as the word black – черный) may be not only black but also red; linen (белье originated from the word белый - white) is not necessarily white, etc. Nevertheless, **the inner form lives in the semantics of its derivative words. The historical traces embedded in a language** give us access to the way in which our forebears saw an object, which colors our understanding of the same object to this day (Nina Mechkovskaya). By correlating with the lexical meaning, the IF creates a unique stereoscopic character of the verbal representation of the world. Associations, shades of meaning and connotations created by the IF have larger natural and national variety than the denotation of a word. Hence the importance of the IF in the transmission of culture.

7. Linguistic-culturology also studies the various stylistic forms a language takes. For example, some languages have strong dialectal stratification, while others have almost no differences between dialects. In some languages stylistic differentiation is only starting to get underway, and in other languages this differentiation is already a deeply engrained feature.

The relation between literary language and its nonliterary forms is determined by the totality of a society's cultural history. This includes the history of its writing systems, schools, literatures, philosophies, and cultural and ideological preferences, etc.

The influence of a people's culture on the character of regulatory stylistic formation is indirect but profound. This is in direct contrast with culture's mirror-like relationship with vocabulary.

8. Another subject of study for linguistic-culturology is **verbal behavior**, or any other behavior expressed in nominative, grammatical, and stylistic units. Alexey Leontiev writes: "The national and cultural specificity of verbal communication in our minds come from a system of factors which determine the differences in organization, functions and methods of mediating the communication processes that are particular to a particular national and cultural community. . . These factors are "attached" to processes at different levels and are themselves different in nature, but they are interconnected to these processes . . . and are primarily purely linguistic, psycholinguistic and generally psychological"[65]. Among these, Leontiev highlighted the following: 1) factors related to cultural tradition (permitted and prohibited types of communication, stereotypical communication, and the me - you - him - grammar); 2) factors related to social situations and communicative functions (functional sublanguage and etiquette); 3) factors narrowly related to ethnopsychology, i.e. the functioning and mediation of psychological processes and other activities. 4) Factors related to the specifics of a denotation; 5) factors determined by the specifics of a language of a particular community (stereotypes, images, comparisons, etc.). Research shows that behavior in every culture is regulated by ideas about how a person ought to behave in typical

---

65 Alexey Leontiev, *Psychology of Communication*, Tartu, 1976. Pages 9-10. 46. (Author's footnote).

situations and in accordance with their social roles (for example employer/employee, husband/wife, father/son, passenger/conductor, etc.).

9. **Speech etiquette** is another subject important research subject of linguistic-culturology (Natalia Formanovskaya[66]). It includes concepts like Osip Mandelstam's "cultural affectations of politeness."

Speech etiquette, the socially defined, culturally-specific rules of verbal behavior for social interaction, is also closely intertwined with social roles. A means to smooth over social communication, etiquette rules arise out of our social and psychological roles and determine how we behave in our role relationships and in our personal relationships when we engage in both formal and informal communication. Eric Berne sees speech etiquette as a way in which national-cultural character colors communication. While etiquette relationships are universal, their particular manifestations are specific to individual cultural groups, making them an appropriate subject f or linguistic-culturology. It might seem as if systems of etiquette are set in stone but violating them can have unpredictable consequences for both the individual and for humanity, as, according to Natalia Formanovskaya, "communicative truth" is more valuable for cultural cohesion than genuine truth.

Thus, linguistic-culturology explores the living communication processes; it examines the connections between linguistic expressions and the culture and mindset of a people, i.e. its mass consciousness, traditions, customs, etc.

This list of subjects examined by linguistic-culturology is not exhaustive or unchanging. We have covered only those areas in which language and culture most actively and visibly interact. In the following sections of this book, we will look more closely at some of the more "culturally relevant" subjects.

Basic Concepts of Linguistic-Culturology

---

[66] Soviet and Russian linguist, specialist in the syntax of modern Russian, functional stylistics, sociolinguistics, psycholinguistics, linguistic pragmatics, linguistic-culturology. Author of several books, including: "Russian Speech Etiquette", "A Reference to Russian and English Similarities", "A Reference to Russian and German Similarities", "A Reference to Russian and French Similarities" and others.

There is a need to form methods of classification for linguistic-culturology, i.e. to define a set of fundamental concepts which characterize the totality of linguistic-cultural reality. This will allow us to better analyze the interaction between language and culture.

Linguistic-culturology, as a special branch of science, has generated many productive concepts in modern linguistics: lingvoculturema[67], the language of culture, cultural text, context of culture, subculture, cultural-linguistic paradigm, precedential names of culture, the key names of culture, cultural universals, cultural competence, cultural inheritance, cultural traditions, culture process, cultural norms and others. Terms such as mindset, mentality, ritual, custom, cultural sphere, cultural type, civilization, paganism and others are also important concepts in linguistic-culturology.

This work requires an understanding of how cultural information is transmitted through linguistic units. It is done through semes, cultural background, cultural concepts and cultural connotations.

Cultural semes are semantic units or features that are smaller and more versatile than words. For example, the following cultural semes can be found in the words "lapti," "samovar," and "shchi": lapti are peasant shoes woven from bast; a samovar is a container with a burner inside used for making Russian tea; shchi is a Russian soup made of chopped cabbage.

Cultural background is a characteristic of nominative units (words and set phrases), referencing social or historical events. For example: missing like a Swede at Poltava, red and brown (about national patriots of Russia).

---

[67] "Complex inter-level unit, which represents the dialectical unity of the linguistic (symbol, meaning) and extra linguistic (concept, object). As a unit at a higher level than the word, linvokulturema accumulates as the actual linguistic representation ("form of thought"), and is closely related to the extra linguistic cultural environment. . . . The term was introduced by Valery Vorobyov (1997) and became widespread in the literature of linguistic area studies and Linguistic-culturology." (Akademic, Electronic Dictionary,dic.academic.ru).

The two types of cultural information described above are found in the denotation. These have been relatively well studied by linguistic regional geography.

Cultural concepts are types of abstract concepts whose cultural information is attached to significatum, i.e. to the conceptual core.

Cultural inheritance is the transmission of significant cultural values and information significant to the culture.

Cultural traditions are a set of the most valuable elements of social and cultural heritage.

Cultural process is the interaction of elements within a system of cultural phenomena.

Cultural space is the way a culture exists in the minds of its representatives. Cultural space correlates with cognitive space (individual and collective), because it is formed by the totality of the entire individual and collective spaces of all the representatives of the particular cultural and national community. For example, Russian cultural space, British cultural space, etc.

The linguistic-cultural paradigm is a set of linguistic forms that reflect ethnically, socially, historically, and scientifically-determined worldview categories. Linguistic-cultural paradigms combine concepts, categorical words, cultural precedent names, etc. Linguistic forms are the basis of the paradigm, as if it was "stitched" by significant points of view.

Mentality is a worldview categorized by forms of the native language. It combines the intellectual, spiritual and volitional qualities of a particular national character. The concept of a given culture is a unit of mentality (see *The Dictionary of concepts of Russian culture* by Yuri Stepanov).

Many studies of mentality exclude the study of language. According to Aron Gurevich, mentality is a way of seeing the world, not at all identical to ideology, which deals with elaborate systems of thought. In many ways, mentality may be even more important, it remains non-reflexive and logically undetected. Mentality is not a philosophical, scientific or aesthetic system. It is a level of social consciousness, where thought is not divisible from emotions or from the latent habits and methods of consciousness. Therefore, mentality is the invisible spiritual unity of the people, without which there cannot be an organization of any society. Mentality of the people is actualized in the most important cultural concepts of language.

Mindset is a category that reflects the internal organization and differentiation of mentality, the make-up of the mind and spiritual constitution of a nation. Mindsets are psycho-linguistic-intellects of multi-scale linguistic-cultural communities. According to the analysis of scientific literature, mindset is understood as a deep structure of consciousness, which depends on social, cultural, linguistic, geographic and other factors. The distinctive features of national mindsets are manifested only at the level of the linguistically naive non-conceptual picture of the world. (Yuri Apresyan[68], Ekaterina Yakovleva[69], Oleg Kornilov[70]). All mindsets are a unique subjective view of reality. They include objects of both direct and mediated reality, consisting of such cultural components as myths, legends, religious beliefs, etc.

Cultural tradition is an integral phenomenon, expressing socially stereotyped group experience, accumulated and reproduced in society.

Cultural reserve is a collection of knowledge and mental outlooks in the field of national and world culture, usually held by the typical representative of a particular culture. However, this is not something that belongs to an individual, but a totality of those basic units that are included in a particular national culture.

Cultural type was one of the first cultural typologies. It was proposed by Pitirim Sorokin, a Russian scientist who in 1922 was expelled from Russia, settled in the United States

---

[68] Head of the Department of Theoretical Semantics at the Russian Academy of Science.

[69] Author of "Fragments of the Russian Language Picture of the World (A model of space, time and perception).

[70] Professor of Linguistics and International Communications at Moscow State University. Author of "The Language Picture of the World as a Product of National Mentality", "Pearls of Chinese Phraseology", "The Language of the Incas. Experimental Textbook on the Quechua Language and Culture."

and became a prominent sociologist. He identified several types of cultures: **ideational culture** - basically religious, **senses culture** - the opposite of the idea culture (beginning with the Renaissance, it is the dominant culture in Western Europe); **idealistic culture** is a mixed type of culture that changes form from one type to another (the Golden Age of ancient culture, European culture of XII – XIV centuries). The type of culture largely (though not always) determines the type of personality of each of its members.

Language culture is a symbolic essence. More precisely, it is system of symbols and their relationship, coordinating values and meanings, and organizing existing or reemerging views, images or other semantic structures. When considering other ethnic cultures, it is understood as a totality of all symbolic methods of verbal and nonverbal communication, objectifying the specifics of an ethnic cultural group and reflecting its interaction with the cultures of other ethnic groups.

Cultural norms are a type of ideal by which a person is categorized as "worthy/unworthy." They are developed through the historical path of a people, staying in the social memory and generating new norms. Along with other factors, we differ from animals because we have agreed upon rules and norms. It is what separates us from the abyss of chaos, regulates our lives and must, therefore, be observed.

Many Russian scholars have attempted to identify the most important Russian traditional structures. The concepts of twentieth century philosopher Nikolay Losskiy are widely known. In his book *The Character of the Russian People*, published in 1957, he highlights the positive and negative structures of the Russian people (collectivism, unselfishness, spirituality, fetishization of the government, patriotism, maximalism, compassionate but at the same time cruelty, etc.

Cultural norms, according to Veronica Teliya, cannot be as obligatory (mandatory) as, for example, linguistic norms. National culture includes everything that may be interpreted in terms of structural values such as "prescriptions (expressions) of folk wisdom" (according to Veronica Teliya).

Cultural values perform a multitude of functions in the workings of human life: coordination between man and nature, stimulation, regulation and others. Axiology includes many value classifications, including the absolute, eternal, social, personal, biological, survival, etc. People do not just perceive the world but evaluate it in terms of its importance in meeting their needs. Linguistic information about value systems is proof of the distinctive ways people perceive the world.

Subculture is a secondary subordinate cultural system (for example, youth subculture, etc.)

Key concepts of culture are determined by core (base) units of the picture of the world, those units having existential significance for an individual linguistic identity as well as for an entire linguistic-cultural community. The key concepts of culture include abstract nouns such as conscience, destiny, will, share, sin, law, freedom, intellectual, homeland, etc.

According to Dimitry Likhachov, concepts arise in a person's consciousness not only as hints of possible meanings, but also as echoes of the entire person's previous language experience - poetic, prosaic, scientific, social, historic etc.

According to Aron Gurevich, concepts of culture can be divided into two groups: the "cosmic" philosophical categories, which he calls the **universal categories of culture** (time, space, cause, change, movement), and social categories, the so-called cultural categories (freedom, law, justice, labor, wealth, property). It seems appropriate to add one more group - the **categories of national culture** (for Russian culture this is will, share, manners, sobornost, etc.). Upon closer analysis of these concepts, one finds that there are more culturally specific concepts in any language than might appear at first glance. For example, potatoes may be considered as a culturally specific concept. For Russians, it is a linguistic model of little food, hence the idiom sitting on just one potato; for Belarusians it is a familiar national food, another type bread even more important than the original.

Key cultural concepts have an important position in the collective linguistic consciousness; therefore, their research is an extremely important issue. -Proof of this is the emergence of dictionaries of the most important cultural concepts; one of the first of these works is the dictionary of Yuri Stepanov, *Constants: Dictionary of Russian Culture* (Moscow, 1997).

Cultural connotations are an interpretation of denotative or figuratively motivated aspects of meaning in cultural categories. This term was introduced by Veronica Teliya in 1993. A special section (the next one) is devoted to this extremely important concept.

Lingo-cultural unit is a term coined by Vladimir Vorobyov. It is a complex inter-level unit, having a dialectical unity of linguistic and extra-linguistic (conceptual or objective) content. According to Vladimir Vorobyov, a lingo-cultural unit is the totality of the linguistic symbol, the content and cultural meaning accompanying this symbol. His understanding of a lingo-cultural unit gives great significance to the deeper meaning, potentially present as part of its content. The term seems quite vague, since it does not reveal the mechanisms of where and how cultural information is attached to a linguistic symbol, how it "works" in a language. It only indicates the fact that it is present in a linguistic symbol, a fact known since the time of Humboldt.

The most important source of cultural markings are the linguistic units in certain types of communication, particularly those concepts directly relevant to linguistic-cultural analysis of text. These are primarily cultural universals, common for all elements of the culture understood as important for a culture and its traditions (the presence of language, making tools, sexual taboos, myths, dances, etc.). Such fragments of reality are found in literary text. As a rule, they serve as a basis for ideological clichés of the era. (For example, the story by Yevgeny Zamyatin "Fisher of Men" contains the culturally universal - the condition of the typical hero. It provides the following maxim: "The most beautiful thing in life is delusion and the most beautiful delusion is love.")

In fact, linguistics has well known language and conceptual universals. Anna Wierzbicka identified several such words, calling them lexical universals: I, you, someone, something, a thing, people, body, this, one, two, everything, many, good, bad, etc. Conceptual universals, or more precisely, their most important combinations, is the cultural universal. Anna Wierzbicka writes: "To conceive of something, we need something more than "concepts": we need sensible combinations of concepts."[71]

The author made some adjustments to the Sapir-Worf theory of linguistic relativity. First, she emphasized the importance of recognizing the fact that systems viewing the world through different languages can be contrasted; second, the identified national-specific concepts can be compared to the extent that they are translatable into the language of "semantic essentials." From her perspective, every language forms its own "semantic universe." "Linguistic and cultural systems greatly differ from one another, but there are lexical and semantic universals indicating the general conceptual basis on which human language, thought and culture are based."[72]

Linguistic-cultural universals can be represented by a single word, as well as by entire expressions that create the core of a cultural image. On the one hand, a cultural universal is addressed to the material world and, on the other hand, to the national and cultural moral problems of an ethnic group. This duality gives them their semantic capacity, the ability to convert the major ideas of the text into symbolic expressions, symbols of a nation and an era. They are the cultural lighthouse of the text. Text is the true junction between linguistic and cultural studies; it is language-based and is its highest tier. At the same time, text is a form of cultural existence. Linguistic-culturology regards language precisely as a system embodying cultural values.

The study of precedent names and key cultural concepts has an important role in linguistic-cultural studies. **Precedential names** include the individual names associated with well-known texts (Oblomov, Taras Bulba), with situations that are known to most of the members of this nation (Ivan Susanin, grandfather Talash[73]). Precedential

71 Wierzbicka A. Universal semantics and descriptions of languages. M., 1971. – page 299. (Author's footnote).

72 Cited above by the author.

73 Grandfather Talas was a famous hero in the famous story by Yakub Kolas "Quagmire."

names of Russian culture include the names of people whose role was great not only in Russia, but in universal culture. For instance, Russian scientists Lomonosov and Mendeleyev, Timiryazev and Vernadsky, Vinogradov and Kolmogorov contributed to the progress of world science. Russian writers like Pushkin, Gogol, Dostoevsky, Leo Tolstoy, Chekhov, Gorky, Mayakovsky, Kuprin, Sholokhov, Solzhenitsyn, Brodsky had an indelible impact on world literature. Russian artists like Rublev and Dionysius, Repin and Vasnetsov, Serov and Korovin, Malyavin and Vrubel bring delight to any admirer of painting. Russian composers like Glinka and Tchaikovsky, Scriabin, Prokofiev, Shostakovich and Schnittke cannot be excluded from the history of world music. Russia has had such a great impact on world culture that getting to know the Russian people and their language implies knowledge of this contribution.

4tation as an Exhibitor of Culture in Linguistic Symbols

Natalia Shvedova highlights 20 general semantic categories in the Russian language: animate, action, condition, subject, measure, place, time and others. These categories form the semantic framework of a language. This is the most abstract level of the linguistic picture of the world. However, each nation has more specific figurative and associative mechanisms to redefine initial meanings into a secondary category. In Russian, for example, a dog is associated with (along with the negative things) faithfulness, devotion, unpretentiousness. This is reflected in idioms, such as a dog's faithfulness, a dog's devotion, a dog's life, etc. In Belorussian, a dog is associated with mostly negative connotations - ушыцца у сабачую скуру, literally 'to get sewn into dog's skin' (meaning "to become a useless, lazy person"), собакам падшыты ("a bad person"). In Kirghiz "it" (a dog) is an obscenity, approximately the same as pig in Russian. In Russian, pig is a symbol of a) filth, b) ingratitude, c) bad manners. For the British, pig means a glutton. For the Kyrgyz, Kazakhs, Uzbeks and other Muslim nations a purely religious connotation is added to this, resulting in *chochko* (pig) becoming a seriously offensive word; in Vietnam a pig is a symbol of stupidity. Thus, the words "dog", "pig" connote different features for different peoples, which indicates that creative thinking of these peoples is specific and individual, affecting the formation of their world views.

From the above given examples, it is clear that each language and each culture is characterized by the appearance of specific additional meanings - connotations.

How exactly are language and culture related to each other? Probably via an interim formation, an ideal implemented as meaning in language. "Such an interim element provides ontological unity of language and culture, meaning that it is an ideal, entering language as meaning into linguistic symbols and existing in culture as an object, i.e. objectified in a labeled form, in an active form, i.e. in the form of an activity, in the form of the results of an activity."[74]

Therefore, if a linguistic unit contains cultural information, there must be a category that connects two different semiotic systems (language and culture) allowing for a description of their interaction. Veronica Taliya believes that cultural connotations perform this function. It has now been established that cultural information may be present in nominative units of a language in four ways: via cultural semes, cultural background, cultural concepts and cultural connotations.

Different researchers have different opinions about how links are formed between language and national culture. Some say it is a national and cultural component (Eugene Vereschagin, Vitaly Kostomarov), others that it from background knowledge (Yuri Sorokin), etc. Like Veronica Teliya, I believe that this relationship is realized via cultural connotations. These culturally designated connotations are the result of associative and figurative interpretations of phraseological units or metaphors, an interpretation done through national cultural standards and stereotypes.

---

[74] E.R. Tarasov Language and Culture: Methodological Problems (Language – Culture – Ethnicity). Moscow, 1994. pg. 107.
(Author's footnote).

Components understood as symbols determine the content of cultural connotations. For example: blood as a symbol of vitality in the phraseological unit: "to suck the blood out of someone", "to the last drop of blood"[75]; blood as a symbol of kinship, "native blood", "blood of my blood"; blood as a symbol of sacrifice, "to spill someone's blood"; blood as a symbol of health, "blood with milk"[76]; as a symbol of strong emotions, "blood rushed to his head", "cold blooded."

If we interpret phraseological units by correlating associative-figurative perceptions to stereotypes that reflect a people's mindset, we reveal the cultural-national essence and character of the phraseological unit. It is here that national-cultural connotations are stored.

The contents of phraseological units and metaphors, as well as the cultural connotations ascribed to them, become knowledge, i.e., a source of cognitive perception. This is precisely why idioms and figurative-motivated words (metaphors) become indexes of cultural symbols.

Why do phraseological units fix themselves in language for centuries, even though they are a clear anomaly of the language, an irregularity? Why are they created again and again in every age? For example, in our period of reforms, unbalanced in every wary, certain idioms have appeared: "nimble as a broom with a whistle" (referring to a fast and noisy person); "a railway station trash bin" (about a dirty, unwashed person); "a level below the stool"[77]; neckline to the knees", and others. These questions may be answered thus: a phraseological unit is a cluster of cultural information that helps to say much while economizing linguistic resources and reaching the depths of the national soul and culture.

There are modern transformations of phraseological units. They are, however, recognizable by the native speaker. The phraseological unit, window to the world, takes on an unexpected interpretation in the following sentence written by a popular contemporary author. "We in Japan make the best

---

[75] To sacrifice everything, including your life.
[76] The picture of health.
[77] A person who's not very smart.

74

televisions in the world, but this doesn't keep us from realizing that television is just a small transparent window into the spiritual garbage chute" (Victor Pelevin).

Culture penetrates these symbols through the associative-imagery of their semantics; it is then interpreted by associating images with stereotypes, standards, symbols, myths, prototypical situations and other symbols of national culture. It is precisely in the system of images, fixed in the semantics of the national language, that cultural information concentrates in the native language.

In this manner, **the relationship between one or another cultural code is stored in national and cultural connotations.** Cultural connotations provide culturally significant indicators not only to the meanings of phraseological units, symbols or metaphors, but also to the meaning of the entire text in which they are used.

The way a connotation emerges is based on giving greater emphasis to a different shade of meaning (often by using the vivid inner form of a word, which is the basis of most stable associations). In this way, associations are a causal basis for the emergence of connotations. The direct meaning of the word is perceived as an internal form in comparison with the figurative one.

Usually, individual symbols are separated from denotations whose images appears in the internal form of the connotative word. Therefore, if a person is called a hare (a cowardly person), it does not mean that he has a gray coat, short tail and long ears; it only shows that this person has been seized by fear, often imaginary, and will manage to flee. Affixing associative characteristics to the meaning of a word, i.e. the appearance of connotations, is a cultural and national process. It is not subject to the logic of common sense (why, for example, is the hare is cowardly but not the fox), so different peoples may have other animals and birds as standards of cowardice.

As a rule, connotations are based on associations arising from the word. However, sometimes they are motivated by properties of the real: ichthyosaur (a backward person), a lamb (about a quiet, gentle man), bazaar (about a noisy place), vinaigrette (about any mixture), cattle-shed (about a dirty apartment), sauna (about any hot place), the Talmud (about tedious reading), etc.

Often, connotations have an evaluative aura, as well as a bright manifestation of national linguistic specificity that creates a picture of the world. For example, according the Russian picture of the world, the combination "old house" connotes a negative meaning. The English regard the same combination as a positive one. For the Kyrgyz, blue eyes (k-k-z) are the ugliest, almost an obscenity. However, "cow eyes" (referring to human ones) are very beautiful. This evaluation is based on a denotation (the cow). Thus, connotations constitute a type of evaluative perception of the world, factors of internal determination of behavior.

Connotations contain potential resources for the linguistic nominative system. This is because the connotative word is able not only to create, but also to retain the deeper meaning, having a complex relationship to the semantics of a word. It is then affixed to language, thus creating a cultural and national language picture.

For linguistic-culturology, "cultural memory" and language units, (words, idioms) are also objects of interest. These are the associations set by linguistic units, originating from previous usage and forming the present meaning. After all, any spoken word has gone through a complex semantic history before obtaining present meaning, leading us ultimately to the initial word-forming efforts of a person. Each word we use bears the heritage not of forty centuries, but of at least forty thousand years. Culture itself is a kind of past, which can be seen through the present. The deeper the past, the higher the culture.

For example, the word "robe" (риза) in contemporary usage is the outer robe of a priest, or an icon frame. However, traces of a wider meaning ("clothing") are found in idioms – "to be so drunk your robes fall down", "to tear your robes"[78] and others. This is the cultural memory of the word, one that is also capable of creating new connotations.

---

[78] Extreme despair.

Linguistic-culturology deals with problems that are not new. Even in the nineteenth century they were being dealt with by Wilhelm Humboldt, Fyodor Buslaev, Alexander Potebnj, Alexander Afanasyev, and later by Edward Sapir, Nikita Tolstoy, Veronica Teliya, Yuri Stepanov, Nina Ariutunova and Vladimir Vorobyov. They were the ones who postulated that language is an instrument of culture, a part of it and the condition of its existence. Linguistic-culturology is based on this postulate.

Today linguistic-culturology is developing through several schools. Its aim is to study how language embodies, store and transmit culture. This aim is realized by determining the following:

1) how culture is involved in the formation of language concepts;

2) the part of the linguistic symbol's meaning a "cultural meanings" attaches to;

3) whether these ideas are perceived by the speaker and the listener and how they influence verbal strategies;

4) whether the native speaker possesses cultural and linguistic competence, i.e. does the speaker have a natural possession not only of the process and understanding of speech but of the cultural norms, etc.

A specific method of taxonomy is forming in linguistic-cultural studies, i.e., a totality of the most important understandings and terms: lingvoculturema, language of culture, cultural context, key names of culture, cultural preferences, etc.

Cultural connotation is an exponent of culture in a linguistic symbol.

Questions and tasks

1. What are the trends in current linguistic-culturology?
2. What schools of linguistic-culturology do you know?
3. Name the main goals facing linguistic-cultural studies?
4. What methods are used in linguistic-cultural studies?
5. What is the subject of linguistic-culturology? How do the subject and the object of study differ?

6. List the basic concepts of linguistic-culturology. Name the most important among them. How do you explain the concept of "cultural universals", "cultural concept"?
7. Define a cultural connotation. Who is the author of the definition? What is the source of cultural connotation?

CHAPTER 3
Language and Culture: Problems of Interaction

Language lays on the surface of a person's existence in culture. This is why from the beginning of the nineteenth century (Jacob Grimm, Rasmus Rask, Wilhelm von Humboldt, Alexander Potebnja) to the present, issues concerning the interconnections and interactions between language and culture have been at the core of linguistics. The first efforts to deal with these questions are found in the works of Wilhelm von Humboldt and its basic concepts can be summarized as follows: 1) language embodies material and spiritual culture; 2) every culture is national and its national character is expressed in language through a specific vision of the world, an inner form (IF) specific to each nation and inherent in the language; 3) the IF of language is the expression of the "national spirit" of its culture; 4) language is a mediating link between human beings and the world around them. The concepts of Wilhelm von Humboldt were interpreted by Alexander Potebnja in his work "Thought and Language" and in the works of Charles Bally, Joseph Vendryes, Jan Niecisław Ignacy Baudouin de Courtenay, Roman Jakobson and others.

The idea that language and reality are structurally similar has also been expressed by Louis Hjelmslev, who pointed out that the structure of language is like the structure of reality, or a somewhat blurred reflection of reality. But how exactly are language, reality and culture linked together?

Evgeny Tarasov noted that language is part of culture. The "body" of the symbol (representation) is a cultural object that has been formed by language and the communicative capacity of the individual. The meaning of the symbol is also a cultural formation that occurs only in human activities. Likewise, culture is a part of language, since it is all represented in text.

Since language and culture are different semiotic systems, the interactions between them must be examined very carefully. Nevertheless, one should in fairness say that as semiotic systems they have a lot in common: 1) culture, like language, is a form of consciousness that reflects the world views of a person; 2) language and culture exist in a dialogue between themselves; 3) the subject of culture and language is always the individual or society, the person or the community; 4) standardization is common in language and in culture; 5) historicism is one of the essential qualities of culture and language; 6) antinomy "dynamic – static" is inherent to language and culture.

Language and culture are interconnected by: 1) communication processes; 2) ontogeny (the formation of linguistic abilities in a person); 3) phylogeny (the formation of the clan, the social person).

The differences between these two entities are as follows: 1) the phenomenon of language is oriented towards the masses, while culture values elitism; 2) although culture is a system of signs (like language), it is unable to structure itself; 3) as previously noted, language and culture are different semiotic systems.

This reasoning leads to the conclusion that culture is not isomorphic (absolutely the same), but homomorphic to language (structurally similar).

The interaction between language and culture is extremely complex and multifaceted. Currently, one notes several approaches in resolving these issues.

The first approach was primarily developed by Russian philosophers – S. A. Atanovsky, Georg Brutyan[79], Elena Kukushkina[80], Edward Markarian[81]. The essence of this approach is that the interaction between language and culture is a movement in one direction; since language reflects reality and culture is an integral component of the reality faced by people, language is merely a reflection of culture.

When reality changes, national cultural stereotypes change; language itself changes. Attempts to answer questions

[79] March 1926, December 2015 — Armenian and Soviet academician. Member of the Academy of Sciences of the Armenian SSR (1982), founder and President of the Armenian philosophical Academy (1987).
[80] Professor at Moscow State University name after Lomonosov.
[81] (1929—2011) Soviet cultural studies professor and writer.

about how individual cultural fragments (or spheres) influence language functions were made by the Prague school of **functional stylistics** and by contemporary **sociolinguistics**.

If the impact of culture on language is obvious (precisely what is studied in the first approach), then questions about the reverse impact, language on culture, remains unanswered. This is the focus of the second approach to questions about the relation between language and culture.

The best minds of the nineteenth century (Wilhelm von Humboldt, Alexander Potebnja) understood language as a spiritual force. Language is a type of environment which surrounds us, outside of which or without which we cannot live. As Wilhelm von Humboldt wrote, language is "a world that lies between the world of external phenomena and the inner world of the person." Accordingly, as our surrounding habitat, language does not exist outside of us as an objective entity; it is found within ourselves, in our minds and in our memories. It changes its form with every movement of thought, with each new social and cultural role.

Questions concerning the second approach have been researched by the Sapir-Whorf School and by various Neo-Humboldtian Schools, developing the so-called hypothesis of linguistic relativity.

This belief is based on the hypothesis that people see the world differently, through the prism of their native language. According to its supporters, the real world exists to the extent that it is reflected in language. But if every language is reflected by reality in ways that are inherently characteristic only to that particular language, then different languages have different "linguistic pictures of the world."

The Sapir-Whorf hypothesis puts forth the following basic propositions: 1. Language determines the way its speakers it think. 2. People's understanding of the real world depends on the language they are thinking in. "We dissect nature along lines laid down by our native language. The categories and types that we distinguish from the world of phenomena are not found there because they stare every observer in the face; on the contrary, the world is presented in a kaleidoscopic flux of impressions that need to be organized by our minds - and this primarily means that it is done by the linguistic systems of our minds. We cut nature up, organize it into concepts and meanings primarily because we are parties to an agreement to organize it in this way - an agreement that holds throughout our speech community and is codified in the patterns of our language."[82]

This hypothesis was supported and further developed in the works of Leo Weisgerber, through his concept of language as an "interim world" between objective reality and consciousness. "Language is a creative force in all areas of spiritual life."

Through the works of several authors, the theory of linguistic relativity began to take on a modern and contemporary sound, primarily in works by Dan Moonhawk Alford, John Bissell Carroll, Dell Hymes and others, in which the Sapir – Whorf concept was significantly expanded. For example, Dell Hymes introduced an additional principle concerning the function of linguistic relativity, according to which the nature of communicative functions differs between languages.

However, it should in fairness be noted that many studies have subjected the linguistic relativity hypothesis to sharp criticism. For instance, Boris Serebrennikov[83] makes the following points about the hypothesis: 1) the objects and phenomena of the surrounding world
are the sources of understanding. The genesis of any language is the result of a person's reflection of the world; language is not a self-contained force creating the world. 2) language is to a large extent an adaptation to the specific features of human physiology, but those features appeared because of a living organism's long-term adaptation to the environment; 3) differences in articulations of the extra-linguistic continuum occurs during the initial naming. It is explained by the

---

82 B. L. Whorf. *The Relation Between Standards of Behavior and Thinking and Language* // New ways in foreign linguistics. Moscow, 1960. Vol. 1. 174 pages. (Author's footnote).
83 March 1915 — February 1989, Moscow. Soviet linguist, academician. Worked on general and comparative historical linguistics of the Ural, Altai and Indo-European languages.

different associations and differences of linguistic material that have survived from earlier eras.

Negative assessments of the Sapir – Whorf hypothesis were also made by D. Dodd, Gennady Kolshansky, Michael White, Revekka Frumkina, Elmar Holenstein[84].

Thus, scientific views concerning linguistic relativity are far from unambiguous. Nevertheless, researchers seriously interested in the interactions between language, culture and thought still turn to the Sapir – Whorf hypothesis, since only with the help of this hypothesis can one understand linguistic facts difficult to explain in any other way. Some examples include the ethnolinguistic works of Nikita Tolstoy, the linguistic-anthropologic works of Jerzy Bartmiński and others.

Further discussion about the interaction between language and culture will be within the framework of the third approach.

Language is a fact of culture because: 1) it is an integral part of the culture inherited from our ancestors; 2) language is the basic instrument through which we learn the culture; 3) language is the most important element of cultural formation. To understand the makeup of culture - science, religion, literature - we should view those phenomena as codes formulated like language. Natural language is the best of all models developed. Only through natural language is it possible to conceptually understand culture.

Therefore, language is both a component and instrument of culture. It is the reality of our spirit, the face of culture, overtly expressing specific features of the national mindset. Language is the mechanism that opened the field of consciousness to humanity (Nikolai Zhinkin[85]).

As noted by Levi-Strauss, *language is simultaneously a product, an important component and a condition for the existence of culture. Furthermore, language is a specific*

---

[84] Swiss linguist and cultural philosopher. "The Atlas of Philosophy", "An Introduction to the Thoughts of Roman Jacobson" are among his most well know works.

[85] July 1893 — October 1979. Soviet linguist and psychologist. Worked on psychological issues of speech communication, understanding of text, speech development.

method for cultural existence, a factor forming cultural codes.

The relationship between language and culture may be viewed as a relationship between the part and the whole. Language may be viewed as a both a component and an instrument of culture (which is not one and the same). However, language is separate from culture and can be regarded as an independent, autonomous semiotic system, as is usually done in traditional linguistics.

According to our concept, since every native speaker is also a bearer of culture, linguistic symbols can also function as symbols of culture and it is precisely because of this that language is able to reflect the national-cultural mindset of its speakers. Culture correlates with language through the concept of space.

Therefore, every culture has keywords, for example, for the Germans they are "attention", "order", "preciseness." To classify a word as a cultural keyword, that word must be: in common usage, frequent, part of an idiom, a proverb, a saying, etc.

Linguistic norms correlate with the cultural attitudes; however, these cultural attitudes are not as prescribed (mandatory) as language norms. The bearers of culture, distributed throughout different social strata, still retain the right to make wider choices.

Thus, culture lives and grows in the "shell of language." If primitive cultures were "material", modern ones are becoming increasingly verbal. Language serves culture but does not define it. Language can create verbal illusions, a verbal mirage that substitutes for reality.

Verbal illusions play an important role in the creation of social stereotypes that form national biases, such as the national stereotypes of a "German", a "Chukchi", "people of Caucasian origin." A verbal stamp is made on the minds of people. It colors the world in the required shade, a bright future, the indestructible friendship of the people, the great achievements, etc. It is no coincidence that leaders of totalitarian states pay special attention to language: Lenin's struggle for making the language "pure", Stalin's article on language, Brezhnev's struggle against "contamination" of the language by foreign vocabulary, etc.

It is precisely through language that a person perceives fiction as reality, experiences and comprehends the nonexistent, suffers and enjoys, experiences catharsis (consider the words of the Russian poet, "I'd shed tears over fiction"[86]). All this is possible due to natural language and other semiotic systems (languages of cinema, colors, gestures). Natural language has a leading place among all other languages because a linguistic symbol can become an exponent of culture. Language is closely related to mythology, religion, science and other forms of understanding the world. Gadamer wrote that philosophy fused with language and exists only in language.

Linguistic Picture of the World and Empirical Everyday Consciousness

Different languages capture the world in different ways, having their own manner of conceptualization. From this we can conclude that every language has its own specific picture of the world. A linguistic personality must organize meanings of expressions in accordance with this picture. Within this appears **a specifically human perception of the world, reflected in language.**

Language is the most important way of forming and preserving human knowledge of the world. People attach onto words the understandings derived from their activities in the objective world. The totality of this understanding is captured in linguistic form, representing something that according to different conceptions is called "an intermediary linguistic world", "a linguistic representation of the world", a "linguistic model of the world", or a" linguistic picture of the world." Because of its more prevalent use, we have chosen the latter term[87].

---

[86] "Elegy", by Alexander Pushkin.

[87] This term is somewhat nebulous in English. It derives from the German word "Weltanschauung" – worldview in English. The author uses the term to expand on

The "picture theory of the world" (including the linguistic picture) is based on the study of human ideas about the world. If the world is the person and the environment in interaction, then the picture of the world is the result of processed information about the environment and the person. Representatives of cognitive linguistics correctly claim that our conceptual system, displayed in the form of a linguistic picture of the world, depends on physical and cultural experiences; cognitive linguistics is directly connected to this idea.

Phenomena and objects of the external world are represented in the human mind as an internal image. According to Alexey Leontiev, there is a special "fifth quasi-dimension" in which the reality surrounding humans is represented; it is a "semantic field" or system of meanings. Therefore, the picture of the world is a system of images.

Martin Heidegger wrote that the word "picture" makes us primarily think about the representation of something, "however, the picture of the world does not essentially mean a depiction of the world, but a world understood as a picture." There are complex differences as to whether the picture of the world reflects the real world or whether it stores this reflection. The picture of the world may be represented spatially (up - down, left - right, east - west, far away - close), as time (day - night, winter - summer), quantitatively, ethically and through other parameters. Its formation is influenced by language, traditions, nature and landscape, education, training and other social factors.

The linguistic picture of the world is not the same as a specialized picture of the world (chemical, physical, and others). The linguistic picture of the world precedes and shapes the latter, because people are able to understand the world and themselves because of language, which stores social and historical experience, both universal and national. The latter defines he specific features of language at all levels. Because of the specific language in the mind of the speaker, a

---

Humboldt's ideas about the interrelationship between language and culture.

specialized linguistic picture of the world arises, and the person sees the world through this prism.

Yuri Apresyan emphasized the pre-scientific character of the linguistic picture of the world, calling it a naive picture. The linguistic picture of the world seems to supplement objective knowledge of reality, often distorting it (compare the scientific meaning and linguistic interpretation of words such as atom, point, light, heat, etc.). By studying the semantics of these words, we can explain the specifics of cognitive (mental) models that determine the specifics of the naive picture of the world.

Since a person's cognition of the world is not free of error and mistake, its conceptual picture of the world is constantly changing, "redrawn", whereas the linguistic picture of the world stores the traces of these errors and mistakes for some time. For instance, if a speaker wishes to indicate and express growing emotions, the idiom "my soul is soaring" is used, not realizing that this type of language is associated with archaic views about the presence of a life-giving substance inside the human body, the soul, conceived in a mythological picture of the world in the form of a vapor and could leave the body and rise to the heavens.

According to Vadim Kasevich[88], the picture of the world is encoded through linguistic semantics and may in time turn out to be a remnant reflecting only past misunderstandings of nature and the lack of any newer linguistic expression; the old meanings serve as building material for new meanings. In other words, there are differences between the archaic semantic language systems and the current mental models of a given linguistic community, as evidenced by their writings and behavioral patterns.

The linguistic picture of the world shapes the way humans relate to the world (to nature, animals and themselves as elements of the world). It sets standards of human behavior

---

[88] Vice President of the Linguistic Society in Saint Petersburg. Vice Rector of Educational Methods at Saint Petersburg State University. Chief Editor of the journal "Language and Speech" (Язык и речевая деятельность).

in the world and defines their attitudes towards the world. Each natural language reflects a certain way of perceiving and organizing ("conceptualizing") the world. These expressions collect and form a uniform and specific system of views, like a collective philosophy imposed on all the native speakers.

Thus, the role of language is not just to deliver a message; its primary role is the internal organization of what the message. A "space of meaning" appears (to use the terminology of Leontiev), i.e. the knowledge about the world fixed onto language, which is certainly intertwined with the national and cultural experiences of a particular linguistic community. A world of those who speak the language is formed, i.e. a linguistic picture of the world as a totality of knowledge of the world, attached to vocabulary, phraseology and grammar.

The term "linguistic picture of the world" is nothing more than a metaphor. The specific features of a national language, to which the unique social and historical experience of the national group are fixed, do not create in the native speakers a unique picture of the world different from the existing objective one. They only **create a particular shade of the world, one that is conditioned by the national significance of objects, phenomena, processes, and a selective attitude towards them that is generated by specific activities, lifestyle and the national culture of the given people.**

One also notes an interest in the language picture of the world in the works of Wilhelm von Humboldt, who wrote that "different languages are organs of original thought and perception for nations."[89] By the end of twentieth century there were many works devoted to this issue: the works of Georg Brutyan, Svetlana Vasilyeva, Gennady Kolshansky, Nonna Sukalenko, Max Black, Dell Hymes, the collective monograph, "The human factor in language. Language and the

---

[89] The author is citing a collection of the works of Humboldt, translated into Russian and published in 1985, by Progress Publishing, Moscow: *Wilhelm von Humboldt – Language and the Philosophy of Culture.*

picture of the world" (Moscow, 1988) and others. The growing interest in this problem is associated with recent cognitive research. Within this framework, attempts are being made to form structures of knowledge by uniting the theory of linguistic gestalt with the theory of framing as structures of knowledge.

The theory of linguistic gestalt was proposed by George Lakoff and was then recognized by other scientists. **Gestalt** is a particularly informative unit of language. In addition to its realization in language, gestalt forms a basis for human perception of reality, directing cognitive processes, determining the specificity and nature of motor acts, etc.

The deep influence of gestalt in language is manifested in several ways. On a superficial linguistic level, gestalt may have different meanings, and only specific research can establish its cohesion. George Lakoff showed that dispute and war are described using the same terms; therefore, they are evaluated in the same way. In other words, they are bound by the same gestalt.

The essence of gestalt is universal representations, belonging to the depths of the human psyche and lying outside of the categorical framework of natural language, in other words, containing great transcendental meaning; gestalt lies directly beyond the limits of the expressed but organically connected to it. Reconstructed on the basis of actual language data, gestalt itself becomes a transcendental value having real meaning.

Humboldt's idea of a "linguistic worldview" was further developed by contemporary neo-Humboldtism. Indeed, every nation partitions and names the diversity of the world in its own way. The uniqueness of the "constructed" picture of the world is shaped by the fact that it objectifies individual, group, national (ethnic), verbal and nonverbal experience. Neo-Humboldtians believe that the nationally unique linguistic picture of the world is not the result of a long historical development, but of the inherent property of language. According to them, with the help of language, people create their own special world, different from the one that surrounds them. The picture of the world of the speaker, in fact, is significantly different from the objective description of the properties, objects, phenomena, or scientific ideas about them. It is a "subjective image of the objective world." However, it is not language itself that creates this subjective image of the world.

The picture of the world, which can be called knowledge of the world, is the basis for individual and social consciousness. Language fulfills the requirements of the cognitive process. The conceptual picture of the world may be different in different people, for example, in people of different epochs, different social and age groups, different areas of scientific knowledge, etc. People who speak different languages may, under certain conditions, have similar conceptual pictures of the world, and people who speak the same language may have different ones. Consequently, the universal, national and personal all interact in the conceptual picture of the world.

The picture of the world is not just "photographs" of objects, processes, properties, etc. It includes not only the reflected objects, but the position of the people that reflect these objects and their attitude to these objects. The position of the person has the same reality as the objects themselves. Moreover, since a person's reflection of the world is active and not passive, the relationship with the object not only forms the object but is formed by it (through activity). The nature of the socio-typical situation, relationships and values, finds symbolic expression in the national language system and has a role in forming the language picture of the world. Hence it is natural that the system of socio-typical positions, attitudes and values, finds symbolic reflection in the system of national language and participates in creating the linguistic picture of the world. For example, the Russian idiom "when crabs whistle in the mountains" is the same as the English "when pigs fly", "when the tail of a donkey touches the ground" in Kyrgyz, etc. Thus, **the linguistic picture of the world generally matches the logical reflection of the world in people's minds.** However, some separate parts of the language picture of the world remain and this, in our opinion, includes a phraseology that is different in every language.

Phraseologies play a special role in the creation of a linguistic picture of the world. They are a "mirror of a nation's life." The meanings of phraseological units are closely connected to the background knowledge of its native speakers, to the practical experience of the individual, and with the cultural and historical traditions of the people who speak the given language. Phraseological units provide meaning to the picture of the world, envisioning an entirely descriptive situation (text), evaluating and expressing it. Phraseological units confer meaning to objects associated with the picture of the world, the picture of the world and reveal their relationship to it. Through their semantics, phraseological units attempt to characterize people and their activities.[90]

These two characteristics can be used to analyze the linguistic picture of the world created by idioms: pejorative, anthropocentric. The anthropocentric picture of the world focuses on the person, i.e. a person acts as the measure of all things: examples of near: *right under your nose, at hand, a skip and a jump, at your elbow;* examples of much: *from head to toe, hands full (worry);* examples of little: *in one sitting; examples of dark: pitch dark;* examples of fast: *in the blink of an eye, at breakneck speed, headlong;* an example of love: *head over heels in love,* etc.

The meanings of a series words and phraseological units are based on anthropocentric understandings of the world: *the head of the column, a bottleneck, table leg, take in hand, not lift a finger, at every step,* and others. Such nominative units create a cultural and national picture of the world that reflects everyday life and customs, habits and behavior of people and their relation to the world and to one another.

The linguistic picture of the world is created in various shades; among the brightest, in our opinion, are mythologems, figurative and metaphorical words, connotative words and others. Our worldview is partially captured by the linguistic

---

90 See Phrasebook of Russian literary language / Ed. A.I. Fedorov. Moscow, 1996; Figurative means of the Russian language / Ed. V.N. Telyia. Moscow, 1995. (Author's footnote).

picture of the world. Each language encompasses a national and distinctive system that determines the outlook of its speakers and forms their picture of the world.

It is precisely within language (and to a lesser extent in grammar) that an ethnic group's picture of the world is revealed, becoming the basis of all cultural stereotypes. Its analysis helps to understand how national cultures differ and how they complement one another at the level of world culture. It would be impossible to study cultural differences if the meaning of all words were specific to one culture. We therefore also consider the universal properties of language units when studying cultural and national features.

A naive picture is reflected in language. A picture that is primarily formed as a response to practical human needs, as a necessary cognitive foundation of human adaptation to the world. Pragmatic egocentrism structures activities so that they are optimally and easily arranged in a person's cognition. Boundless space, labor, intellectual activity and torrents of feelings are measured in human dimensions (*as far as the eye can see, head in a muddle, nose to the grindstone, a full heart*), taking it all in and going out into the world. The linguistic picture of the world preserves the image of such anthropocentrism even when the role of man has been diminished or values have changed.

In all probability, the totality of objects and events that the stereotypical image represents is the one that people encounter most often during the course of their lives. Generally, it forms a stable linguistic picture of the world that represent an objective reality.

The naive picture of the world is very pragmatic, but it is a special type of pragmatism. Purporting to be the absolute truth, knowledge of this type may arbitrarily deviate from what traditional science considers objective truth. Its standards are not formal and logical consistency, but the completeness and universality of the model, its ability to serve as an explanatory (often – quasi explanatory) matrix for structuring experience.[91]

---

91 See: V.B. Kasevich Buddhism. The picture of the world. Language. Saint-

External comparisons to visual images are often based on everyday classifications that identify objects based on similarity as opposed to scientific classification. For example, the Russian idioms: up to my ears, (in love up to my ears)[92], up to my neck, a good head on your shoulders, are somatic, i.e. they name important life functions after various parts of the body and can be classified into one thematic group "indicating physical demarcations." Everyday consciousness selects attributes typical to these parts of the human body, "location at the top" and combines them into a single group. These attributes are recorded in the linguistic picture of the world.

The commonality of practical daily functions performed by people can be united into groups and stored in their consciousness; for example, the common functions of organs such as the mouth and eyes are used to express a person's surprise, as is indicated by the idioms open-mouthed and fix your eyes on.

The various functions can even distinguish between objects having very similar scientific classifications; for example, in the phraseological unit, stand on your own legs, means "to gain independence" and to get on one's knees means "to express one's submission." Knees, as parts of the legs, are nevertheless opposite the legs. This is because, as a part of a somatic idiom, knees acquire the quasi-symbolic meaning, "unacceptable form of support" in contrast to the meaning of legs, "a kind of necessary support."

In the naive linguistic picture of the world it is possible to expand concepts found within the scientific picture of the world; for example, idiomatically the word heart means not only the organ of blood circulation, but also the "center of emotional experiences", the "source of feelings" (for example, to take to heart, with a pure heart, etc.).

Each linguistic picture of the world may have arbitrary lacunae in the lexical model that cannot be logically explained; for example, in Russian there is a standard for size

---

Petersburg, 1996. (Author's footnote)
[92] Head over heels in love.

which uses a vertical line (tall as a pole, tall as Kolomna's Milestone), but the model of horizontal length is rarely represented (in Arabic as long as a river, as long as a snake). When using entire images as models, without specifying the basis of the comparison, the approving or disapproving emotional attitude of the speaker towards the listener is usually revealed.

The world, reflected through a prism of secondary sensations, imprinted in metaphors, similes and symbols, is the main factor determining the universality and specificity of any national linguistic picture of the world. An important point here is the differentiation between universal human factors and the national specificities in different linguistic pictures of the world. Although genetics is a universal factor in bodily sensations, it is intertwined with human activity, both universal and national-specific. Invariably, these interactions are factors in the creation of the linguistic picture of the world, in common characteristics and in individual characteristics.

Apparently, attributing the storage of emotions to particular organs is one of the universal features of the linguistic picture of the world. For example, in traditional Chinese medicine and belief, the liver was considered a focal point of all things bad: anger, rage, lust. In the Russian idiom, "sits on the liver" conveys the idea of something very annoying, as if traumatic, almost as if the essence of the human nature is traumatic: "Well Dron, Dron-Dronushka, get ready, fop, dance floor polisher, I have you tightly bound to my liver." (Yuri Nagibin); in Japanese and several other languages the word "liver" symbolizes a sense organ; in Italian idioms the word "liver" has the symbolic meaning "courage" (in Milan dialect also "envy, tenderness").

Frequently, the empirical properties of objects humans observe, such as the hand's ability to grab and hold, are not just "photographed" into the mind but are refracted through the prism of certain anthropocentric scenarios and imprinted in idioms, "it's in your hands", that is, in your power, "snatched up" i.e., get quickly, "empty-handed", i.e. to have nothing, not to bring anything, etc.

The cumulative image of reality in everyday consciousness includes recurring empirical data from everyday experience as well as from a symbolic universe. Every type of culture, including the Slavic one, develops its own symbolic language and "image of the world", in which elements of this language acquire meanings. Oswald Spengler even suggested the term para-symbol to characterize culture within a spatial context. If the Egyptian soul sees itself walking along a predestined path, its para-symbol is the road; the para-symbol of the Arabic culture is the world-cave; this worldview led to the invention of the arch and dome (the first domed structure is the Pantheon in Rome which was built by a Syrian architect); the para-symbol of Russian culture is the endless plain. Perhaps this is why in Russian, even time (the age of man) appears as space: "To live a life is like crossing a field" (Boris Pasternak).

Units of natural language acquire additional meaning through the semantics of culture. So, within the linguistic consciousness of the members of Slavic culture, the word "head" not only includes the semantics of "the upper part of the body" but is also a verbal symbol of the center of reason, intellect and higher values. This cultural semantics is based on a magical and mythological understandings of features that verbally signify body parts: "the top spot", "in the heavens", "opposite from the bottom", "area of regeneration", "leading actions", "retention and replication of useful information", etc., which are included in the core definition of the word head. The indicator "top location" is mythologically reinterpreted by such idioms as: "head on fire", "spinning head", "to walk on one's head"[93]. These idioms establish a connection to the symbolism of the Slavic microcosm, in which all that pertains to the upper part of the body is associated with the sky and its primary objects - the sun, the moon and the stars.

Another important symbol is the "management of actions and deeds", which associates the word "head" within the context of various traditional beliefs and rituals. Traces of

---

[93] To be full of mischief; go wild.

these are stored in idioms such as "to sprinkle the ashes upon one's head"[94] and others.

As a rule, there are reasons why models or symbols in a naive picture of the world are chosen. The reason depends on the characteristics of the entire conceptual system and may occasionally be detected within the linguistic picture of the world. Idioms themselves may, according to Veronica Teliya, "serve as models, stereotypes of cultural and national worldviews, or point to their symbolic character and as such act as linguistic exponents (carriers) of cultural symbols."

Thus, the study of the linguistic picture of the world is closely connected to the study of the conceptual picture of the world, which reflects the uniqueness of people and their everyday life, their relationship to the world and the conditions of their existence. The linguistic picture of the world explains differences in various pictures of the world and reflects a universal picture of the world.

Human activities, including component and symbolic, i.e. cultural and universal, are both universal and national-specific. These properties define the unique linguistic picture of the world as well as its universal character.

The naive picture of the world, encompassing everyday consciousness and dominated by subject specific modes of interpretation, includes an interpretive element. Language captures these group stereotypes and standards, objectifies the mind's interpretations and makes them available for study.

One of the more interesting concepts explaining the relationship between language and culture belonged to Wilhelm von Humboldt. He put forth the idea that language reflects the national character of a culture by means of a special world vision. Language and culture, being relatively independent phenomena, are linked through the meanings of linguistic symbols that provide the ontological unity of language and culture.

---

[94] Old Testament reference to the ancient Jewish custom of dusting their heads with ashes to mourn misfortune.

We experienced a boom in linguistic-culturology at the end of the twentieth century, when issues about the interactions between language and culture were identified as among the most urgent problems in modern linguistics. In the last five years, almost every European country has had several conferences on cultural-linguistics. A great amount of material on this topic has been and continues to be published.

The explosion of interest in this problem is due to a cognitive revolution in language, which according to Rebeca Frumkin began when a kind of dead end became apparent; the study of mankind did not include the most important element, the thing that created the human intellect: culture.

Each culture has its own keyword. A full list of the keywords of Russian culture has not yet been made, but several have been very well described: the soul, the will, fate, longing, intelligentsia, etc. To be considered a keyword of culture, the word should be of frequency and common usage and it should be part of idioms and proverbs.

Consequently, every particular language is a distinct system that leaves its mark on the consciousness of its speakers and shapes their view of the world.

Questions and tasks
1. According to Wilhelm von Humboldt, how are language and culture related?
2. What are the basic tenets of the Sapir – Whorf hypothesis?
3. Provide an explanation of the linguistic picture of the world. What is the difference between a conceptual and a linguistic picture of the world?
4. What does gestalt mean in cultural linguistics?

CHAPTER 4

Linguistic-Cultural Analysis of Linguistic Concepts

Description of a regional language from the perspective of linguistic-culturology

Let us consider the constructive role a language plays in the formation of a people's spiritual culture. We'll use the example of a small region, the Belarussian Lakeland (the Vitebsk region), a kind of buffer zone between the Smolensk region, the Pskov region (they are Russian regions) and the Belarusian-speaking part of western Belarus.

Nikita Tolstoy wrote that Slavistics still has no description of language that includes the ethnic history of its native speakers. This work is one of the first attempts to provide such a description.

What is the description of a language from the perspective of linguistic-culturology? We will try to demonstrate through examples.

One of the research objects in linguistic-culturology is the stylistic method of different languages, the forms in which a particular language exists. For instance, there are languages with strong dialectal stratification, and languages where there are almost no differences between dialects; there are languages with stylistic differentiations that have only just begun and, on the contrary, languages in which these differentiations are deep and multifaceted. If in the first parameter there are almost no differences between Russian and Belarusian, the stylistic stratification within Russian is much greater, and this must to be considered when describing a linguistic-cultural situation.

We know that language varies. It includes literary language and dialects, vernacular and jargon (an incomplete, reduced, abbreviated word usage of a language subsystem). Nikita Tolstoy regarded culture based on four aspects: elite, rustic, urban and professional. Accordingly, four similar elements, correlating with linguistic ones, can be identified in Slavic culture: "the culture of the educated class, learned or elite culture, popular or peasant culture, transitory culture, corresponding to a vernacular one, which is usually called 'the culture of the people' or 'third culture', and ... traditional and professional subcultures."[95] The latter includes, for example, beekeeping, engineering cultures, the culture of "river commerce", etc. They are dependent and fragmented cultures which makes them like jargon.

Thus, we have the following parallel guides:

literary language - elite culture;

dialects and parlances - popular culture;

vernacular - "third culture", i.e., culture of the people;

jargon - professional subcultures.

Here we see that the structure of culture reveals a certain similarity with the structure of language. The world outlook of a particular social group is conditioned by its culture: the same phenomena of reality are perceived and interpreted differently by different groups. The problem before us is to determine how the language used by a given social group reflects its understanding of the world.

At present we have a fair description of the spiritual life of the youth of the Belarussian Lakeland. It is determined by a number of negative factors:

- the nation's youth are exposed to the enormous influence of "mass culture" and other inhuman phenomena, for example, various sects of Satanism and fascism;

-there is insufficient support for traditional Belarussian culture (not only in the popular but in the classical form);

- there is a lack of maturity, expressed in consumer ideology and morality (the state must not only feed, but also entertain ... and so on);

---

[95] N.I. Tolstoy: Language and Popular Culture: Essays on Slavic Mythology and Ethnolinguistics. - Moscow, 1995. - p. 16. (Author's footnote)

- social disorientation expressed in eclectic views, blurred criteria, romanticizing the criminal world, etc.

These negative factors are reflected in the language of the young; the main trends include:

1) students naturally forming new dialects based on a "combination" of traditional and professional social dialects (to lather up at the shake[96] – to go to the disco, to hang out at the lobby[97] – standing in the stairwell, wipe the scoreboard - smack in the face);

2) the tangible influence of criminal social dialects (for example, cabbage – money, humanizer, democratizer - police baton);

3) the revival of certain Belarusian expressions, mixed with professional vocabulary and dialect (to hop – to be taken to the police station, to stroll with a drunk woman[98] – to go on a drinking binge).

We will later describe the linguistic-culturology of the Belarussian Lakeland using the above-mentioned framework.

Literary Language - Elite Culture

The speakers of literary language are the elite of a society - the creative and scientific-technical intelligentsia. This language of the cultural elite is characterized by a rich vocabulary, logically connected syntactic constructions, perfect pronunciation, etc. Literary language not only signifies fluency in all features of a language, but its creative use as well. It is the art of speech (oral and written), which not all the educated population possesses, only the elite native speakers, whose numbers are few.

It follows that not all those who speak a literary language are members of elite culture. Valentin Goldin[99] and

---

[96] намылиться на булкотряс

[97] потусоваться в тамбуре

[98] в бутыльбол пагуляць (Belorussian)

[99] October 12, 1935 – November 9, 2017. Professor at the Department of General and Slavic-Russian Linguistics at Saratov State University. Author of several publications, including: "Etiquette and Speech", "The Russian Language

Olga Sirotinina[100] developed the concept of intermediate literary culture, i.e., a failed elitist culture. Its speakers include educated citizens taking greater liberties regarding literary norms of pronunciation, a certain stylistic carelessness, misuse of foreign words, the occasional violation of language norms. An observation of the speech of Vitebsk intellectuals shows that verbal culture has worsened noticeably, even in the speech of academic economists (not to mention local TV hosts). Many incorrect tautologies have appeared: service help, trade market, etc. Vitebsk journalists disseminate and introduce intermediate literary culture to the masses through mass media. For example, on the front page of the newspaper "Vitbichi" (№ 21) an article offering invitations to a mathematical tournament ends unexpectedly: "C'est la vie", an article in the same issue of the newspaper contains the absurd tittle: "Every woman should have an affair."

To this day one notes fairly extensive use of Soviet-style language: evaders[101], defectors, disenfranchised[102], cosmopolitans, promoted worker[103], renegade, signer[104], tamizdat[105] and so on.

Literary language is now being greatly influenced by spoken language, which is not just changing journalistic speech, but literary and even scientific speech, (for example, the following phrase cannot be considered correct in a

---

Today" (Published in Russian).

[100] Professor at the Department of Russian Language and Speech at Saratov State University. Member of the Russian Academy of Science. Along with Valentin Golding, coauthored *Russian Language and the Speech of Culture* (Published in Russian). Author of *Conversational Speech, Russian Language and Cultural Speech*. Coauthored *The Language of Mass Media*.

[101] Уклонисты. As in draft-evaders. Note the term "Национа́л-уклони́зм", (nationalist-deviants), introduced by Stalin in reference to the efforts of nationalist groups to gain autonomy from the party.

[102] From the Russian лишение, "deprivation". I this context "disenfranchised." A person stripped of the right of voting in the Soviet Union of 1918–1936. Enemy of the working people.

[103] Выдвиженцы, in the USSR, during 1920 – 1930, a worker promoted because of socialist background.

[104] Подписанты. (informal) someone who signs a joint petition.

[105] Tamizdat, literally, published over there. Similar to "samizdat", self-published in the West. Boris Pasternak is the best example.

syntactic or stylistic sense: Literary data shows an improvement in the physiological condition of insects when their food crops are weakened. - Journal of Voronezh State University, 1999, № 1, p. 96).

The concept of *idiolect*, developed by the academician Aleksey Shakhmatov, is extremely productive for linguistic-culturology. In the second half of the twentieth century, it was supplanted by the notion of "individual style" but reappeared at the end of the century; an example may be found in the works of Nina Ariutunova, and in the ideolect of Fyodor. Dostoevsky.

The Vitebsk region also has ideolects: well-known writers, poets, scientists and cultural leaders.

In folk culture they may include story tellers, chastushkas[106], fortunetellers, psychics. It is important to know the status of the speaker of an idiolect in their particular culture, because as Edward Sapir said, "there are as many cultures as individuals in the population."

Dialect and vernacular are part of popular culture. The way literary speakers use language is different from the way those who speak dialects use it. Alexander Peshkovski claimed that if one compares speech to ordinary body functions such as walking or breathing, then intellectual "language" would be as different from the language of a peasant, as walking on a tightrope is from walking normally, as different as normal breathing is from the breathing of a fakir. But this is somewhat theatrical and seems to be the precise condition for literary dialect. "Clearly, given this situation, the dialect and speech of people cannot be ignored by linguists, just as a botanist will always prefer the study of meadows to greenhouse. On the contrary, dialect makes up the principal and most exciting element, containing research objects having the most revealing secrets of linguistic life"[107].

---

[106] Traditional Russian folk poetry.

[107] A.M. Peshkovski "Objective and Normative Points of Views on Language //. The History of Linguistics in the XIX and XX centuries, essays and excerpts / Ed. V.A. Zvegintsev. - Moscow, 1960. - Part 2. - P. 233. (Author's footnote).

Nevertheless, the idea that regional dialects deteriorate language has been spreading since the 1930s. This view still has active support and has resulted in conflicts concerning the acceptance of dialects. However, it is precisely the study of dialects that can provide invaluable and inexhaustible information for understanding the laws of language development. This is true because the linguistic characteristics of any local dialect are due not to the carelessness of its speakers but to specific historical factors.

Dialect (in Greek dialektos – a talk) is a kind of language used to communicate within a community that is united on a territorial or social basis. Dialect is a basic and essential form of existence for language, a means of everyday routine and work communication of the peasantry. A speaker's dialect creates a type of linguistic personality, which is a fundamental principle of a national linguistic personality.

The individual is the subject of social and cultural life. Linguistic personality establishes the individuality of this culture's representatives, the various linguistic characteristics and skills used by a person most often. Studying the linguistic personality of the speaker of a dialect is important for the preservation of the past, which supports the present and the future of a language: "The linguistic material inherited from older generations contains the opportunities and speech trends of future generations, the heirs of this treasure." It is within this context that interest in the study of linguistic identity presents itself. (Lev Shcherba, 1974, p. 136). This is precisely why studying the linguistic personality of those who speak dialects is interesting for us.

According to Nikita Tolstoy, all folk culture is a dialect. Folk cultures, their sayings and dialects, are rather broadly represented within the territory of the Vitebsk region. They include Belarusian dialects, mixed dialects of the Vitebsk-Smolensk and Vitebsk-Pskov border regions, and purely Russian dialects such as those used by Old Believers. In the Vitebsk region today, there are about 100 villages of Old Believers - speakers of a Russian dialect well preserved to this day. Fourteen communes of Old Believers have not closed, continuing in Latvia, the Pskov region and other areas of Belarus (for example Mogilev).

The language of folk culture and the literary language of elite culture peacefully coexist as language-cultures, influencing and feeding of one another.

Folklore, a concentration of the figurative in dialect, brings together various elements of a people's spiritual culture: myths, beliefs, popular philosophy, popular teachings, aesthetic views and ideas, artistic tastes, morals and ideals, etc.

Scholars have different opinions concerning how oral poetry and dialect interact. Some researchers believe that a dialect has no stylistic differentiation; therefore, the language of folklore is above dialect. Others see a literary form of dialect in the language of folklore. We tend to lean towards the latter point of view.

A full linguistic-cultural study of the Vitebsk Lakeland should include a compilation of several dictionaries: 1. The Dictionary of the Rituals of Vitebsk Region; 2. Legends and Fables of the Belarusian Lakeland; 3. Regional Dictionary of Dialects; 4. Dictionaries of Dialects of Border Areas of Russia. Materials for these dictionaries have been partially collected at Vitebsk State University.

Vernacular is a "third culture", i.e. the culture of the people. There is literary and non-literary vernacular. Literary vernacular is the term coined by Yuri Sorokin; it is the lower stratum of a language, partly composed of non-literary vernacular, partly of dialects and jargons (bro, piteous, belly, fancy man, get up to, etc.; Nikita cheated on me. \ I barely caught a breath, \ Bought a "Smirnoff" - \ Vanya tapped on it - Vitebsk ditty).

In our opinion, proof of the influence of a "third culture" and colloquial language includes the following: a) extensive use of phrases without a subject and passive constructions (*Your comments and suggestions will be analyzed and, if necessary, appropriate action will be taken* ("Vitbichi"[108], №21); the number of similar phrases in one small article of 100 words is 8); b) greater use of the plural form collective noun, (*Life became unbearable \ even Aquarian . . .*)[109]; c) an increase in the number of indeclinable nouns (I've put on a white dress[110]. \ *If I make a mess, I'll wash it.* \ *I am giving away my friend in marriage,* \ *My favorite!* A Vitebsk ditty); d) the use of declinable nouns as indeclinable ones (I went on a tour \ and I will ask for a cabin. \ There isn´t a minute to live peacefully on tour– a Vitebsk ditty); e) more frequent use of word-formations referencing the unproductive (addict[111], somber[112], a little porn[113], gangbang[114]); e) the abundance of truncated forms of the vocative in morphology (Banya! Sing!)[115]; f) phonetic idiosyncrasies: although the set of phonemes is the same as in literary language, their implementation is different. There are contractions (вапще vapshe- as opposed to вообще vobshe), loss of consonants (кода koda – когда kogda), тады tadi – тогда togda), etc.

The "third culture" is characterized by a certain massiveness: mass celebrations, festivals, entertainment events. An analysis of Soviet mass spectacles and festivals indicate that they are connected with the carnival traditions of other European countries.

The third culture greatly "blurs" the strict rules inherent in literary language and, as a result, we note the penetration of non-normative language common speech (love to haggle[116], soul is under lock and key – A Vitebsk saying). Literary language has been heavily influenced by the jargon of the criminal class (*атас* warning, *бабки* money, *беспредел* mayhem, *бухарь* drunk, дубарь meathead, кореш buddy, крыша protection i.e. against the police, кусок great, легавый

---

[108] "Vitebsky City Journal"

[109] (*Стало жить невмоготу \ Даже Водолеям...*). *"Водолей"* - watercarrier was declined in the plural *Водолеям*.

[110] Я одела бело платье. Бело, a noun, would normally be белое, an adjective.

[111] Наркота (narcotics addict) slang,

[112] Чернуха (from black, черный and the ending of girl, девушка, ушка) slang.

[113] Порнуха

[114] Групповуха

[115] Short for the folk tradition "don't' sing in the banya."

[116] Торгаша, from торговать to trade or engage in commerce.

nark, лимон one million rubles, мусор cop, наезд shakedown, по жизни actually, разборка shoot out, хаза home); We must admit that today these words are no longer just part of the criminal class.

A feature of the "third culture" is the abundance of nicknames given not only to one another, but to major political figures as well, (The Gypsy – Alexander Lukashenko; Elkin, Garantor, BEN, Benny – Boris Yeltsin; Rusty Tolik, Redhead, Voucher, the Iron Lumberjack – Anatoly Chubais; Stakanych; Emergency Force – Viktor Chernomyrdin; Primus – Yevgeny Primakov; Birch, BAB – Boris Berezovsky; Cap, Kolobok – Yuri Luzhkov, etc. "Arguments and Facts in Belarus", 1999, № 52).

The act of naming starts the creation of language in general and continues to the particular political language of the times. The phenomenon of Soviet era proper names is one example, the new trends seen during the 90's in the Vitebsk region is another, (Wilen, Ville, Vladlen, Vilor, Kim, Cam, Lenmaren, Mylena, Oktiabrina, Revmira, Stalina and so on). Artificial names almost disappeared, but many abbreviated names (Iana from Ianina) and colloquial variations appeared (Arina from Irina, Nastasya from Anastasia) as did English names (Arthur, Michael, Ernest and others).

Social upheavals affected the sphere of spiritual culture, "undermining" the mentality of the people. Now, it has become fashionable to use "semi-language." Even an elderly person might say: It's like I'm in a violet cloud, (indifferent). One student theater in Minsk ran the play "Arnad the Botanic[117]" ('Woe from Wit).

There is no longer a borderline but an abyss between literary language and the language spoken by particular social groups. This situation is very similar to the one so artfully depicted by Victor Pelevin in his novel *Chapaev and Void* (about Nietzsche): "It's so damn gaudily written so that the normal person won't be able to understand, but it's still very clever. Vovchik hired a hungry professor on purpose and gave

---

[117] Botanic is slang for "nerd."

him the lad who thinks for himself. In a month, the two of them improved it so that everyone could read it. They translated it into normal language."

A huge number of foreign words have entered the spoken language, i.e. its Americanization has begun. Now our youth (and others) say: *wild trouble*[118], *golda* (gold chain)[119], *oldovy* [120] old, etc.; The words *stoned* and *cool*[121] have become part of the Russian language.

The language situation is further complicated by the fact that the Belarussian language is influencing spheres that were previously served only by the Russian language – politics, business, and often education. This proliferation has led to strong fluctuations of standards, to the point where the under-educated part of the population has long ceased to understand proper speech: dollar or dolyar, computer or camputar, gorcom or gorcam[122]. This fact gives scholars the right to use the terms *semi-language* or *tryasianka*[123]. Tryasianka has become fashionable among officials and has even penetrated FM-radio station, where entire programs use it.

The most common mistake made by speakers is confusing words that are formally identical or partially overlap but having different semantics: interlanguage homonyms, interlanguage paronyms, Russian-Belarussian parallaxes: сварка - svarka[124] (Rus) and сварка svarka [125](Bel), соучастник [126](Rus) and сучасьнік[127] (Bel), беспечность -

---

[118] дикий трабл - dikij meaning wild, and trabl taken from the English word "trouble."

[119] Golda – taken from the English word "gold."

[120] Олдовый – oldovyj, taken from the English word "old."

[121] *кайф и приколно*

[122] Горка - hill. The dative plural should be горкам.

[123] The everyday language of people in many areas of Belarus, consisting of a mixture of Belarusian and Russian vocabulary.

[124] Welding.

[125] Quarrel

[126] Accomplice

[127] Сучасьнік - modern

bespechnost[128] (Rus) и бяспека - bjaspeka [129](Bel), речь - rech' [130](Rus) и рэч rjech [131](Bel) and so on.

Accordingly, the most important language problem in the region is to increase the use of the Russian and Belarusian languages, clearly differentiating between them when used by speakers of both languages. But this problem can be solved only when a national mentality is formed.

Jargon as a professional subculture.

Even members of elite culture have long had high hopes for technical improvements in our lives, believing technology would free us from physical labor and spiritually liberate us. But it turns out to be the path to our dehumanization. It is precisely the other path that can free us – in the beautiful imagery of folkloric language

Computer use extends to many areas of our lives and its users have created a special professional language. For computer users, there are mens[132] (those who do not use computers), teapots[133] (those who are just beginning to use it), hackers (those who break into computer programs), coders (those who just click the keys) and programmers (those who make programs, the creators of the original product). A very bifurcated language has appeared, which is used to discuss the possibilities of pisyuk, pentyukh, zuhel[134], etc. (PC computers, "Pentium", etc.). The phrase the mother crashed and I barely managed to sell the brains, means the motherboard crashed but I managed to sell the operating system's memory. The expressions to the limit ("to the end")[135], to polish off (meaning "to kill")[136] etc. were derived from professional speech.

---

[128] беспечность - carelessness
[129] Бяспека - security
[130] Speech
[131] Thing
[132] мэны
[133] Чайники – tea pots. The slang meaning is "dummy".
[134] Modem, from the company ZyXEL.
[135] до упора
[136] Мочить

The conflict between the "land" and "hardware", nature and technology, leads to a destruction of the connection between man and nature. The Russian language was first filled with "industrial" vocabulary, and then (at the end of the millennium) with Anglicism, professionalisms, syntax was simplified, the profoundness of phrases and thoughts was gone, i.e. general language simplification took place.

The study of language in the Vitebsk region shows that it is heterogenous, like the culture of the region, and has four interacting linguistic-cultural models. Each language reflects the cultural realities of the society in which the language functions while serving the needs of culture.

According to the sociolinguist Leonid Krysin[137], most modern industrial societies are not characterized by rigid differentiation of language in a fairly self-contained subsystem. This view is confirmed by a linguistic-cultural analysis of the Vitebsk region, where socially and culturally conditioned variants of one language coexist with each other, serving communication needs in different areas.

At the turn of the millennium, the Vitebsk region is a multinational region with a predominantly Belarusian population and wide use of the Russian language in official communications, education and record-keeping. However, in mass communications and domestic relations, the Belarusian language is becoming more widespread.

Linguistic-Cultural Aspect of Russian Phraseology

Phraseological units, reflecting within their semantics the long process of cultural development of a people, record and transmit cultural attitudes and stereotypes, models and archetypes, from generation to generation. Idioms, according to Fyodor Buslaev, are a kind of a microcosm; they contain "both moral law and common sense, expressed in short

---

[137] Specialist in lexicology, semantics, stylistics, lexicography, sociolinguistics. Deputy Director of educational projects, head of the Department of Modern Russian Language at the Russian Academy of Sciences. Author of "The Russian Word, Us and Them."

sayings bequeathed by ancestors for the guidance of their descendants."[138] They are the soul of every national language, in which the spirit and identity of the nation are uniquely expressed.

When considering Russian phraseology, we put forward the following hypotheses.

1. Most phraseological units contain "traces" of national culture that must be identified.

2. Cultural information is stored within the internal form of phraseological units. It is a figurative view of the world and provides phraseological units with a cultural and national quality.

3. The most important thing when identifying cultural and national specificity is to reveal cultural and national connotations.

Phraseology is a fragment of the language picture of the world. Phraseological units always focus on the subject, i.e., they are there not so much to describe the world, but to interpret it, to evaluate and express subjective attitude towards it. This is what distinguishes phraseological units and metaphors from other nominative units.

Since humans are strongly influenced by common generic features, idioms should be common to all mankind and universal, but not cultural and national. In fact, the opposite is true. Some scholars are even inclined to say that, for example, idioms are endowed with a certain cultural and national specificity. Is this true? It seems that this does not apply to all phraseologies, because if the meanings of all phraseological units were culturally specific it would be impossible to study their cultural differences.

Veronica Teliya writes that the phraseological makeup of a language is "a mirror where the linguistic-cultural community identifies its national consciousness." It is precisely phraseologies that imposes a particular vision of the

---

[138] F.I. Buslaev Russian proverbs and sayings collected and explained. Moscow, 1954. - p. (Author's footnote).

world on the native speakers. For example, information about the everyday life of Russian people (red corner[139], rub elbows[140]), about behavior etiquette (to walk before you can crawl[141]– as sure as death[142], empty-handed[143], to come cap in hand), about traditions and customs (without intermediaries[144], to expose[145]), etc.

The internal forms of most idioms contain meanings that give them a cultural and national quality. For example, the phraseology "сбоку припеку"[146] - a fifth wheel (something unnecessary, optional) originated from a prototypical (real) situation of baking bread, when dough that cannot be eaten comes out for the side of a loaf. The semantics of such phraseology can be interpreted from the standpoint of attitudes and stereotypes inherent to the mindset of a nation, i.e. in terms of the national culture. The fact that the dough is separated from the main loaf is bad; moreover, it cannot be used as food, because it burns and crusts; therefore, side growths on a loaf are not needed.

One should keep in mind that different types of phraseological units reflect culture in different ways, as has often been pointed out by Veronica Teliya.

It is easiest to understand and explain cultural elements of phraseologies if denotations play an important role in their meaning. For example, let us analyze phraseological units where the names of cultural objects are included in one or more components: щи лаптем хлебать - *gulp down cabbage soup with a bast shoe* (about a very simple person), как с писаной торбой носиться[147] - (to give too much attention).

---

[139] Icon corner. A small worship space prepared in Eastern Orthodox homes.
[140] печки-лавочки.
[141] садиться не в свои сани – literally, to get into someone else's sled.
[142] как пить дать – literally, like giving water. The expression originally meant that a person will surely die from poison as soon as any drink is accepted.
[143] несолоно хлебавши.
[144] из полы в полу, literally from one hand to another. Selling a horse to another without intermediaries.
[145] вывести на чистую воду, literally – to put somebody in clean water.
[146] Literally, baked on the sides.
[147] Literally, to treat someone like a painted feedbag.

The vocabulary of these idioms contains an indication of the material culture – cabbage soup (shchi), bast shoe (лапоть), feedbag (торба). Their meaning and negative connotation is partly formed due to the meanings of these lexical terms. For example, cabbage soup is very simple food for common people; simple shoes, bast shoes, are used instead of a spoon. Bast shoes are unworthy for eating, hence the negative connotation; feedbag is a type of bag previously used by beggars and other common people. It is not a thing of valuable, because even if it's ornamented, it is still just a feedbag. Therefore, those who wear them are subjected to disapproval. This may also include idioms, which reflect the history of the people, national proper names – Mamay's battle[148], a mile marker to Kolomenskoye[149], orphan from Kazan[150], like a Swede at Poltava [151], to show Kuzka's mother[152]. These contain cross-cultural information and their understanding relates to specific historical facts.

It is rather simple to explain phraseological units like "pansy"[153]. Their original definitions do not come into play, because it detracts from a current understanding. But the question remains, who or what is a pansy? And for this reason, the original definition is the only the way to identify "a specific definition." Cultural information in such idioms is closely related to the parameter of denotation and it is the denotation (pansy) which is the carrier of cultural information here.

---

[148] мамаево побоище, In English, it is more commonly known as the Battle of Kulikovo.

[149] Refers to a tall person, a bean pole.

[150] poor soul (thing) (a person pretending to be poorer (humbler) than he/she is); whimperer; whiner; moaner.

[151] как швед под Полтавой - one who was or is about to be destroyed or ruined; in a hopeless, disastrous situation. Refers to the 1709 battle at Poltava, in which Russian troops won a decisive victory over the Swedes.

[152] показать кузькину мать, to give someone hell.

[153] анютины глазки, literally Anna's eyes. In Russian, it is one of the names for the Viola flower. In English, it is also known as a "pansy" or as "love in idleness." The term is found in Roman mythology and in many of Shakespeare's plays.

However, in mass culture, the majority of phraseological information is connected to other things, primarily to figurative and emotive idioms where the original image is extremely important. To understand what part of these phraseological units carries cultural information, let us look at how these idioms are formed in general.

Initially, a certain prototypical situation appears in the world, i.e., a situation corresponding to the literal meaning of an idiom; for example, a man slipped and sat on his galoshes. Meaning is attached to this, which is then rethought, i.e. the idea of an idiom is formed based on the original meanings of words in the prototype situation. These original words leave their trace in the image. In this way, an internal form (IF) appears, which contains basic information related to the culture. Cultural information can be obtained from the IF of an idiom, because there are "traces" of culture in it - myths, archetypes, customs and traditions, reflected historical events and elements of material culture.

Thus, the very formation of the phraseological unit, which starts with the selection of the image, is connected to cultural-national stereotypes and standards. This information is then resurrected as connotations, which reflect the associations between the original image and culture (standards, symbols, stereotypes). Naturally, these idioms are the most interesting for us in terms of identifying national cultural specificity, because they have cultural origins or culturally significant implications.

Idioms depicting typical situations and ideas begin to play the role of symbols, standards and stereotypes of culture (for example, to wash dirty linen in public[154] meaning "to disclose information about some troubles related to a small community of people").

However, not all idioms can incorporate cultural and national information. Slavic languages have many idioms that relate to the universal knowledge of real properties included in the original meaning – get to the root of something; between

---

[154] выносить сор из избы - literally, to take the argument out of the hut.

the devil and the deep blue sea[155]; keep your chin up[156], and others. The fact that the idioms of other languages are different can be explained not so much by cultural uniqueness but by a mismatch in the secondary nominations in different languages. Consider the Chinese expressions, *flowing water does not rot* (referring to useless, purposeless actions) and, *the worm does not grow on the door hinge* (meaning hope for a successful outcome, confidence in it). In Russian this might be, *one needs it as much as a dead man needs a poultice*, and *as simple as ABC, a mosquito hasn't touched the nose*[157]. There is a different figurative base in the Russian linguistic consciousness.

These idioms are based on figurative-metaphorical ideas and, therefore, play a role in the formation of the language picture of the world that varies based on culture and nationality. Hence the conclusion that, with some reservations, they can be considered carriers of cultural information.

General human knowledge about the world can also be found in idioms. They unfasten language, tie it hand and foot into semantical knots, having a magical effect, i.e. national culture is revealed through connections with mythology, which is also quite general, at least for the Slavic people.

For us, the phraseological units of greatest interest are the ones where national culture is reflected through its connection with cultural and nationalistic connotations, models, symbols and stereotypes. Examples include: *to suck the blood out*[158] or *to fight to the last drop of blood*. Here, blood is a symbol of vitality. In the idiom *native blood*, blood is a symbol of kinship, etc.

According to the data we collected, many phraseological units relate to mythologems and archetypes; for example: *like looking into a crystal ball*[159], *like in a mirror*.

---

[155] между двух огней – literally, between two fires.
[156] не вешать нос – literally, not drop your nose.
[157] комар носу не подточит – hard to find fault with.
[158] пить кровь – literally, to drink blood.
[159] как в воду глядел – literally, like looking into water.

For Slavs, a mirror is the borderline between the earthly and the other world; therefore, its function is similar to other borders: a boundary, a threshold, a window, a well, etc.

The mirror as an actual item appeared after its deeply archaic semantics and symbolism.[160] A mirror is a dangerous thing, forbidden, created by the devil, a means of contacting him. Brides wearing a wedding dress cannot look in the mirror, nor can pregnant women or newborns, because they are in transition from one world to another. Mirrors are covered up during burial rituals, allegedly to prevent the dead from coming through the mirror from the other world.

The world behind the mirror is an inverted world of the living. Fortune-telling with the help of a mirror was popular because a mirror supposedly reflects the visible world, as well as the invisible world, and even the other world. A mirror is like *a window into the other world.* According to Slavic belief, you cannot look into a mirror at night, because the night is a time of dark unholy forces. A person is particularly vulnerable at night.

Looking into the mirror for a long time is harmful; it can abduct parts of the human soul, sending it to the world behind the looking glass, where the soul dies. A mirror is like a clone of the person who is reflected in it. This is why people believe that breaking the mirror causes trouble, because the copy of ourselves within it breaks as well.

Contemporary psychics recommend washing and wiping mirrors frequently, because they collect all the information from the outside world, including negative things, and therefore they can become a storage of negative information, which can provoke a person to do take inappropriate actions and create dark moods.

Accordingly, the mirror is 1) a way to contact the devil; 2) a communication channel with the other world; 3) a means of closing the borders of the world; 4) a means to

---

[160] See S.M. Tolstaya The Mirror in Traditional Slavic Beliefs and Rites // Slavic and Balkan folklore. - Moscow, 1994. - p. 111.
(Author's footnote).

reflect the unseen other world; 5) able to steal the human soul, making the person empty and soulless; 6) a storage of information about the world; 7) our clone.

The symbolism of the mirror is also found in the number "two", in the concept of parity and pairing. The Belarussian expression "two pock marks", meaning "both are equally bad", forms the negative connotation by using the word "two (both)" and the word "pock marked" - "changeable, fickle, false." Many restrictions are motivated by the danger of doubling, repetition of actions.

The idea of a doppelgänger is most clearly expressed in myths. It was believed that the number 1 was something whole, unified and perfect, the peace of the Absolute and nonliving. This could only be God and the Cosmos. The number 2 is the beginning of the creative act, the separation and pushing away of one from the other, withdrawing from non-life, not forgetting about the abandoned perfection.

In Plato's "Symposium", Aristophanes speaks about the first people. They were round, four-legged and four-handed, until Zeus cut them like an egg is cut by a hair. The two halves have been seeking to find each other since then, love and marriage being an attempt to return the former unity, i.e. to the recovery of human nature. Love is not about reproduction; it is of spiritual and religious significance. Love is a unique way of improving oneself, a path towards immortality. According to the writings of Vladimir Soloviev, and continued by Blok, life is a search for your other half, souls are doomed to eternally search for one another: "The soul is silent . . . And, being anointed in silence, struggles relentlessly to catch the distant call of another soul" Vladimir Soloviev.

The birth of twins always aroused fear in ancient people, mixed with reverence: twins were considered a symbol of fertility. Twins were considered rivals and allies; one was associated with good, nice things, and the other one - with bad, imperfect, sly things; it was the balance of good and evil, light and darkness. It was implied that twins and their mother

116

had come into contact with supernatural powers and became its bearers. Sometimes they were either separated from their tribe or killed; people were afraid of the doubling effect, a phenomenon which was not understood.

The idiom *to call somebody to the carpet means* that a subordinate is being called for censure at the superior's office. The term *carpet* creates a vivid imagery. The idiom is simultaneously a localization of the situation and a marker of national culture: a carpet in the office of the big boss is a sign of Russian (half-Oriental) culture.

Thus, most features associated with cultural and national standards, stereotypes and mythologems attach onto language and become idioms. This is precisely what forms the meaning of the idiom. Looking in a mirror means seen very clearly (its meaning is based on the mythologem "reflects the invisible, and even the other world"). And in the process, idioms themselves become cultural stereotypes. The clarification of national and cultural identity in phraseology is closely linked with the problems of human awareness of the world ("living" in historical memory), an awareness is reflected in the language.

A mythologem is what a people have forgotten but kept in the hidden depths of words and consciousness. Mythologems may not fully controls the semantics of idioms, but they surely direct and adjust its actual usage. This begs the question about whether language is a storage of culture? Despite the cumulative function, i.e. accumulation and storage of information, language does not become a storage of culture. A unit of language, the word, is just a signal whose function is to awaken human consciousness, to evoke certain concepts that are ready to respond to this signal (Alexander Potebnja, Lev Shcherba, Alexander Luria, Alexey Leontiev).

Language is only a mechanism that facilitates the encoding and transmission of culture. The true storage of culture is text. Not language, but text reflects the spiritual world of a person. It is text that is directly connected with culture: it is penetrated by a multitude of cultural codes. Text stores information about history, ethnography, national psychology, national behavior, i.e. about everything that constitutes culture.

Text is a set of specific signals that automatically cause the reader, brought up in the traditions of the culture, to not just feel the immediate associations, but to many circumstantial ones as well. It therefore follows that the rules of textual construction depend on the cultural context where it occurs. Text is created from the lower levels of linguistic units which, if appropriately chosen, can enhance the cultural signal. Idioms are precisely such units.

From our point of view, every idiom is text, i.e. it stores cultural information. But if we hear a phrase like "language remembers and keeps secrets . . .", we should understand that it is nothing more than a metaphor. Phraseological components of language do not just replicate the elements and characteristics of cultural and national worldviews but forms them as well. Every idiom, if it contains cultural connotation, contributes to the overall mosaic picture of national culture.

Idioms directly (in denotation) or indirectly (through the correlation of an associative figurative base with the standards, symbols or stereotypes of national culture) contain cultural information about the world and society. Therefore, an idiom is like a nation's *well of wisdom,* preserving and reproducing its mindset and culture from generation to generation.

The Metaphor as a Representation of Culture

The meanings contained in idioms and metaphors, as well as the cultural connotations attached to them, become knowledge themselves, i.e. a source of cognitive assimilation. This is precisely how idioms and figurative expressions (metaphors) become exponents of cultural symbols. We will examine the metaphor from this perspective.

The metaphor is now understood as a more complex and important phenomenon than previously imagined. It permeates language, culture, science, life and the entire world.

It has been shown that metaphors are universals of consciousness. Modern psychologists are inclined to associate a metaphorical vision of the world with the genesis of human beings and, accordingly, with human culture. Most likely, protolanguage was metaphorical, and proto-communication itself was carried out on a metaphorical level.

Metaphors are a universal linguistic phenomenon, inherent in all languages. Its universality is manifested in space and time, in the structure and operation of language. Many linguists even claim that all languages are merely a graveyard of metaphors. The metaphor is a productive concept for science. Mikhail Bakhtin noted that he introduced the scientific term "chronotope" as "a metaphor." Many of the most successful scientific terms are metaphors: "internal history of a language", "cultural connotation", "Aqua vitae" and so on.

Metaphors are one of the most mysterious phenomena of language. Despite the various definitions of a metaphor almost all of them date back to Aristotle: " "Metaphor consists in giving the thing a name that belongs to something else; the transference being either from genus to species, or from species to genus, or from species to species, or on grounds of analogy."[161]

Although issues related to the metaphor have been stimulating the intellect for the past two thousand years, it is often regarded as either a stylistic tool or as an artistic technique. Only in the last decades has the attention of linguists and philosophers shifted to the study of the ontology of metaphors (Nina Ariutunova, Veronica Teliya, B. Black, George Lakoff, Mark Johnson and others).

Most of contemporary work dealing with the study of metaphors deals with the cognitive role metaphors play in the formation of meaning: "you are last century's aging crop" Evgeny Onegin", a massive cloud of air stood before me (Anna Akhmatova); century-wolfhound, a deep swoon of lilac and sonorous steps of color (Osip Mandelstam); She had imagination - the muscle of the soul (Vladimir Nabokov).

---

[161] Aristotle. Poetics. - Leningrad, 1927. - p. 39. (Author's footnote).

According to Marvin Minsky, a connection of two concepts in speech or thought occurs during the displacement of one frame or scenario (range of concepts) by other meanings, for a metaphor functions as a name for something that has no name. A second point of view is that metaphors synthesize "fields of images", "a spiritual act of analogy where two semantic regions mutually bond" (Veronica Teliya).

Metaphor embraces the world and humanity:
"Shine on the sad crop, lantern of today's sadness, shrug your shoulders in the dark and grieve for all" Joseph Brodsky.
The birth of the metaphor is coupled with the conceptual system of the native speaker, with his/her standard conceptions of the world, with a system of valuation that exists in the world itself and is only verbalized in language. Hence the conclusion: a metaphor is a model for conveying knowledge, a model for hypothesis.

The mechanism for creating a metaphor is to take two different objects from different logical classes and match them based on common characteristics and properties; for example, a dark sorrow (the feeling is sorrow and the state of the world is dark – darkness is common to both. Joy is bright, but sorrow and sadness are dark and gloomy).

A metaphor is formed from a categorical, taxonomical (classification) error. It is as if the person creating a metaphor (usually a poet), lives in a world of qualities and properties, logical classes and their substitutions. This person is in a field of holistic meaning and in the events that created this meaning. According to Nina Ariutunova, a metaphor does not reveal abstract signs or qualities; it reveals the semantic image of the very essence of the object. When Osip Mandelstam calls the piano "a wise, kind indoor beast, he is not just taking items from different logical classes. The point here is not about real objects, but about images of objects manifested in consciousness. This is how the essence of the whole is created.

Charles Bally wrote: "We compare abstract understandings to tangible world objects because for us it is the only way to get to know and share them with others. This is the origin of metaphors: a metaphor is no more than a comparison, where the mind's tendency of bringing together abstract concepts and concrete objects combines them into one word."[162]

Why does a person compare feelings to a fire? Expressions like *the flame of love, a warm heart, the fire of desire, burning with love, hot love, burning hatred, the flames of passion, a warm friendship, a flicker of hope, to have warm feelings*. These images are widespread throughout Russian poetry: Where is the sultry heat of desire? (Innokenty Annensky); and insomnia's melting fire... And the blue fire of my eyes (Anna Akhmatova); Oh, reason how you've burned \ (Alexander Blok).

Why is the back thought of as protection? (to have one's back means to provide protection, broad shoulders - reliable protection, "sponge"[163] – a kept person, living at somebody else's expense). Such metaphors can be called kernels, i.e. they develop in language according to images having encyclopedic, cultural, national or purely personal information.

In creating their theory of metaphors, George Lakoff and Mark Johnson noted: "metaphor is pervasive in everyday lives, not just in language, but in thought and action. "Our ordinary conceptual system, in terms of which we both think and act, is fundamentally metaphorical in nature."[164]. According to their theory, people use metaphors to more accurately implement in their minds an "abstract" concept – both existing and nonexistent. Scientists call the metaphor a basic sense for understanding the world, a means of processing the reality. Metaphors are a powerful means of perceiving; a new concept is understood through comparisons with the known. The mechanisms of analogy are introduced through the principle of fictitiousness. The metaphor "starts" from this principle, it lives there and dies there if it is no longer felt in the internal form of the denomination" (Veronica Teliya).

---

[162] Charles Bally, French Stylistics. - Moscow, 1961. - p. 221. (Author's Citation).
[163] Захребетник, someone who stands behind the back of others.
[164] G. Lakoff, M. Johnson Metaphors We Live By. - Chicago; L .; 1980. - P. 3. (Author's citation).

Olga Freydenberg wrote about the appearance of metaphors: "Figurative meaning! Who could have thought up such semantic obstacle, if it was not in human consciousness due to objective epistemological laws." There are other views about the emergence of metaphors. According to Max Muller, metaphor appeared as a result of the lexical poverty of the ancient language. Vocabulary was limited, and humans had to use one and the same word to describe different objects and phenomena. According to Alexander Afanasyev and Alexander Potebnja metaphors did to appear because of need or the poverty of language. Metaphors arose due to an affinity between objects that produce similar impressions. They appeared spontaneously, drawing from a rich source.

Hence, a metaphor is a way of thinking about the world. Metaphors use previously acquired knowledge to obtain new knowledge, derived from some still unclear, not "thought out" concept. A new concept is formed by using the initial meaning of the word together with its numerous accompanying associations. The metaphor is also interesting because, after creating new understanding, it contrasts the different entities through the individual, measuring the world on a human scale of knowledge and understanding, and through a system of cultural and national values. As previously stated, man is the measure of all things: a whispering brook, speak your conscience, awakening hope, etc.

Thus, metaphors are anthropometric by nature, and the ability to think metaphorically itself belongs to homo sapiens only, which means that the comprehension of metaphors is, in some measure, our comprehension of ourselves. It is metaphor that makes the abstract easier to perceive and understand (metaphor's basic path is from the concrete to the abstract, from the material to the spiritual).

The metaphor has the following key characteristics: it is an instrument of thought and cognition; it reflects fundamental cultural values, because it is based on cultural and national worldviews. According to Veronica Teliya, metaphors act as an effective prism through which people see the world, since they manifest through national specific patterns in the internal form of language, mythologems, archetypes, etc. Many foreign and Russian researchers are "focusing" on figurative and conceptual metaphors (Nina Ariutunova, Veronica Teliya, Elena Oparina, Michael Apter, D. Center and others).

Scientists are intrigued by the ability of metaphors to express ideas, distant from the direct meaning of the linguistic symbol. In February 1978, a special symposium in Chicago was devoted to this topic, "The metaphor: a conceptual leap." The Metaphor has other mysteries: it slips away from reality, as if hiding from thought. Here, the deeper more critical role of metaphors in cognition emerges. We need metaphors not just for naming and expressing our thoughts - no, we need it for ourselves. It is impossible to think about particularly difficult subjects without metaphors. It is not only a means of expression, but one of the principle methods of cognition. Metaphors convey ideas that are beyond the threshold of purely logical understanding, formulating a method to understand them.

We believe that studying poetic and figurative speech will help unravel the mysteries of the metaphor, for it is in poetic texts where the creative function of language is most clearly manifested. Figurative metaphors, which we also call poetic, are found in literary texts and realize its creative and figurative potential.

For example, the following metaphors are characteristic of European poetry: May subdued winter, bringing to the forest its summer clothes; day is the son of night, forever circling the world in a chariot; damnation hovers in space, until attacking its victim, etc. The metaphor of a bird's soul is inherent to Russian poetry: "There I go, and somewhere you are flying, I live there, and somewhere you are screeching and excitedly beating your wings." Joseph Brodsky

The metaphors in the above given examples are not literary decorations, but a natural expression of thought and cognition. Even the Italian political philosopher Giambattista Vico emphasized that the metaphor, as the language of myth, is a knot that binds language with thought and culture.

The metaphor is the principle way new concepts are created in the modern Russian's language picture of the world. When communist censors heard the scholars of Aesop's language, they declared that it was sheer metaphorization, the emergence of a kind of "winking" language. And even now metaphors are created in abundance: *out of the barracks democratic socialism,*
Stalinist dinosaurs, bloody bacchanalia, super-power conceit. Metaphors appear not only in the socio-political field, but also in everyday life: *belted with a crowbar*[165] (about a strange man), *a stub of happiness*[166] (about a young, hapless, inept person), to sculpt a humpback[167], to take the Netherlands[168] (to lie).

Metaphors are the basis for neologisms and proverbs (*Living Speech. Dictionary of Colloquial Expressions*, Valerie Belyanin): a *flying stumble*[169] (about a drunken gait), *to move the furniture* (to make love*), that is not the stump* (it is not the point), don't smell like fish (shut up), the world is small and the layer is thin[170] (about unexpectedly discovered connections), spit in my ear[171] (about strange hairstyle), etc.

"Winking" metaphorical language has filled all socio-linguistic space, including fiction.
We are not interested in the metaphor in and of itself, but its role in culture, or, more precisely, in the creation of image (in poetry and prose). Let us examine this function.

We cite several examples from contemporary Russian writers of the twentieth century: Galina Shcherbakova, Lyudmila Ulitskaya, Mark Kharitonov and others.

"... She was shoved into the raspberries, where some other aunties were nesting" (Galina Scherbakova. *Mitin's Love*). The isolated use of the word "nest" is neutral.

---

[165] ломом опоясанный – 1 a man though as flint, strong-willed 2. Criminal, unbending, has his/her own opinion, lives his/her own principles
[166] огрызок счастья
[167] лепить горбатого
[168] нести голландию
[169] летучий спотыкач – спотыкач (spotikach) is also an alcoholic beverage made from berries.
[170] мир тесен, а прослойка тонка
[171] плюнь мне в ухо.

However, given its context, it acquires an additional emotional and evaluative tone, that women ("aunties") were apparently already gathering raspberries and jealously guarding them. This metaphor appears as a comparison to the way a bird guards its nest. And the use of a word with reduced stylistic nuance (aunties) provides an ironic tone to the statement as a whole.

"Oh, poor Sonechka, her bright youth, spent in the highlands of world literature! Oh, oh! - fiction, only fiction... was read by her humanitarian-innocent daughter" (Ludmila Ulitskaya. Sonechka). The entire metaphoric context here is based on situational metonymy: the highlands are inaccessible, sitting on high – the highlands of world literature are something inaccessible, high, inaccessible to most. *Humanitarian-innocent daughter*: innocent means pure, unadulterated (here, meaning a lack of knowledge), innocent in the field of the humanities - not having any knowledge about the humanities. Thus, the metaphors here are based on features, motivated by extra-linguistic, social reality.

"Robert Viktorovich smiled, flashing the dual steel of his eyes and teeth." (Ludmila Ulitskaya, Sonechka). Here, the eyes are metal, i.e. a cold and colorless + the material that the crowns on the teeth are made of.

"Ice pellets swished in the rough wind, filling it with a dry rash" (Mark Kharitonov). The chain of semantics shifts within the framework of this micro-text, creating a metaphorical shift: snow, consisting of pellets becomes ice pellets, and then a dry rash: pellets - dry – rash – dry rash.[172]

Double meanings of the same realities are inherent to poetic texts; there is the direct and the metaphoric meaning: Two forget-me-nots, two sapphires – Her eyes' welcoming glance (Afanasy Fet); The pine was stung by a bright serpent (Afanasy Fet). The duality of naming determines the dual nature of the semantic connection, derived initially from literal meaning and then from metaphor, ultimately, doubling the semantic depth of the poetic text. If in the previous example a

---

[172] Сыпь means rash. There is a play on word here with the word сыпать, which means to rain or to pour.

bright snake means bright lightning, stung by a bright serpent becomes a multi-faceted image.

A metaphor tries to impose its will not only on the verse, but on the entire poetic text. For example, the metaphor "a lizard of inspiration" plays a key role in the poem by Evgeny Vinokurov "Inspiration", and almost the other language in the poem merely "works" the metaphor, developing and supplementing the image:

No, not proud! . .
She seems plain and simple:
A lizard of inspiration
Slips away, leaving her tail...
to take daily strolls again
looking forward to seeing you -
To – slippery, and nimbly –
sneak up again.

Metaphor may combine with other types of tropes, complicating and intensifying the effect produced. Most often, it is superimposed on comparisons: yonder the moon, like a clown . . . making faces at me... (Alexander Blok) – a moon making faces = the moon is a clown. But, a metaphor may be combined with a paraphrase, an oxymoron or other tropes: The moon, lonesome rider, let the reins fall (Sergey Yesenin); the delicate ice of a stranger's hand (Osip Mandelshtam); the sky sows shallow drizzle (Anna Akhmatova), etc.

There are lasting poetic metaphors, symbols and images in text, however, as a rule, we see the numerous variations of the authors. At times, metaphors are close to the lasting traditional ones, but at other times, they are so far as to be almost unrecognizable. Lasting metaphors include: all world is a stage, the world is a book, the world is a temple, love is a fire, time is a river, a family branch, and others. Their variations include: I wrote the words of the river's surge (Velimir Khlebnikov) – this is based on the metaphor *the world is a book*; gentle branching legs (Maximilian Voloshin) - the original metaphor is a family branch; To the open temple of the earth, heavens and seas \ I come again, pleading and yearning (Ivan Bunin) - the original metaphor here is the world as a temple.

In time, metaphors lose their aesthetic value; their freshness and surprise "wear off" – *a table leg, a bottleneck,* etc. And then such metaphors are no longer used to create imagery; new bright, personalized images appear instead, in an endless process.

Bright metaphors, individualized by their authors, are of value because they host a great number of diffuse and changing and associations.

This semantical vocabulary creates a metaphorical context in the mind of the reader. From this vocabulary, purely subjective additional associations arise that are linked to a particular perception, psychological makeup or intellect.

The use of apparently similar metaphors, but in different texts, creates different types of texts, which can be classified according to their use of the metaphor: poetic texts (but few remain in Russian poetry), words with direct meaning using rare metaphors (for example the famous "I remember a wonderful moment ..."[173]); in other text, by contrast, metaphors use few words with direct meaning.   and among them there are rare inclusions of words in the literal sense (many poems by Boris Pasternak, Boris Grebenshchikov and others). The rest of poetic text is found between these two examples.

Poetic metaphor needs no interpretation. It would destroy the poetry. The cultural-national personality understands the poetic metaphor because its mechanisms are universal. But every metaphor of this kind is a poetic discovery in which the world appears from an unexpected position, from an aesthetic perspective.

For these reasons, the metaphor in now understood as a more complex and important phenomenon than previously realized.

The Symbol as a Stereotyped Cultural Phenomenon

---

[173] Tittle of poem by Pushkin.

Among the many human needs, there is one that distinguishes humans from animals – the for symbolization. Humans live not only in a physical environment, but in a symbolic universe as well. The world of the senses in which humans lived at the dawn of history was defined by rituals. Rituals acted as symbols, a knowledge that determined a person's level of cultural mastery and social importance. So, from the very beginning, from the moment humans first appeared to now, symbols have not existed on their own, but as the product of human consciousness. People, as a microcosm, create an image, a picture, a symbol of the macrocosm - the world.

The ties between people are closely linked to the word "symbol." Initially, this Greek word denoted a pot, a sign of friendship. A host would hand departing guest a piece of broken pottery and kept another piece. No matter when this guest returned to this house, he would have been recognized by the broken pottery. The original ancient understanding of the word "symbol" was as an "identity card."

The interest in symbol is great not only in linguistics, but in philosophy, semiotics, psychology, literary studies, myth-poetics, folklore, cultural studies and others. We are in absolutely agreement with Alexander Potebnja's understanding that only in terms of language is it possible to arrange symbols in a way that corresponds to a people's views and not to the arbitrariness of the writer. A result of this interest has been a rather independent understanding of symbols: 1) a symbol is a concept, identical to a sign (in artificial languages); 2) a universal category that reflects the details of how art has assimilated a specific image (in the aesthetics and philosophy of art); 3) a cultural object having conventional meaning (i.e., it can be found in dictionaries) that is analogous to its meaning in another subject (in cultural studies, sociology, and a number of other humanities); 4) a symbol as a sign that uses its original understanding as a basis for further understanding (the broad understanding of symbol existing in much of the humanities - philosophy, linguistics, semiotics, etc.). Immanuel Kant, Friedrich Shelling, Georg

Hegel and Johan Goethe all spoke about the symbol as a way of knowing the true divine essence.

For our purposes, the most interesting views about symbols, which will be discussed in more detail later, are those found in the philosophy of language (Aleksei Losev, Elena Shelestyuk[174])

.

A number of dictionaries have been published based on the interdisciplinary works of linguists, historians, archaeologists, art historians, musicologists, psychologists, theologians, folklorists and other study areas (Jose Cirlot *A Dictionary of Symbols*, Moscow, 1994; Vasily Bauer[175], Irmtraud Dyumotts, Sergius Golovin, *Encyclopedia of Symbols*, Moscow, 1995; Hans Biedermann *Encyclopedia of Symbols* - Moscow, 1996; Jose Cirlot *A Dictionary of Symbols*. 2nd edition – New York, 1971; Hans Biedermann Knaurs *Lexikon der Symbole*. - Munich, 1989; *An Illustrated Encyclopedia of Traditional Symbols,* Leipzig, 1986, and others). Today there are numerous institutes and centers where various aspects of the symbol are studied: Warburg Institute in London, study of icons; C.G. Jung Institute in Zurich; Ludwig Kayser Institute of Basel, etc.

Our interest in symbols focuses on culture; from this perspective, the symbol can be categorized as a stereotypical phenomenon, characteristic for any culture. The context of symbols encoded in various cultures has different meanings in each of them. We will examine literary symbols of East Slavic cultures. Therefore, we will rely on the fourth understanding of the symbol – the symbol as a sign, where the original content is the basis for a new one.

To understand the symbol, it is essential to understand its cultural content. Aleksei Losev wrote that the symbol includes the principle that stored semantic content continues to develop, i.e. the symbol can be viewed as a specific element that encodes socio-cultural information and, simultaneously,

---

[174] Professor at Chelyabinsk State University, Department of the Theory of Language. Author of several books including, "Impact of Speech" ("Речевое воздействие" published in Russian only).
[175] Vasily Bauer December 1833 – November 1884, Dean of Historical-philological faculty at St. Petersburg University (1880-1882).

acts as a mechanism for its transmission. Yuri Lotman also emphasized these properties in symbols; he noted that, on the one hand, culture was defined by a certain amount of inherited text and, on the one hand, a certain amount of inherited symbols.

The term "symbol" does not mean the same thing to literary scholars that it does to linguists. Yuri Stepanov, for example, claims that the understanding of symbol is not a scientific concept; it is a poetic concept whose genuine meaning always occurs within the limits of a particular poetic system. And, there are many such symbols: Gogol's road, Chekhov's garden, Lermontov's desert, Tyutchev's smoke, the use of the blizzard by Pushkin and the Symbolists, the use of a wing and of a house by Marina Tsvetaeva, the use of borders and threshold as symbols. Yuri Lotman called these symbols "gene-plots."

Additionally, there are language symbols that are created during the evolution and operation of language. These symbols are of a mythological or, more precisely, an archetypal nature. For Russian the rainbow is a symbol of hope, wellbeing and dreams, i.e., it has a very positive meaning; hence the expressions: *rainbow colored dreams, rainbow mood, rainbow hopes,* etc. This symbol dates to the Bible. After the flood, God gave the people a rainbow, promising that the flood would not reoccur.

These metaphors, influenced by cultural connotations, become symbols. Furthermore, these metaphors frequently combine to create symbols.

In the "Encyclopedic Dictionary of Literature" (Moscow, 1987, p. 378), Sergey Averintsev provides the following definition: "the symbol in art is a universal aesthetic category, revealed through comparisons to related categories: artistic imagery is contrasted with the allegorical." The "Updated Philosophical Dictionary" (ed. L. Rodionova, Moscow, 1999) provides the following rather broad definition of a symbol: "a concept with the ability of recording material items, events and sensual images, and of expressing the ideal content rather than their direct sensory and physical properties."

130

Leaving aside the discussion about the essence of a symbol, it should be noted that the role of a linguistic symbol is to replace the meaning of a linguistic essence and turn it into a symbol. A symbol is a kind of conglomerate of equivalent meanings, and this makes it different from other tropes. The literal meaning of symbol is abstract: an abstract idea is encoded in a concrete content in order to express the abstract, but the concrete is encoded by the abstract as well, showing its ideal, abstract sense. The meanings of the abstract and the concrete are both enriched: the sun is a symbol of gold, but gold is a symbol of the sun. Their unity produces a new amalgamated essence.

The word-symbol is a type of "data bank", which can be imagined as a spiral, i.e., circles seemingly hidden within one another and passing through one another. The symbol's semantic spiral includes a wide range of meanings, starting from the implicit ones (hidden, potential), i.e., those which are not explicit, but which are an integral part, becoming semantic substitutes (alternates), i.e. the programmed replacement of one meaning for another. For example, Belarusians say: "What's red is good, what's licorice is savory", in other words, the symbolic meanings of sweet are good, tasty, love, happiness. The same applies to death and the symbols of evil: a snake, a wasp, a prickly plant, things that sting and burn; for the Slavs, fire is the symbol of anger and malice. The sun is a symbol of beauty, love, joy. Alexander Potebnja believes that the word «хорошъ» (good) is the possessive form of the archaic word «хръсъ»[176] (the sun).

Yuri Lotman wrote that the most common understanding of a symbol is associated with the content that is the basis for expressing another, usually more valuable, cultural content. Therefore, the substantive base (carrier) of the recreated meaning is founded not only on the tangible reality, but on the intangible name. For instance, in the expressions *right hand*, and *a cross to bear*, the words *hand* and *cross* are symbolic. The word hand signifies power and the cross signifies a sacrifice uniting heaven and earth; the

---

[176] The pagan god of the Slavs.

spiritual height of cross is vertical, the material world is horizontal; crossing oneself during prayer signifies agreement with Christ, i.e. a symbol of the Christian faith. Perhaps one should not search for the exact meaning of a symbol. One should focus on readily available perceptions and general meanings (conventional), and on the intersection of meanings in a symbol. For example, a dove is a symbol of the Holy Spirit, a symbol of peace, but also a symbol of the other world (They are ravens in Marina Tsvetaeva's "Alleys"). Thus, the most significant feature of symbols is their inherent ambiguity and blurred boundaries. The same symbol can have several meanings.

According to Veronica Teliya, the types of examples cited above are quasi-symbols. The different meanings of quasi-symbols, as well as of symbols, are because of their culturally meaningful content. For example: the cross on the dome of a church is a symbol, the word "cross" (name) is a quasi-symbol.

Levi-Strauss initiated the use myth to study symbolism. He believed that the symbol had a set of paradigmatic relation with the symbolic and the logical meaning. Mythology was one such type of semiotic code, denoting universal images and ideas. For example, according to the archaic Slavic world picture, fish were a symbol of the lower cosmic area, large animals were symbols of the middle cosmos, and birds were symbols of the upper cosmos.

The most important property of a symbol is its imagery. Therefore, many scholars study the concept of the symbol through image. Many definitions contain a set of concepts "images - symbols – signs." Symbols and signs, comprising most of the semiotic vocabulary, have much in common: both are based on a conventional three-component model (signified - signifier and semiotic connection). However, the meaning of the sign, unlike the meaning of the symbol, cannot just be conventional; it must be concrete as well. For example, road signs need to be specific in order to avoid accidents. According to Nina Ariutunova, signs become conventionalized, but symbols become canonized: the cross becomes a symbol of the Christian faith, of suffering, of unification of space, etc. The symbol, unlike the sign, does not provide a direct reference. "Signs regulate movement on the Earth, on the water and on the air. Symbols guide you along the paths of life." [177]

If the essence of a sign is to indicate (George Gadamer), then the essence of a symbol is to be more than an indicator, combining different aspect of reality into a whole during the semantic activities of a particular culture. One such example includes phraseological units having separate components that become symbols. For example, a nose is a symbol of a person's vulnerability, hence the idiom to wipe your nose, to lead by the nose, tweak someone's nose, even if your nose bleeds[178]. Other symbols of the nose as an instrument of response can be found in the following idioms: not according to the nose[179] (I don't like it), turn one's nose[180] (to disagree), turn up one's nose[181] (to express contempt).

The image is the core of the symbol. Every symbol has an image, but an image can be considered a symbol only under certain conditions. Herman Frye identified the following criteria for "symbolic" image in poetry: 1) the abstract symbolic meaning is explained (shown) in context; 2) the image is presented in such a way that a literal interpretation is impossible or insufficient; 3) the image has an implied (hidden) association with myth, legend or folklore.

It seems that a sign becomes a symbol when its use assumes that there will be an effect not on the symbolized object itself, but on the entire spectrum of secondary conventional meanings.

Signs need to be understood, but symbols require interpretation. Symbols have the properties of signs and all its features, unless the sign is very specific. Ferdinand de

---

[177] Nina Ariutunova, Language and the World of Man. Moscow, 1998. - p. 342. (Author's Citation).

[178] хоть кровь из носу, (colloquial). Must be done despite any difficulties or obstacles; no matter what; even if it kills me; come hell or high water; by hook or by crook.

[179] не по носу (colloquial) beyond someone's ability (to do, get, handle, attain etc.): too much for me; out of you league.

[180] крутит носом (colloquial) to express dissatisfaction, disdain, reject.

[181] воротить нос (colloquial).

Saussure compared symbols and conventional signs, pointing out that iconic elements are inherent in symbols. He wrote that scales are a symbol of justice because they contain the iconic idea of equilibrium, which other things, such as a cart, do not have. Thus, symbols do not have a straight forward indication of meaning, but they can establish an external or deep internal similarity with the object.

The symbol is a concept akin to the image; this why one often hears the term symbolic image. The symbol has higher meaning, while image can be associated with objects of any level. If the transition from image to metaphor is due to semantic and literary needs, the transition to a symbol (both from an image, and a sign) is determined by factors of an extralinguistic nature.

The image is psychological, but the metaphor is semantical; the symbol is functional, meant to unite social, tribal, and national groups (Ariutunova, 1998, p. 338). From this perspective, the symbol has higher semiotic status than the image, because the symbol is often interpreted in terms of culture (in the Russian culture, a hand is a symbol of power and a symbol of help - first-hand, to be one's right hand, to have a hand in something. But it is also a symbol of punishment – a hand doesn't tremble[182], hands are itching[183], to raise one's hand at somebody).

Symbols should be distinguished from gestalt. Primarily, they differ in function.
As mentioned, at a superficial linguistic level, the same gestalt may have different meanings and only a special examination can establish its unity.

Yuri Lotman wrote that at the heart of a literary idea there is no rationally formulated theme, but a symbol: "the text's seed for future growth." He claims that the function of a symbol is to provide cultural memory.

For example, the number seven is a Christian symbol that is widespread throughout various cultures, (in Germanic

---

[182] РУКА НЕ ДРОГНЕТ (colloquial) Determined, resolved to do something, often cruel or harmful, to another person.
[183] руки чешутся spoiling for a fight.

cultures the number nine served as the prototypical number, but was later replaced by the number seven); in Russian culture the number seven is a symbol of something excessive: behind seven locks (seals) - very hidden, strictly classified; to have a forehead seven spans wide[184] – to be very smart; to slurp kissel seven miles away[185] – to go on a wild goose chase; seven sweats fell[186] - very tired; seven versts to heaven and all the forest[187] – talk a lot of hot air; seven Fridays in a week[188] - to often change one's mind; to be in seventh heaven[189] - to be very happy. Therefore, here it is hardly possible to say that the symbol "seven" has national characteristics - this symbol can also be found in the Germanic languages. However, the symbol *forty*, meaning "a lot" is found only in Russian culture, so the idiom *forty times forty*[190] is culturally specific.

Another important property of a symbol is its motivation, which establishes itself between the concrete and the abstract elements of the symbolic content. It is through motivation that symbols and signs can be distinguished, where the link between the signifier and the signified is arbitrary and conventional. The motivation of a symbol can be explained through analogy, which is the basis of semantic transpositions (transfer), such as those found in metaphors, metonymies and synecdoches.

It is motivation that unites symbols with metaphors and metonymies. Ernst Cassirer was one of the first to mention the role of the metaphor in the symbolic construction of reality (Cassirer, 1970). A metaphor explains the similarities in myths; metaphors connect the concrete and abstract aspects of symbols: the goddess - earth - mother; a snake crawling on the ground is a symbol of the earth (a metonymy) and a symbol of the underground deity (a metaphor). Therefore, we can conclude that symbols can be metaphoric or metonymic.

---

[184] семи пядей во лбу.
[185] за семь верст киселя хлебать.
[186] СЕМЬ ПОТОВ СОШЛО sweat blood. Knocked out.
[187] семь верст до небес и все лесом.
[188] семь пятниц на неделе.
[189] быть на седьмом небе.
[190] сорок сороков.

Human nature allows us all to speak and understand the language of symbols. Erik Fromm noted that the language of symbols does not need to be taught and its reach is not limited to specific groups of people, because symbols are archetypical by nature and transmitted to us at an unconscious level.

According to Carl Jung, and as we understand it, archetypes are ancient images and socio-cultural ideas, inherited from the "collective unconscious" and recorded in our genes; these archetypes are the basis for creativity. Jung believes that an archetype is a hypothetical model, an unconscious aspiration whose existence can be studied through its manifestations. But an archetype is also the original image of the unconscious, repeated throughout history in motifs. These basic images and ideas are embodied in the symbols, myths and beliefs that are found in literature and art. All poetry is imbued with archetypes, original images found primarily in nature: a forest, field, sea, birth, marriage, death, and others. The purest archetypes are found in mythology and folklore. So when we speak of the mythologems in idioms or other linguistic phenomena, the term "mythologem" is usually synonymous to "archetype."

The principle archetypes highlighted by Carl Jung are: shadows, heroes, fools, wise old men (old ladies), Prometheus and others. The primary characteristics of these archetypes includes the: involuntary, unconscious, autonomous, genetically determined (Jung, 1991).
Symbols embody many archetypes. Therefore, one can speak of archetypal symbols, such as the world tree, the cosmic egg, the holy mountain, etc. The archetypal symbol is their most important feature. It is twofold. On the one hand, symbol reflects the images of the unconscious, most of which are archetypes. The archetype, on the other hand, includes consciousness and is part of our reality, often strongly transformed.

Many symbols are national-specific. The Chinese draw a picture of a toad and a hare (symbols of immortality) on the moon, of a crow in the sun (a symbol of filial piety). In Slavic culture, these symbols have a different meaning: a hare is a symbol of cowardice; a crow is an ominous bird that brings misery to the home, etc.

Having analyzed different concepts of the symbol, we concluded that a symbol is a thing that has been given meaning. For example, a cross, bread, a sword, blood, a circle, etc. Bread is real and visible, having shape, color, weight, taste, etc. But when we say, "Give us this day our daily bread" or when we read the words of Christ "I am the bread of life ..." (John 6:35), the bread becomes a symbol of life, or rather, food necessary for the spiritual life.

According to Yuri Lotman, symbols form the core of culture. They usually come from ages past, for example: twisting and curling is understood by us as a symbol of happiness and joy (Twist the mustache, curl the mustache: you will find a piece of meat[191]). But some have emerged relatively recently: a dove as a symbol of peace (the "father" of this symbol is Picasso), shaking *multicolored hands* has become a symbol of friendship between diverse people, etc.

Why are symbols part of culture? According to Alexander Potebnja, they appear because of the need to restore the forgotten inherent meaning of words: the Kalina flower came to symbolize a young girl because both are beautiful[192]. He believes that there are three types of relationship between the original word and a symbol: to compare, contrast, and a causal relation (causality). To this day, people apply a red rag to certain skin rashes[193] because rashes are red.

A symbol has no particular addressee; it is addressed to every native speaker. It performs the function of storing texts in a concentrated form. For example, a nest is a symbol of family, of home. The title of Ivan Turgenev's novel, "Nest of the Gentry" stores an entire layer of Russian culture.

---

[191] Вейся, у сок, завивайся, усок: будет мяса кусок.
[192] In the Russian, the word red (красный) is etymologically related to the word beautiful (красивый). The Kalina berry is red and the young girl is beautiful.
[193] In Russian, the skin rash St. Anthony's fire is named Рожа, from the Latin word for red. A rash, рожа is similar to both fire and the color red.

Poetic language, metaphors and other figurative devices use symbols extensively. In fairness, we should mention that Valery Bryusov, claimed that primitive art was realistic rather than symbolic: "The tendency towards symbolism and conventionalism is not by force, but because of the artist's weakness. The primitive artist paints a king or leader bigger than others not because such a figure is more beautiful in shape, but because of an inability to express the status of a "royal person"[194]. However, in studying the high level of cultural development in certain ancient cultures, such as in the Aegeans and Mayan cultures, Bryusov acknowledges a high level of symbolism. Poetic symbolism, as well as poetic metaphor, is individual, changing from era to era and from poet to poet. In poetic texts, these two phenomena are rather closely related. Any element of a poem – a grapheme, a phoneme, a lexeme – having penetrated the forcefield of the text, acquires multiple connotations, capable of becoming part of a poetic symbol.

The poetry of the Symbolists is of particular interest in this regard, where a poet creates a series of images that have not yet become a complete picture. This is why symbolist theorists called this poetry "the poetry of hints." The reader of these works should possess a sensitive soul and a fine imagination to recreate the mental image envisioned by the author.

There are literary works that can be understood only by penetrating the deeper meaning of the text's symbolic images. For example, in *Sign of Misfortune* by Vasil Bykov, we come across several important symbols that, like knots, connect the entire work: the symbols of Calvary and ashes (a ruined and abandoned farm). The images partially overlap: Calvary is a mountain not in Palestine, but in occupied by Nazis Belarus. Bykov's Calvary symbolizes the people's, suffering, caused by troubles not of their making. This symbol appeared earlier in the text (in the description of the pre-war period), but the war begins, normal human life is destroyed, and the ashes begin to

---

[194] Valery Bryusov, *Collected Works*. -- Moscow, 1975. -- T. 7. -- C. 320. (Author's citation).

appear. Calvary lives and dies with its heroes. Ashes survive to tell the story, recalling the trials that the characters survived, heroes on a path to immortality.

Literary text embodies the unique world views of a people. It is for this reason that Ernst Cassirer calls human beings symbolic creatures. For the symbols are natural attempts to reconcile and unite opposites within the psyche.

Carl Jung wrote: "It is inherent in the nature of symbol to connect opposites; it connects the opposites of real and unreal; on the one hand, it is psychological reality. . . on the other hand, it does not correspond to the physical reality. Symbol is a fact and an illusion."[195] According to Friedrich Schiller, literature is the art that lets you see, selecting a symbolic foundation to build a personal fictitious reality. Luis Buñuel's symbols are dark and cannot be expressed in words. Alexander Blok also believed that at their deepest level symbols should be dark.

The symbolic use of a word can be formed from a particular text (or from the many texts of a particular author), or it may be culturally introduced. A symbol appears to grow from the direct meaning of the corresponding word, without replacing or modifying it, becoming part of a broader cultural context. Tropes can also interact with symbols and contribute subtext; a symbol is a universal trope and can blend with any literary device to create textual imagery.

Symbols are deeply national. Victor Pelevin provides a humorous example in *Chapaev and Void*, sarcastically emphasizing the national character of a symbol-archetype: Gangsters and "New Russians" who put huge winch like ornaments on the hood of their cars: "Anthropologists studying 'New Russians' believe that such winches are used during shootouts as battering rams, and some scientists even see their widespread propagation as indirect evidence of a long-hoped-for revival of national spirit - from their point of view, winches perform the mystical function of figureheads that once adorned Slavic ships."

---

[195] Carl Jung, *Archetype and Symbol.* -- Moscow, 1991. -- Pages 213. (Author's citation).

Let us examine a few symbols (universal and national) by using Russian poetry. Sleep is an important symbol commonly used in poetry. Pagans believed that you go to the other world when you sleep, to the "other." In a sense, dreams were real for pagans. In Christianity, there is no evil other world; evil is spiritual emptiness, a place that lacks Light and Goodness. Evil cannot and does not have a rightful permanence in the world: it is rooted in the spiritual world, in the human soul. Dreams are a natural phenomenon of humans, revealing their inner evil to the world. Andrei Tarkovsky sees it like this:

I'm dreaming of some kind of sea,
Some kind of unfamiliar ship,
And sorrow, a kind of sorrow,
A black heart oppressing me.

Any word can become a symbol in the particular text of a particular author. For instance, in the poetry of Sergey Yesenin, the word light blue became a symbol of home, near and dear to the poet's heart - his native country. The word blue acquired a similar meaning in his poetry:

Predawn, blue, gentle...
I have left my native home,
I have left blue Russia

Symbols are not created exclusively through language units. In the 1920s, Pavel Florensky wanted to write a "Dictionary of Symbols" (Symbolarium), which would have consisted of geometric shapes. As a matter of fact, according to the well know principle, an infinitesimally small and negligible point was the origin of the universe. This point symbolizes the center, the initial cause, the place where everything begins and where everything returns, the point from which a beam emanates, from the God-creator who made the universe and provides Unity, etc.

Colors often become symbols. According to Ludwig Wittgenstein: "color inspires us to philosophy." For millennia, scholars have been trying to solve the questions of color. Recent research has shown that humans have a set of 10 gene pigments responsible for color. Each person has their own particular set. Therefore, two people can be looking at the same object, but perceive the color differently. Studies of people with permanent brain lesions indicate that the concepts of colors, words expressing these concepts, and the connection between the concepts and words depend on its different systems (brain systems). This may explain why different cultures react differently to colors (in the U.S. "green" means it is safe, in France it means crime; for the Chinese white is a symbol of mourning and sadness; for Europeans these functions are performed by the color black). Consequently, color is truly mental in nature and has meaning for people.

The names of many colors are directly associated to light. Alexander Potebnja, citing Lavrenty Zizany[196], writes that the word "scarlet" is interpreted through the word "white." Thus, a squirrel[197] gets its name not because in the northern regions its color is almost white, but because the red and white have the same underlying understanding. *Day* has two persistent meanings in popular culture - red and white, and both, as it turns out, were initially the same; they can both be traced to the god Yarila, guardian of the sun and fire. White and red are symbols of beauty, but white is also a symbol of love – to wash white means "to love." Red signifies not just beauty, but a brightness associated with fire.

Black originated from fire, symbolizing disgrace, hatred, sorrow, death, i.e., a symbol opposite to light. Night too is a symbol of grief as well; it is dark and black. Green is associated with light but also symbolizes youth (young and green).

Sergey Yesenin's description of a birch tree includes two colors - green and white. Here, one should pay attention to the symbolic meaning of colors, noting that there is some difference of opinion as to their significance. Traditionally,

---

[196] 1570 – 1633, Western Slavic linguist, translator, teacher, preacher. Credited with writing the first Slavonic grammar book.
[197] Белка is squirrel, белый is white.

green is associated with life and prosperity; white is associated with light.

In her research of Jungian psychology, Jolande Jacobi writes that green is the color of the earth, tangible and immediately perceived from the plant kingdom. Anna Wierzbicka provides an interesting theory: concepts about colors are linked to "universal elements of the human experience." Perception of color occurs when we link our visual categories to a universal pattern or model accessible to human senses. According to her, these patterns and models include fire, sun, flora, world, sky, earth (as well as day and night). Therefore, when referring to colors we must focus our perception on the surrounding environment. For example, green often used to describe birch trees, is the color of vegetation. But green can also symbolize youth (the word *green* is often used when referring to *young*). This linking of representations can be the initial formation of another connection: a girl as a birch tree, where the starting point for comparing a bride and a birch tree links the concepts "young and green." This probably explains why for Russians a birch tree is not just a symbol of the motherland and of Russia itself, but also of a girl and bride, young and innocent. Sergey Yesenin writes in the poem *My Way*:

With green pigtails,
In a white skirt,
A birch tree standing by the pond.

Green also symbolizes beauty and joy (spring is described as bright, glowing and joyful; interestingly, the words joyful and spring sound similar, and may be related[198]). Alexander Potebnja notes that *green* signifies joyful and that this is confirmed in Germanic languages. Thus, we see an adjective denoting color changing from the visual to the evaluative. Researchers have also noted that evaluative meaning is very persistent. Therefore, we conclude that color symbolism is archetypical in its structure.

---

[198] Веселье – joy; весна – spring.

White also symbolizes beauty and has an evaluative definition "good, beautiful." White is synonymous with the words *ardent*[199] and *flamboyant*[200], which in turn come from the name of the god of light and fire in Slavic mythology - Yarila. Therefore, *white* should have meanings similar to color and light (gold and fire). Everything associated with the sun and light was perceived as positive and beautiful. And as mentioned above, the color white was a symbol of love. Hence Yesenin's metaphor "birches with white faces." Through color symbolism, a birch tree also appears as a symbol of graceful beauty and purity.

A birch becomes a symbol of Russia, a symbol of Russian nature. It is worth noting Yesenin's metaphor: white birch trunk = milk (the poem "I will go wearing the skufia of a humble monk...", "Hooligan"). When viewed from a distance, a birch grove looks like a permanent milk-white stain. But this symbol has a deeper subtext, which is based on a metaphor. Milk is usually associated with a cow. And, as is known, the Slavs were extremely reverential towards cows. Cows provided food, clothing and shelter from the cold; these were gifts from the goddess Mati Syra Zemlya[201]. This is evidenced by the fact that nature's creative forces, herds of sheep and cows were all similarly named. A cow was considered a symbol of fertility, and this is reflected in comparisons of dairy cows with rain clouds (milk is a metaphor for rain). Therefore, milk is a connecting link between people and the earth, between people and the sky. The cow embodies ideas about life and the cycles of nature. Milk is closeness to mother.

Sergey Yesenin used this metaphor in broader analogies: the milk of birches connects him to the land, the motherland, old Russia, his mother. Sergey Yesenin's motherland is drawn closer through words linked to concepts of "mother" and "earth." In folk tradition, this link between

---

[199] Яры.

[200] Яркий.

[201] мать сыра земля – literally, mother damp earth, a goddess from Slavic mythology.

motherland, the cult of rod[202], and the cult of the earth is a fixed archetype.

Gray symbolizes the resurrection of the dead, a symbol of the universal unconscious. People identified gray as a primordial color of the universe (an infant and animals lives in gray world). Gray is the color of mourning, so the ancient Jews sprinkled ashes on themselves (an expression of grief and mourning).

There are also popular-poetic symbols: autumn is aging, a kalina blossom is a girl, clouds signify unhappiness, winds are enemies, a nightingale is love, an eagle of the steppes is a dashing Cossack, rain means tears, spring is the beginning of love, winter means dying, etc.

In the near future, the task of philosophy will be to identify the structure of word-symbols in twentieth century poetry. A dictionary of these poetic symbols should be compiled in order to reference information about the content of a particular symbol, its use and its origin.

Only a person who has mastered the cultural values of a nation, who is familiar with the poetry of his own people, is rewarded with the ability to use poetic symbols and images.

Stereotypes as a Phenomenon of the Cultural Environment

The phenomenon of "stereotypes" is studied by linguists as well as in the works of sociologists, ethnographers, cognitive science, psychologists, ethno-phycho linguists (Walter Lippman, Igor Kon, J. Collen, Yuri Apresyan[203], Yuri Sorokin, Vladimir Ryzhkov, Yuri Prokhorov, Victoria Krasny[204], Pyeter Shihirev[205], Alexey Mikheev[206], Svetlana Tolstaya[207],

---

[202] Supreme god of the Slavic native faith.

[203] Soviet/Russian linguist. Member of the Russian Academy of Sciences. Author of several books on language and dictionaries.

[204] Professor at Moscow State University. Author of "Linguistic-Culturology, Theory and Practice."

[205]December 1936 – January 2004. Professor of Social Psychology at Moscow State University, author of

Jerzy Bartmiński, Albert Baiburin[208], Genady Batygin[209], Stanislav Silinsky[210] and others).

Representatives from each of these fields of study emphasize the properties of stereotypes that they see from their academic perspectives; therefore, there are social stereotypes, communication stereotypes, mental stereotypes, cultural stereotypes, ethno-cultural stereotypes, etc. For example, social stereotypes manifest themselves as stereotypes of individual thought and conduct. Ethno-cultural stereotypes are a generalized representation of the typical features that characterize a people: German punctuality, Russian "maybe", Chinese ceremonies, African temperament, short tempered Italians, Finnish stubbornness, the slowness of Estonians, Polish chivalry. These stereotypes about a people are applied to each of its representatives. Stereotypes serve as a basis for most of anecdotes about national character. For example: "Members of different nationalities were sent a film of the following: a red-hot desert and scorching sun. A man and a woman struggle to walk. Suddenly the man gets out a juicy orange and gives it to the woman. The viewers are asked: what's his nationality?" A French viewer says: "Only a Frenchman could have treated the lady so gallantly! A Russian: "No. This is a Russian: what a fool! He should have

---

"Psychology of Mutual Relations", "Contemporary Social Psychology in Western Europe" and others.

[206] Russian writer and journalist. Editor of the "Dictionary of the XXI Century." Author of "Meaning and Categorization", "Reading Letter by Letter, a Roman-Album" and others.

[207] Director of the Department of Ethnolinguistics and Folklore at the Institute for Slavic Studies of the Russian Academy of Sciences, author of "The Semantic Categories of the Language of Culture: Features of Slavic Ethnolinguistics", "The Space of a Word. Lexical Semantics from a Slavic Perspective."

[208] Professor of Ethnolinguistics at the European University of Saint Petersburg, Director of the Museum of Anthropology and Ethnography, Kunstkamera. Author of "Ritual in Traditional Culture", Coauthored "Half-Forgotten Words and Meanings: Dictionary of Russian Culture XVIII-XIX Centuries."

[209] February 1952 – June 2003 – Soviet/Russian Sociologist, Professor at the Department of Sociology of the Russian Academy of Science. Author of "Social Sciences in Post-Soviet Russia."

[210] Head of the English Department at St. Petersburg State University, Author of "Russian – English Dictionary of Colloquial Expressions."

eaten it himself." A Jew: "No, it's a Jew: who else could have gotten an orange in a desert?" Here are the stereotypes - the French chivalry, the recklessness of a Russian, Jewish resourcefulness.

There are **self-stereotypes**, reflecting what people think of themselves, and then there are **hetero-stereotypes**, about other people, the latter being much more critical. For example, what one nation thinks is prudence, another views as greed. People perceive ethnic and cultural stereotypes as models, which must be met so that "people won't laugh." Therefore, stereotypes have rather a strong influence on people, stimulating the formation of the traits reflected in the stereotype.

Experts of ethnic psychology who study ethnocultural stereotypes note that economically developed nations emphasize qualities such as intelligence, efficiency and initiative, but nations with a developing economy emphasize kindness, warmth and hospitality. A study by Svetlana Ter-Minasova[211] confirms this: according to her results, in English society professionalism, hard work, responsibility, etc. are given greater value, while in Russia its hospitality, sociability, justice (Ter-Minasova, 2000 p. 255).

Natalia Ufimtseva distinguishes ethnic stereotypes and cultural stereotypes: ethnic stereotypes are not subject to the self-reflection of a "naive" member of an ethnic group; they are behavioral facts of the collective unconscious and cannot be specifically taught. Cultural stereotypes, however, are behavioral facts of individual consciousness and unconsciousness, subject to self-reflection and to being taught.

The concept of stereotypes was first used by Walter Lippman in 1922. He believed that a stereotype was a culturally determined sketch, a "pictures of the world" in the human mind. Stereotypes minimize the efforts needed to understand the complexity of the world. This understanding of a stereotype focuses on two of its more important elements

---

[211] President of the Department of Foreign Languages and Area Studies at Moscow State University. Author of several English language learning textbooks.

– that stereotypes are determined by culture, and that they are meant to economize effort; and therefore, the focus is also on language. If mathematical algorithms are a more efficient form of human thought, then stereotypes are a more "efficient" form of individuality.

In cognitive linguistics and in ethnolinguistics, the term stereotype relates to the contents of language and culture, that is, it is understood as mental stereotype that correlates with the "naïve picture of the world." This understanding of stereotype is found in the works of Jerzy Bartmiński and his school. In his works, the linguistic picture of the world is to the linguistic stereotype what the part is to the whole. Linguistic stereotypes are understood as an opinion, or several opinions, about an object in the extralinguistic world, a subjective deterministic representation of an object, where descriptive and evaluative features coexist, an interpretation of reality within the framework of social cognitive models. I, however, believe that a linguistic stereotype is not just an opinion, or several opinions, but any fixed expression consisting of several words, such as set comparisons and clichés, etc.: *a native of the Caucasus, as gray-haired as the moon, a new Russian*. The use of such stereotypes makes communication easier and simpler, saving the energy of communicants.

Yuri Sorokin defines stereotypes as a type of cause and effect in communication (conduct) based on specific semiotic models. The numbers of stereotypes are limited by the semiotic-processing in a particular society. This semiotic model is implemented on the social, and socio-psychological level (values) or on the linguistic, psychological level (norms). Values and norms exist in two forms: as a stock-phrase (overly explicit complex symbol), or as a cliché (insufficiently explicit complex symbol).

Victoria Krasny divides stereotypes into two types - stereotype-image and stereotype-situation. Examples of stereotype-images include: a bee as a hard worker, a ram is stubborn; stereotype-situations include: a ticket – punch, a stork – a cabbage.

Stereotypes are always national; if there are equivalents in other cultures, they are quasi-stereotypes because, although they generally coincide, they differ in nuance and details of crucial importance. For example, every culture stands in line in different ways. Therefore, stereotyped behavior is different as well. In Russia we ask, "Who's last?" or just get in line. In many European countries, they tear off a ticket from a machine, and then follow the number indicated over the counter, as in a post office.

Accordingly, a stereotype is like a fragment of a conceptual picture of the world, a mental "picture", a persistent national-cultural view (according to Yuri Prokhorov, "super-persistent" and "super-fixed") about an object or a situation. A stereotype is a culturally-deterministic understanding of an object, phenomenon or situation. However, a stereotype is not just a mental image; it is a verbal structure as well. whether one belongs to a particular culture is determined by the presence of basic stereotypical knowledge, which repeats itself during the socialization of the individual in a given culture. Therefore, stereotypes a considered to be a precedent (important representations) for the identification of a culture. Stereotypes are a phenomenon of language and speech, a stabilizing factor that can store and transform some of the dominant features of a given culture; additionally, stereotypes let you identify and be with "your own kind."

The basis for the formation of ethnic consciousness and culture, regulating human behavior, is both innate as well learned during socialization. Cultural stereotypes are absorbed from the moment a person begins to identify with a particular ethnic group or culture and feel a part of this element.

Because stereotypes perform many cognitive functions, the mechanisms that form stereotypes consists of cognitive processes such as schematic functions, simplification, formation and storage of group ideology, and others.

We live in a world of culturally imposed stereotypes. The set of mental stereotypes of an ethnic group is known to all its members. For example, a member of a rural peasant

148

culture might describe a bright moonlit night as a light is so bright that you can sew by it, while an urban dweller in this typical situation might say that the light is so bright you can read by it. Similar stereotypes are used by native speakers to communicate standard situations. Almost any feature may become a dominant stereotype, not just obviously apparent ones.

The cultural sphere of a particular ethnic group contains many stereotypical elements which, as a rule, are not perceived by members of other cultures. Yuri Sorokin and Irina Markovin call these elements lacunae: everything the reader of foreign text has noticed but not understood, everything that seems strange and requires interpretation. These gaps are an indication that the text has national specific cultural elements.

The influence of a culture, its vitality, depends on well-developed structures establishing unity and integrity, and this integrity requires a formulation of cultural stereotypes, of a general picture of the world, including: stereotypes of goal setting, behavior, perception, understanding, communication, and others. The frequency of certain objects and events in people's lives, often prolonged interaction, results in the stereotyping of such objects and events.

Stereotypes of behavior are the most important stereotypes, because they can become rituals. Generally, stereotypes have much in common with traditions, customs, myths and rituals. However, they are distinguishable by the fact that traditions and customs are have an objectified significance and accessibility for others, but stereotypes remain a hidden mindset existing only among "your own people."

Accordingly, stereotypes are specific to the mentality and language of a people's culture. Stereotypes serve as the base of culture, its brilliant ambassador and, therefore, the base for others in a dialogue with cultures.

For purposes of linguistic-culturology, we will use the ethnolinguistic methods used by Nikita Tolstoy to describe the language of a particular region: literary language corresponds to elite culture, dialect and vernacular to popular culture, etc.

This method can be used to describe the language and culture of any region.

The most striking linguistic features reflecting the culture of a people are its idioms and proverbs, its metaphors and symbols. Language has absorbed these mythologems, archetypes, models, stereotypes, customs, rituals and beliefs.

The national-cultural specifics of idioms, metaphors, symbols are shaped by cultural connotations. Nevertheless, we still maintain that language is not the repository of culture.

The unit of a language is the word, a mere signal whose function is to stimulate human consciousness, awakening certain concepts upon this signal's command. And language is just a mechanism that facilitates the encoding and transmission of culture. But the true keepers of a culture are its texts. It is text, not speech, that displays the spiritual world of human beings. Text is directly connected with culture. Imbued with a multitude of cultural codes, text stores information about history, ethnography, national psychology, national behavior, i.e. everything that constitutes a culture. And in turn, the rules of textual construction depend on the culture from where it originates.

Text is created from lower level linguistic units that, if chosen correctly, can enhance the cultural signal. These units are primarily idioms.

Questions and tasks
1. What is the relationship between natural language and culture?
   Complete the diagram:
   Literary language - .... culture;
   Dialects and proverbs .... culture;
   .... – is a "third culture", i.e., a culture for the people;
   .... – is a professional subculture.
2. Name several aliases (nicknames) you know (friends, politicians). In what type of culture does this phenomenon occur.

3. Provide 5 Russian idioms and 5 idioms from foreign languages you study. Which ones reflect national specificity?
4. Find 10 metaphors in the poetic texts of Boris Pasternak that describe a) the world, b) nature, c) human feelings, d) human emotions.
5. What definitions of a symbol do you know? Provide examples of numeric symbols and color symbols. Which one of these are national symbols and which are universal symbols?
6. What are the roles of stereotypes in culture? What are their functions?

CHAPTER 5
Human Existence in Culture and Language

The Person as Bearer of National Mentality and Language

Our era, the beginning of the twenty-first century, is characterized by uneven scientific development. There has been a sharp leap in technical civilization. However, there has been a slower development in the humanities, the primary object of study being a person's deeds and actions, thoughts and aspirations, fantasies and emotions.

Civilization has made it possible to create powerful destructive and enslaving forces, and the humanities are not yet able to save us because we have insufficient knowledge to understand and perfect our behavior. Only one of the many humanitarian fields is now actively growing, propaganda and its influence on the masses. Proof of this weakness in human intellect is the fact that with each new ruler we have the illusion that a more intelligent, strong-willed, kinder person has come to power.

The thinking of modern technological civilization has given rise to a new language - a language of primitive, malformed, overly pragmatic technical thinking, where life is expressed in military or medical terms: *the battle for the harvest, operations in Chechnya*, etc.

There has been a recent trend in philosophy, cultural studies, linguistics, and linguistic-culturology towards a more complete study of the person by including the person's nature, appearance, inner world, mentality, etc. And, there is a growing conviction that understanding the phenomenon of man lies not in natural sciences, but in natural languages.

Our goal is to show how one can learn more about a person based on his/her language. After all, language is not merely a way to communicate, transmit and express thought. This approach focuses on the use of language, rather than on its origins, and language use is determined by its primary function: the formation of the conceptual image of the world.

We understand a person to be the bearer of a specific national mentality and language, someone who participates in joint activities (most importantly, speech acts) with other representatives of the national community.

The focus of interest for modern science is not just on the person, but on the person's identity: the person's consciousness, the native language of the speaker's complex inner world, attitudes towards fate and the material world. A person has a special position in the Universe and on Earth, being in constant dialogue with the world, themselves and others like this person. Man is created in the image of God, having free will but, nevertheless, being social by nature, "The humanity in human life is created under culturally established terms" (Alexey Leontiev).

This work does not focus on people in general, but on people in language. The fact is, language is the only means that can help us penetrate the mental sphere hidden from us; it determines how a particular culture divides the world. It tells us things about a person that are unknown to that person. In a letter to Ekaterina Naryshkina[212], Ivan Goncharov wrote: "Language is not just speech and words; it is the image of the whole inner person: the mind, what we call the heart. Language is the spokesman of education, of all mental and moral forces."

We were created by the Word, and so was the world, and maybe that's why we find the word so interesting. Wilhelm Humboldt wrote: "Learning a language does not have an ultimate purpose but, as with similar fields, it serves the higher more general purpose of obtaining knowledge about humanity and its relation to everything around it, both visible and hidden."[213] But it took more than one hundred years to fully understand the great linguist's idea.

---

[212] May 1789 – December 1841 Daughter of privy councilor Baron Alexander Stroganov. By birth, member of Moscow's highest nobility.
[213] Wilhelm Humboldt. *Selected Articles on Linguistics* -1984 - Pg. 119.114. (Author's citation).

In the second half of the twentieth century, philosophy began developing through to a scrupulous analysis of language. Language for the philosopher is not just a means of expressing philosophical concepts but, it is also a means of knowing the world and the person. So, if in the beginning there was the Word, then it is the most important source of knowledge. It contains all the information about the world and the person.

The object of philosophical thought is the person: known through semiotic activity and presupposing the existence of "another." It is probably based on this that the famous Jewish philosopher Martin Buber established a new object of study: the *I – Thou* relationship in which the person lives. It is in fact a dialogical relationship in which, without the *Thou,* the *I* is impossible; the path of the person is always with another person, a life in common. When an individual perceives the world, it is done together with another individual. Ludwig Feuerbach wrote that the human essence is present only in interaction, in the unity of one person with another, a unity based only on the reality of the difference between *I* and *Thou.* The relationship of this universal dialogue includes the study of the person: his/her place in the world, his/her relation to God, nature, and other people. Of primary importance is the relationships between people. Martin Buber points to a trinity in the relationships of a man's life: to the world, to man, to God. The essence of a person's relationship with the world is through art; the relationship with a person is through love; the relationship with God is through religious revelation. The *I – Thou* relationship between one person and another is revealed in dialogue, formed in speech. *Thou* is an address to God. It is our answer to a call we do not hear but feel. True dialogue with God is silent but generates speech.

Martin Buber writes: "We will get closer to answering the question 'What is Man?' when we learn to see within the person a creature whose dynamic nature and organic ability to be with another is done and understood through One and the Other." [214] In "The Problem of Man," he notes that the object of study should be the holistic and specific human personality. This study should include information from other sciences: psychology, ethnography, biology, etc., with linguistics playing an important role. Man is the main object of research in many literary genres: biographies, chronicles, autobiographies, epistolary works, obituaries and sermons.

In an article written in the 1960's and published in Russian in 1974, Emile Benveniste wrote that language is enclosed in the very nature of the person, therefore it cannot be an artificial invention: "In the world there is only a person with language, a person speaking with another; therefore, language must be part of the very definition of man . . . It is in language and through language that a person is created as a subject, for only language imparts reality, its own reality, which is the property of being . . . "[215]

At the turn of the millennium, interest in studying man has grown. In 1990, the magazine *Man* began publication. At the end of 1991, the Institute of Man was created in the Russian Academy of Science; In 1990 the journal *Man and Culture* began publication, and at the end of 1991 the anthology *On the Human in Man* was published. A major contribution to the study of the problem, *Man in Language,* was made by Nina Ariutunova, in 1998, she published the book *Language and the World of Man*, and in 1999 she edited the book *Logical Analysis of Language The Image of Man in Culture and Language.*

The works of Natalia Ufimtseva and Yuri Sorokin are of great interest for cultural studies, particularly with regards to the interaction of national mentality and language. Representatives of one nation are shown through the prism of perceptions of another nation, for example, Russians through the eyes of Americans, Japanese, etc. Russians give themselves the following characteristics (given in order from higher to lower frequency): hospitable (5 answers), cordial (5 answers), kind (4), sincere (4), patient (4), generous (3), open

---

[214] Martin Buber. *The Problem of Man.* - Kiev, 1998. (Author's citation).

[215] Émile Benveniste. *Problems in General Linguistics.* – Moscow, 1974. Page 293. (Author's citation).

(2), trusting (2), talented (2), inventive (2), sympathetic (1), intelligent (1), ill-bred (1), thoughtful (1), well-read (1), sincere (1), hypocrites (1), smart (1), limited (1), dashing (1), reserved (1), optimistic (1), desperate (1), funny (1), unhappy (1), tired (1), gray (1), gloomy (1), greedy (1), angry (1), no initiative (1), witty (1) great (1) to lazy (1) rioters (1), etc.

Americans see Russians as: materialists (7), friendly (4), extravagant (3), loud talkers (2), liking entertainment (2), free (2), proud (2), individualists (2), business like (2), competitive (2), hardworking (1), goal oriented (1), motivated (1), ambitious (1), aggressive (1), greedy (1), nasty (1), arrogant (1), coarse (1), lazy (1), inventive (1), kind (1), happy (1), etc. The set of qualities that make up the portraits and self-portraits of Russians is a controversial but holistic entity where the authors identify the core and the periphery.

Using the methods proposed by Yuri Sorokin, we conducted an experiment in which we tried to establish the national identity of Belarusians from the point of view of Russians and Ukrainians. The following results were obtained.

Belarusians through the eyes of Russians (120 subjects who visited the following countries: Armenia, England, Belarus, Hungary, Germany, Holland, Canada, China, Latvia, Poland, Uzbekistan, Czech Republic, Estonia): hard-working (27), kind (16), thrifty 11), hospitable (11), bulb eaters (7), good-natured (6), peace-loving (6), inactive (6), outgoing (6), open (6), self-conscious (6), cheerful (5) , love Russia (5), tight-fisted (4), speak Russian (3), greedy (3), closed (3), decent (3), agricultural (3), economical (3), talkative (2), mild (2), naive (2), nationalists (2) unwelcoming (2), affable (2), hard-working (2), "gray" (2), cute (2), secretive (2), calm (2), patient (2), orderly (1), polite (1), Disciplined (1), homebodies (1), lazy (1), not harmful (1), laconic (1), collected (1), cohesive (1), fair (1), clever (1), cunning (1), hospitable (1), clean (1).

Belarusians through the eyes of Ukrainians (110 subjects who visited the following countries: Belarus, Hungary, Kyrgyzstan, Latvia, Lithuania, Moldova, Poland, Russia, Turkey, Czech Republic, Estonia, Yugoslavia): stingy (12), patient (11), industrious (11), complaisant (10), good-natured (9), greedy (9), economical (8), hardworking (4), soft (3), calm 3), like feasts and songs (2), sometimes "gray" (2), chatty (2), like us (2), modest (2), polite (2), nationalists (2), charming (2) , submissive (2), benevolent (2), simple (2), human (1), harmful (1), sympathetic (1), cordial (1), stubborn (1).

Therefore, if from the point of view of Russians, the Belarusians are hardworking, kind, thrifty, hospitable (the four most frequent reactions), Ukrainians consider them to be stingy, patient, hardworking, agreeable. A small pilot experiment allows us to characterize the leaders of a nation not through self-observation and opinion, but through the perceptions of other peoples, less influenced by the media. Of course, self-understanding is important for establishing the true state of things, but even more important is how neighboring people see you. Such knowledge helps anticipate many ethnic conflicts and, in some measure, to prevent them. Thus, national mentality is reflected in language and can be studied with the help of simple psycholinguistic experiments.

Language is one of the most important means of human identity. Therefore, sharp changes in the language can be viewed as violence against the linguistic personality. It takes away a person's usual means of self-realization and self-understanding. Although life creates language, it breaks away from life (for words are filled with a different meaning) and starts to create it.

Linguistic Personality

As is known, human personality creates culture and lives there. It is precisely within personality that the that the social nature of man comes to the forefront, with the person acting as the subject of social and cultural life.

There are other concepts of personality. According to the famous American psychologist Abraham Maslow, man has an inner being that is practically independent from the external world, and that this is the basic premise in all of psychology. Furthermore, a life in harmony with this internal nature is believed to be the source of mental health. The development of personality, according to Abraham Maslow, is movement towards the ideal, where personality acts as a path towards full self-realization. He writes: "The human being needs a framework of values, a philosophy of life, a religion or religion-surrogate to live by and understand by, in about the same sense that he needs sunlight, calcium or love."[216]

Personality should be examined from the perspective of a nation's cultural traditions and ethnicity (Anatoly Piskoppel[217], 1997); the individual requires a cultural-anthropological prototype to become part of humanity, and the prototype is culture. Categories of culture include: space, time, fate, law, wealth, work, conscience, death, etc. They reflect the particular existing system of values and establish models of social behavior and world perception. This is a unique system of coordinates that shapes linguistic identity.

The German scholar Leo Weisgerber was the first to use the term linguistic identity. In Russian linguistics, the first steps in this area were made by Viktor Vinogradov, who developed two ways of studying linguistic personality — the personality of the author and the identity of the character. Alexey Leontiev also contributed to the study of speaker personality. Georgi Bogin[218] developed the notion of linguistic identity, creating a model in which the person is considered from the perspective of " being ready to produce verbal acts, to create and receive speech."

Yuri Karaylov introduced this as a concept for wide scientific use. He viewed linguistic personality as a person's ability to create and understand texts that differ in: "a) the degree of structural-linguistic complexity; b) the depth and accuracy reality is described; c) specific target orientation." Karaulov developed a tiered model of linguistic identity that

---

[216] A. Maslow. Toward a Psychology of Being. — M., 1997. — S. 250. 118. (Author's citation).

[217] 2009- professor at the Philosophy Department of Moscow State University; Director of the Cultural and Natural Heritage Research Institute. Author of *Conflictive Synergy*, Coauthored *Engineering Psychology*.

[218] December 1929 – October 2001, Soviet and Russian philologist. Founder of the Tver Hermeneutics School, Author of over 300 publications, including the book, *Acquiring the Ability to Understand*.

focused on literary text (Karaulov, 1987). In his opinion, linguistic personality has a three-tiered structure. The first tier is verbal-semantic (semantic-level, unchanging), reflecting the level of mastery of everyday language. The second tier is cognitive, keeping up-to-date and recognizing relevant knowledge inherent in society (linguistic identity), and being able to create collective and (or) individual cognitive space. This level reflects the language world model, vocabulary and culture of the person. The third and highest tier is the pragmatic. It includes the identification and characterization of the motives and goals that drive the development of a linguistic personality.

Accordingly, the encoding and decoding of information occurs during the interaction of the three levels of "the communicative space of personality": the verbal-semantic, the cognitive, and the pragmatic. This concept of a three-level structure of linguistic personality is in some ways correlated to the three types of communication needs: establishing contact, information, influence. It also correlates to the three-level process of communication: communicative, interactive, perceptual.

This tiered model of linguistic personality reflects a general type of personality. However, there could be many kinds of specific speech personalities in a given culture, made different by the various meanings at each level comprising the personality. Thus, linguistic personality is a multilayered multicomponent paradigm comprised of speech personalities. Speech personality occurs within a paradigm of real communications and activities. It is precisely at the level of speech personality that the national cultural specificity of language personality and interactions appear.

Linguistic personality usually includes the following components:
1) values, world outlook, educational factors, i.e. a system of values, or life expectations. Language provides an elemental and profound view of the world. It forms a linguistic image of the world and a hierarchy of spiritual representations that are the basis for the formation of national character. All this is implemented during linguistic interactions;

2) cultural component, i.e. the extent culture has been assimilated as an efficient means of increasing interest in the language. The cultural facts of the language being studied, including the rules of speech and nonverbal behavior, allows for the formation of adequate skills and for an effective impact the communication partner;

3) the personal component, i.e. the in-depth individual in every human being.

The parameters of linguistic personality are only beginning to be developed. It is characterized by a specific amount of vocabulary and frequency of use in an abstract syntactic model. If the model is sufficiently representative of this linguistic community, then the lexicon and speaking style may indicate the person's social group, level of education, character type, gender, age etc. The linguistic repertoire of this personality, which involves the performance of dozens of social roles, must consider the speech etiquette of the society.

Linguistic personality exists within culture and is reflected in language at the various levels of social consciousness (scientific, every day, etc.), as behavioral stereotypes, norms, cultural artefacts, etc. The values of the nation define the culture and provide meaning. Cultural values represent a system in which meaning is separated into universal and individual, dominant and secondary. These meanings are expressed in language or, more precisely, in word meaning, units of syntax, phraseology, paremiology, and precedent setting text (according to Yuri Karaulov). For example, all cultures condemn human vices such as greed, cowardice, disrespect for elders, laziness, etc., but in every culture, these flaws have different combinations of indicators. Each culture can develop parameters that are peculiar to its coordinates. These parameters will be considered as sources that indicate values.

Today, there are various approaches to the study of linguistic identity; these approaches determine the status of linguistic identity within general linguistics: polylectal (many people) and idiolectal (single person) personality (Vladimir Neroznak[219]), ethno-semantic personality (Sergei Vorkachev[220])

, elitist language personality (Olga Sirotinina, Tatiana Kochetkova[221]), semiotic identity (Alexei Baranov[222]), Russian linguistic personality (Yuri Karaulov), language and speech personality (Yuri Prokhorov[223], Luba Klobukova[224]), linguistic personality of Western and Eastern cultures (Tatiana Snitko[225]), the vocabulary of language personality (Vladimir Karasik[226]), emotional language personality (Victor Shahovsky[227]), etc.

There are additional understandings of linguistic personality. Victoria Krasny highlights the following components: 1) the personality of the person speaking is a type of speech activity 2) the actual linguistic personality of the person engaged in speech activity, the person's knowledge and understanding of the language; 3) speech personality is realized through communication, choosing and implementing particular strategies and tactics of communication, a repertoire of methods; 4) the communicative personality is a specific participant in a particular communicative act, a genuine activity of real communication.

In this textbook, we will focus on only two components of linguistic personality — the strictly linguistic and the communicative.

---

[219] November 1939 – November 2015. Linguistics professor at the Russian Academy of Science. Author of, *The Names of Ancient Russian Cities*, and *Paleo Baltic Languages*.

[220] Philology professor at Kuban State Technological University. Specializes in theory of translation and international communication, linguistic-culturology, Author of over 200 works, including *Country, Mine and Foreign; Love as a Linguistic-Culturological Component*, and others.

[221] Philology professor at Saratov State University.

[222] Russian educator and Privy Counsellor (1844-1911).

[223] Dean of the *Pushkin State Russian Language Institute* in Moscow. Author of "We're Alike, But Different", "In Search of Concept".

[224] Head of the Moscow State University Department of Russian Language for Foreign Students.

[225] Professor of the Department of General linguistics of Rostov-on-don Institute of Foreign Languages.

[226] Head of the research center laboratory "Axiological linguistics" at Volgograd State Pedagogical University.

[227] Founder of the school on emotive language, speech and text. Author of over 375 publications.

Linguistic personality is a social phenomenon, but it has an individual aspect. The uniqueness in language personality is formed through a personal relationship with the language, a relationship that forms individual linguistic meanings. However, we should remember that language personality influences the formation of linguistic traditions and is formed when a specific person assimilates all the linguistic wealth created by those who came before. Therefore, the language of a specific person is more of a common language having few individual linguistic features.

According to Nikolai Alefirenko's[228] vivid description, personality is a unique kind of "knot", tied to the relationship network of a specific ethno-cultural community in joint activities. In other words, the most important factor transforming the individual's linguistic identity is socialization, and it involves three aspects: a) including a person in certain social relations, where linguistic personality is like a realization of society's cultural-historical knowledge; b) speech activity established by the norms and standards of an ethno-linguistic culture; c) assimilating the laws of a people's social psychology. The second and third categories play a critical role in the formation of linguistic identity, since the process of assimilating one or another national culture and the formation of social psychology is possible only through language. In the words of Stanislaw Lem, language is to culture what the central nervous system is to human vital organs. Linguistic-cultural identity is enshrined in the language (vocabulary and syntax) of the native speaker's basic national and cultural prototype, constituting a timeless and invariant part of the personality structure.

Man and Woman in Society, Culture and Language.

---

[228] Professor at Belgorod State University, member of the Russian Academy of Social Sciences, author of several publications, including: *Linguistic-Culturology, The Values-Understanding Space of Language.*

There are two forms of people - man and woman. The "male-female" opposition is fundamental to human culture. There is abundant proof of this. One is rooted in an ancient idea about the world: the soul is the father of creation, and matter is the mother. The result of their universe is the universe and everything in it.

In the anthropomorphic model of the universe, a woman was equated with the abyss, which the pagans believed was be primary source of all living things in the universe. Woman was the embodiment of fate and language preserved this idea; in the Old Russian, "kob" was destiny (compare Polish kobieta - woman). However, woman is also a symbol of the lower world: sinfulness, evil, corporeal and perishable.

Historians have been unable to distinguish gender differences in archaic societies, where survival and work were extremely complex. However, when women entrusted men to graze cattle, men became providers. The subsequent "sexual" division of labor allowed man to establish himself as the absolute in history. It was precisely male activity conquered nature, and woman. Man recognized woman, but only as a half. The second half was like an appendage; his "other me." Accordingly, gender inequality entered culture together with social progress.

Classical culture and philosophy also juxtaposed woman and man. Woman was the keeper of the gene pool, having the most valuable quality in nature - the ability to reproduce life, to continue the genus, i.e. reproduce traditional values, providing the mechanism for preserving community life. Despite this, society associates her to the irrational (Aristotle), immoral (Schopenhauer), sensual (Kant), a creature with a mass of flaws (Freud), etc.

In our culture, woman is a chaos that gives man order. Pythagoras believed that a positive principle created order, light and man, and a negative one created chaos, twilight and woman. In the Gospel, Jesus never uttered a word of humiliation towards women. But the Apostle Paul, in his epistles and sermons, reduced woman to a subordinate position, and these views became the basis of Christianity. Eve emerged from the rib of Adam as his friend and helper; this

163

was the purpose of her being. In the Old Testament, man's morning prayers began with, "Blessed is the Lord, who did not make me a woman." It was upon this postulate that history, philosophy, language, religion, etc., were built.

Unlike the English language, Eastern Slavic, German, French and other languages, do not differentiate "sex" (biological) and "gender" (as a sociocultural category) as distinct concepts. However, the understanding of sex as a mere biological phenomenon impoverishes and simplifies the categorical concept. This is because masculinity and femininity are, on the one hand, phylogenetically conditioned properties of the psyche, and on the other, ontological sociocultural formations. Modern sociologists and philosophers view the concepts of "sex" and "gender" as opposites. Gender is a sociocultural category that does not assume traditional views about sex roles.

Initially, masculinity and femininity were fixed in mythology as the main binary dichotomy through which the entire world was interpreted. This is evidenced by Slavic notions of Mother Earth and Heaven-Father, the ancient Chinese concept of Yin and Yang, and the ancient Greek myth about Androgynes.

A scientific interest in this phenomenon was noted at the end of the 18th century, when a rapid development in the natural sciences led to masculinity and femininity being viewed from a perspective of natural laws. Thus, Charles Darwin argued that male aggression and intellect have a physiological substratum of predominantly male traits. His contemporary followers consider *masculinity - femininity* as genetically predetermined forms of behavior or *biograms*.

The term "women's issues" is a question of women's participation in politics that originated in 1791 during the French Revolution. The French writer Olimpia de Guja stated: "If a woman has the right to ascend the scaffold, she must have the right to rise to the rostrum." The followers of de Gouges, who believed that femme (woman) was also a person, received the name of feminists. The founder of modern feminism was the French writer and philosopher Simone de Beauvoir, who in her classic work, *The Second Sex* showed

164

that the man is the creator of history and woman the mere object of his power. For women, the 19th century became a struggle to establish social and political equality. But if achieving social equality was easy, political equality was more difficult. Women won the right to run for office in Denmark - 1915, Russia - 1917, Germany - 1919, France – 1944. The first decrees of the Soviet government gave the Russian woman both social and political rights.

At the end of 19th century, the phenomenon of masculinity - femininity began to be viewed as a phenomenon of social order, where social differentiation is based on sex and results in natural divisions of social functions. If at the beginning of the twentieth century femininity was viewed as two opposing poles - the role of a respectable woman and the role of a prostitute, then at the beginning of the twenty-first century roles have changed (the role of a housewife and the role of a woman seeking career advancement). Other female roles include the vamp, the guardian of sexual morality, mother, victim, housewife, etc. Woman was once assigned the role of housewife and mother, but the family and economic balance that completely excluded her from the decision-making process has now changed. However, instead of emancipation, a post-Soviet woman now has a double and overwhelming burden.

Sociology now generally includes the subcategory feminology: the science of the status and roles of women in society. The term "feminist" is viewed negatively by modern society, being somewhere between "lesbian" and "nymphomaniac." Examples include the common terms such as: rabid feminist, frenzied feminists. Feminist theories are commonly only referred to as: specialized theories, female theories, etc.

The birth of boys in the family was always preferable. The reason for this was the patriarchal nature of family relations, where man is the head of the family and breadwinner. The following parable is applicable here. A peasant sifts through rye and says: "I'll throw one part into the wind (pay taxes), throw another part into the water (give the daughter away to another family), I'll take the third one for myself, I'll use the fourth to pay a debt (give to parents), and the fifth as a loan (to the son who will feed them when they are old)."

These socio-gender roles and behaviors, which develop and deepen gender differentiation, are imposed by culture. The polarization of the sexes began to be seen as a manifestation of the "natural" qualities of men and women. Accordingly, the dichotomy of the sexes is shaped by society and culture. Simon de Beauvoir's renowned statement is absolutely correct: "Women are not born, they become women." German researcher Karin Hausen also attributes the formation of sex role stereotypes to family work-life divisions. Indeed, there are no "naturally prescribed" social roles. A woman's second-class status is forced by society.

Gender is a large complex of social and psychological processes, as well as cultural attitudes generated by society and influencing the behavior of the national language personality. Gender is a complex intertwining of cultural, psychological and social factors, of interest not only for philosophers and sociologists, but for members of several sciences, including linguists. Therefore, there is a gender psychology, gender linguistics and gender poetry.

In this work, gender is viewed as a phenomenon of culture and language, i.e. part of linguistic-culturology. Our task is to see what is unseen in everyday language and poetry. We will try to show how this category is refracted in language. In traditional Western culture (and others) culture is heterosexual but focuses on the masculine. This is primarily manifested in language. Several nations associate the very notion of a "person" only to a man: in German das Man, in English - man, in French - un homme. A person is a man.

Even the very word woman has a negative origin. In Russian, all words ending in *"щина"* have a negative connotation (contempt or disdain) – *деревенщина (*farmer), *казенщина (*red tape), *групповщина (*factionalism), *чертовщина* (devilish). The word *женщина* (woman) came from the Slavic *жено* and had the connotation of contempt. As civilization developed, the word lost this overtone.

Male culture teaches us to emphasize action and not posture, ends not means. Some sentences are even structured from masculine positions: "I came, I saw, I conquered!", "sink or swim" etc. The feminine point of view is constructed through question or "doubt."

In the mid-1960s gender began to play a greater role in linguistics, resulting in three main areas of research:
1) the social nature of male and female languages;
2) the features of speech conduct;
3) the cognitive aspect of the differences.

This text is mostly interested in the second and third areas of research. One of the first works on gender linguistics was the work of Otto Jespersen *Language.* In includes the chapter "Woman"; however, there is no chapter "Man", because the female language is considered specific, and the male language is viewed as the appropriate literary standard. In English dictionaries, words about women generally have negative connotations. In Roger's Thesaurus, under the heading "untidy", all the words refer to a woman: slut, frump, bitch, etc. Under the heading of education - all the words are about men, except for two, expressing a pretense to education: pedantic, bluestocking.

In 1987, the German scholar Senta Trömel-Plötz published the book *The Language of Women*, in which she argues that discrimination of women in terms of language is expressed not only in speech behavior, where the man is always the leader of the dialogue, but also in using masculine words for women (the author, the passenger, the doctor), and the use of masculine pronouns in a generalized sense.

Since gender speech behavior is built on historically established stereotypes, fixed in language, one can say that gender stereotypes are a system of ideas about how men and women should behave. It has been established that there are differences between male and female strategies of behavior and speech. Friedrich Nietzsche noted that the happiness of a man is "I want!", and a woman's happiness is "he wants!" The speech strategies of men and women are built on this.

We agree with the understanding of speech behavior described by Adam Suprun (1996)[229]; it includes the whole complex of relations in the communicative act, i.e. verbal and non-verbal information, para-linguistic factors, place and time of the speech act, the situation in which the act occurs, etc. Accordingly, speech behavior is the speech action of individuals in typical situations reflecting the specifics of the linguistic consciousness of their society.

Since a man and a woman belong to different social groups and perform different social roles, society expects specific models of speech behavior from them. There is indeed a gender dichotomy in speech behavior. The male type of communication is less flexible, but more dynamic and not as oriented towards conversational communication. The most common genre of communication among men is informational conversation, with women it is private-conversation. Women often provide feedback, supporting it with the word "yes", which does not mean agreement. This "yes" confuses men who often complain that the women constantly agree during a conversation and suddenly say the opposite in the end. The female type of communication is more focused on the interlocutor, on a subordinate role in dialogue, where as the man chooses and changes the topic.

On the one hand, society has developed stereotypes of behavior where a woman plays a subordinate role to a man; she must be a good mistress, able to perform any work, be kind, patient, obedient, tender, faithful, beautiful, and always desired. The absence of a husband in this model is a departure from the norm, a rebellion. The norm is a family with man at the head and a division of roles. A woman, on the other hand, is always negatively evaluated by male society, as evidenced by philosophical, historical, literary discourses and political events.

To study gender speech behavior, we conducted an associative experiment. Words of femininity, masculinity, beauty, strength, weakness, tenderness, reliability, infidelity, and fornication were chosen as stimulus words. There were 400 test subjects - 200 girls and 200 boys aged 16 to 20 years

---

[229] Adam Suprun (October 24 - August 18, 1999). Soviet and Belarusian linguist.

(students from the 10th to 11th grade of schools in Vitebsk and first and second year students of Vitebsk State University. The working hypothesis was that language has a cumulative function that records certain gender stereotypes. The purpose of the experiment was to identify specific features of the linguistic consciousness of native Russian speaking men and women. The experiment indicated that the Russian language consciousness of both sexes primarily associated femininity with beauty, tenderness, charm, elegance and grace.

Women's self-evaluation emphasized internal personal qualities (refinement, charm, intelligence, elegance, gentleness, wisdom, poise, originality, politeness, tact, etc.), while men, for the most part, focused on the external features of women (beauty, hair, legs, love, sex, eyes, shape, figure, clothing).

Women are more critical of men than men are of themselves. Masculinity for them is not only strength, courage, bravery, reliability, fearlessness, nobility, but also cruelty, war, and lies. Such harsh assessments of masculinity are not typical of how men see themselves. Their answers had no negative words, only words such as strength, dignity, endurance, determination, and confidence. Women had more varied and original visual images of the mind.

Beauty is also evaluated differently by men and women. If women's evaluations include a relatively wide range of objects (attractiveness, woman, nature, youth, girl, femininity, etc.), then men most often evaluate a particular woman (woman, girl, hair, face, body, figure, individuality).

The strength of men was evaluated in more detail and more carefully than the strength of women. Men provided 92 answers, but women only provided 61, most of which were synonymous with power: strength, energy stamina, health, etc.

Men and women regarded betrayal and licentiousness differently. For a woman it is primarily associated with: treachery, lies, meanness, deception, resentment, revenge (love being the only positive word, marriage and mystery being the only neutral words). However, men used more positive and neutral words: love, homeland, loyalty, home, family, friends, etc.

The experiment revealed significant differences in the images of linguistic consciousness between men and women.

In Russian culture there are many associations related to gender, even moral associations. For example, the concept of shame is more closely associated with the weaker sex: maidenly shame; to lose shame (most often referring to a woman). Decency is also most often associated with women and for Russians a woman's decency is obedience to her husband, modesty, loyalty.

Our observations allow us to say that it is not only the female language that is considered labeled, but also pairs of opposing words; in "man-woman" the word "woman" includes labels. Similar pairs of apparent equality have one term that is always perceived as more significant, and the second as derivative and labeled: light-darkness, day-night, male-female. A non-labeled member always leads the pair: the bride and groom, the grandfather and grandmother. Of course, linguistic labeling cannot be recognized as the one and only factor reflecting gender relations in language, but we cannot fail to see this as a cultural tradition reflected in the language.

The fact that the gender issues are reflected in language is confirmed by the following observations: families with boys use dialect more often, whereas families with girls use literary language more often; women and men have different attitudes to humor: in the first group laughter and joke are aimed at integration in the group, and in the second for individual confrontation (George Lakoff).

We are also interested in comparisons; they are the oldest type of intellectual activity. Based on comparison and other intellectual techniques, each person develops their own stereotypes and symbols. So, a Russian woman is compared with a birch tree, a flower, a rowan tree; Belarusians make comparisons to kalina bushes; Lithuanians cannot compare a woman to a birch, because the genus of a noun influences the formation of a symbol, and for Lithuanians the birch is masculine in gender. Chyngyz Aitmatov compares a woman to the mare.

Language establishes patriarchal policy of firmly entrenched stereotypes in which a woman has many vices.

Therefore, the comparisons of men to women are always negative: she is talkative, curious, coquettish, narcissistic, capricious, hysterical as a woman, female logic. Compared to men, a woman is a mere adornment. Men have intelligence, reach, character. A woman is described as unable to be a friend and keep secrets, stupid, illogical: a woman's path is from the oven to the front door[230], a woman's mind ruins homes; where a woman rules, the devil is commissar. Numerous proverbs and sayings about women use a disdainful and patronizing tone: *it's not my business and my husband is right; A husband sins outside the house, but the wife brings everything inside; a woman's flattery has evil intent.*

Woman has negative connotations even in the role of wife and mother: *to show Kuzka's mother to someone[231]; Drink wine, beat your wife, no problems; Married like a sunset behind the clouds. Marry[232] once and cry for a century.* Everything good in women comes from men, such is the stereotype of Russians. Therefore, if a woman has a man's intelligence, she is smart; a man's grasp refers to a successful woman; a man's character is about a woman with a steady character, etc. Nekrasov's description of a Russian woman, "will stop a horse at full gallop to enter a burning hut"[233] is not just masculine behavior; the phrase is strengthened by the prototype of throwing oneself into the fire, a male element.

These are linguistic and folk stereotypes. But, what is the speech behavior of a woman? Deborah Tannen explored speech strategies in her book, *That's Not What I Meant! How Conversational Style Makes or Breaks Relationships*, showing that men and women use language for different purposes: a woman treats conversation as an important part of interpersonal relationships; a man, on the other hand, uses

---

[230] Old Russian saying, when it was believed that a woman's main duty was to care for the home and keep the family fed.

[231] Show someone who is boss, to fix someone's wagon.

[232] In Russian, there is a verb for when a man marries and a different one for when a woman marries. Here, the saying uses the verb женишься, meaning when a man marries a woman. There are no similar sayings for when a woman marries a man.

[233] From the poem ""Grandfather Frost the Red Nose" by Nicholai Nekrasov.

conversation to show that he is in control of the situation; the conversation helps him to preserve independence and raise his status. The reasons for this, in the author's opinion, lie in communicative styles. She identified two of their most important characteristics - involvement and independence. Men are independent; women are a secondary part of the communication.

Our observations, and that of other researchers, make it possible to establish that men are more adaptable to changes in language, their speech having more neologisms. The speech of a woman is more neutral and static; her vocabulary more often includes outdated words and phrases. Female speech is much more emotional, as expressed in the more frequent use of interjections, metaphors, comparisons, epithets and figurative words. Her vocabulary has more words describing feelings, emotions and psychophysiological conditions. Women are more likely to use euphemisms. They try to avoid elements of familiarity, nicknames and invective vocabulary.

While studying the use frequency of individual parts of speech, it was found that women used more complex adjectives, adverbs and conjunctions. A woman's speech often uses specific nouns, while men's speech is more abstract. Men often use active verbs while a woman uses passive ones. This can be explained by the more active roles of men. At the same time, it was found that higher education diminished these differences in speech.

Gender differences are also reflected in literary fiction, where gender is represented from two perspectives: 1) female topics; 2) women's literature. At the end of the nineteenth century, the intimate lyricism of a woman's perspective increased dramatically: female poetry removed itself from topics related to social problems. Examples of this may be found in the works of Mirra (Maria) Lokhvitskaya, who at the beginning of the century was known as the Russian Sappho, a title that was also later awarded to Marina Tsvetaeva. Their main theme was love's devotion, not abstract or romantic, but fatal, passionate, carnal and sensual:
I crave sultry pleasures, unearthly caresses, immortal words, indescribable visions, incomparable moments.

She sings of a liberated love, of an anguished love:
And if you have a wish to write but are destined to drag the yoke of a slave, bear your cross with the grandeur of a goddess, learn to suffer!

This type of poetry is a protest against traditional female poetry (themes of Christian and romantic love, family happiness, motherhood). For Marina Tsvetaeva, poetry "grew" from life. But, the life of Mirra Lokhvitskaya differed sharply from the lyrical heroines she wrote about: Lokhvitskaya was a sensible housewife and mother of three children. Valery Bryusov noted that "a poet is not attracted to sin as a goal, but as a violation of truth, and this creates a truly demonic poetry" (Valery Bryusov, 1912).

The female is portrayed with great diversity in the poetic picture of the world; woman is a flower: "I remembered her as a festival of Snowdrop flowers" Igor Severyanin.

George Lakoff found that men and women distinguish colors differently. Men make significantly less distinctions. Our observations made it possible to supplement this idea; a woman not only has a wider color spectrum but uses more names for exotic colors: "moire", "azure." Women poets transform color distinctions into symbols more often than men do. Male colors are more specifically grounded: "the color of pressed strawberries" (Herzen, *Notes of a Young Man)*; "the eyes were insolent and multicolored, the colors of a bee"; "a neck the color of a mummy"; "a skirt the color of partridge" (Bunin); "Sobakevich's coat was truly bear colored" (Gogol). It seems that all color designations, such as ash, honey, emerald, lilac, cherry, milk, pistachio, coffee with milk, ivory, etc. were invented by men.

In the nineteenth century, parlor speech included terms such as the color of snake skin, the color of downcast eyes, a bonnet the color of victory, a scarf the color of a newcomer; these are typically female designations.

Of course, male writers also use a variety of color designations, but most of them are grounded: "Men's suits for sale. There is one style . . . What color? Oh, a huge selection of colors! Black, black-gray, gray-black, blackish-gray, grayish-black, slate, emery, the color of pig iron, coke color, peat, earth, trash, press cakes, and the color that in old days was called *a robber's dream*" (Ilf and Petrov); "He was in something that looked like a stage jacket, the color of cafe ole, and trousers the color of chocolate-ole, and in shoes the color of creme-brule, with wine-red socks" (*The Holy Well*, by Valentin Kataev).

And this is how Marina Tsvetaeva uses color. In the poem "Side Streets", azure symbolizes paradise, a heavenly temptation:

Azure, azure,
precipitous mountain!
Azure, azure,
a second Earth!
dawns of Azurevna,
blue Ladanovna
azur-azur,
my cool one!
a dawn![234]

Marina Tsvetaeva plays on azure, turning the word around its different facets, fearlessly experimenting with color, turning it into a symbol of a steep mountain, then a symbol of the earth, then a symbol of coolness. Imitating folklore, complex names such as dawns of Azurevna and azure Ladanovna.

In verbal behavior, women are oriented towards "obvious social prestige," i.e., on generally accepted norms of social and verbal behavior, while man gravitates toward so-called hidden prestige - to deviation from established norms and rules of communication. Therefore, a woman's speech is softer and has less conflict. Women are less categorical in expressing and defending opinions, making them more suitable for performing many social functions. Realization of this fact has caused a revaluation of women's obviously low social status. Women are finally becoming full legal partners

---

[234] In Russian, Лазорь (azure) is similar to зорь (dawn).

in all aspects of social life. Several modern social scientists use male and female equality as a factor in assessing social development.

The male-female attraction is the law of life in the Cosmos. According to Clement of Alexandria's apocrypha, a disciple of apostle John once asked Jesus about the coming of the Kingdom of Heaven, and Jesus answered: "When the two are one and the male will be feminine and there will be neither male nor female" (The Mystery of the Three, Egypt and Babylon, by Dmitry Merezhkovsky). Therefore, gender relation issues should be of the highest cultural importance; otherwise, the decay of morals will lead to the death of nations and civilizations (Sodom and Gomorrah).

The image of man in myth, folklore and phraseology

At the center of the world stands the individual, having a body, soul and speech, i.e. a person of feelings and status, thoughts and words, actions and emotions, a person who is good, evil, a sinner, a saint, a fool, a genius, etc.

In the mythological consciousness, man was at the center of the universe; the ancients saw the person as an anthropomorphic embodiment of the universe: the vertical position of the person was a striving towards the sky, with which his "higher" thoughts were connected, and the horizontal in man was all that was earthly and perishable ("heavenly" and "worldly" in the Bible).

The external appearance of man as embodied in myth and language

The outward appearance of a person consists of three components: the head and its parts, the body, the legs. How is this represented in mythology and language?

If in modern understanding the head is the center of information processing, then for the ancients everything related to the head corresponded with the heavenly constellations: the sun, the moon, the stars. The mythologem for the head was "the sun", which formed the basis of such phraseologies as: spinning head, hot head, head swirls.

Another mythology of the head was "God, above all, important" reflected in the phraseology of the godhead (important), the golden head (about an intelligent person). Most Russian phraseologies with the component "head" were formed later and have lost practically all connections with these mythologems. Now these phraseologies mostly refer to the intellectual abilities of a person, qualities, physical condition, etc. For example, *a good head on her shoulders, his head is screwed on right, head is boiling with ideas* - about a clever person; *without a king at the head, a green head, a hot head, a block head, a straw head* - about a stupid person man.

Denoting the most important part of the person, the word "head" forms phraseologies that characterize a person from the most varied perspectives: like snow on your head[235] (unexpectedly), even if you carve the head with a stake (a stubborn person)[236], an unbowed head (a defiant person), a swollen head (the wealth of a person), a bowed head (a person without hope), a hot head (an impetuous person), a talentless head (a destitute person), etc. Most phraseologies using the "head" component have a positive connotation, which is explained by the presence in Russian mentality of the archetype: "head = sun, divinity."

The parts of the include eyes, nose, mouth, tongue, ears, teeth, etc. These organs have their own appearance and very broad but clear functions: to look, smell, taste, talk, etc. Eyes are the most important part of the head and face of a person. The most ancient mythology, from which many metaphors survive to this day, is "eye = deity." Quasi-synonyms for "eyes" include the mind's eye and the mind, which are stylistic expressions of the neutral word "eyes", the organ of vision of any living being. Human eyes can be beautiful, large and expressive. The eyes characterize not only

---

[235] как снег на голову, appear out of the blue; come like a bolt from the blue; as sudden as an April shower

[236] *хоть кол на голове теши* (old Church Slavonic).

the physical, but the spiritual abilities of man to comprehend phenomena, i.e. inner vision. They are the organ of intuition: to see with my mind's eyes, to see with the inner eye, the mirror of the soul, the eyes of the heart, the spiritual eyes, the person in contemplation, "you present me with the eyes of my very soul" (Fyodor Tyutchev).

Language accurately notes the unusual capacities of the eyes; its pupils in motion. This is why many verbs of motion are combined with the word "eye": "to make eyes at someone", "to keep an eye on", "to take your eyes off of something", "skim with your eyes", "measure with your eyes", "devour with your eyes", "follow with your eyes", "fix your eye on." The eyes are an organ-instrument, an organ of "vision." Therefore, our eyes "spin in surprise and amazement", our eyes open wide when we unconsciously try to get as much information through them; we screw up our eyes during close observation or with a high concentration of thought, we turn our eyes away from the condemning gaze of others, thereby protecting our brain from the negative impact of the speaker, etc.

In many people's mythologies, the sun and the moon were believed to be the eyes of a powerful deity. Related to this mythologem are the phraseologies: "through the eyes of the owner" (reliable supervision of something),"no eyes" (without supervision).

Another mythologem is "eye = person", which gave rise to many phraseologies: "a good eye" (about an experienced person), "easy on the eyes" (about a physically attractive person), "eyes are smiling" (visible joy), "the eyes deceive" (about doubting what is seen), "he has eyes for her" (about a strong desire for a person), and there are metaphors such as "the eyes speak", "wandering eyes", "eyes of shame"; and sayings such as "covetous eyes", "hands like a rake" (about the insatiability of human nature), etc.

Since 80% of the information about the world comes through the eyes, they are considered the most important organs; magical powers are attributed to them. In ancient Rus, a side glance was considered "evil." Faith in the evil eye was born when, according to the ancients, the world was inhabited by spirits. However, to this day, when we have a bad feeling about something, we still say a bad eye has looked on it[237]. Phraseologies that include the word "eyes" have recorded and preserved ancient behavioral stereotypes. "don't take your eyes off", "eye wash and others."

Deception interferes with someone's perception of the world, hence the phraseology, "to throw the wool over your eyes", "throw dust in the eyes"[238].
Amulets, long used against curses, were made of precious metals and stones and in the form of an eye, hence the phraseology, "eagle eye" (the ability to see the important or fundamental), "the apple of your eye" (loved), "keep your eyes open" (be careful), "the aided eye" (more common is the naked eye), etc.

Hair is regarded differently by various peoples. In ancient times, The Rus gave hair tremendous significance. Pregnant women were forbidden from cutting their hair, because it had a protective function. This is confirmed by surviving folk traditions – do not to cut a child's hair until it's one year old. In folk poetry, a girl with cut braids was disgraceful; she could not marry without braids. Only recently has popular scientific literature begun to explain this.

Language has retained many phraseologies that use archetypes of *hair* to gather the forces of experience: grey haired experience; experienced to the roots of one's hair. Hair is a receptacle of memory and will – "hair stood on its ends" (about a fright that paralyzes the will). At a subconscious level, these archetypes continue to guide our actions. Convicts are shaved so as to paralyze their will; another archetype is at "work" here: "haircut = change of life." Ancient Slavs performed "tonsure" on boys who reached adolescence, and this ritual is still used by monks, although the hair is not cut. Army recruits, however, are thoroughly sheared.

In Rus, cut hair was burned. Throwing hair into the fire was a kind of sacrifice to the hobgoblins. There was one more

---

[237] недобрый глаз поглядел.
[238] замазать глаза, пускать пыль в глаза (Russian); замыльваць вочы, сляпщь вочы, жвір у вочы сыпаць (Belorusian).

custom: hair left on a comb could not be thrown away. It was believed that if birds used it for their nests or if it was near tools, if would affect a person's wellbeing. To this day, natives of the Pacific Ocean attach an enemy's hair to water plants in order to ruin his health in the tides. To prevent hair from falling into the hands of enemies, locals often cut their hair short.

The phraseology, "you won't lose any hair over it" is from Church Slavonic, meaning that the person will not suffer any harm. It includes the archetype, "hair = human health." The archetype, "hair = person" corresponds to the Belarusian phraseology "hair and hair" (about similar people).

The nose is also an important part of the face. The word "nose" has become a component of a rather large number of metaphors and phraseologies where the archetype, "nose = man" is evident (for example, in Gogol's novel *The Nose*, the nose behaves like a human being): "stick your nose in" (about a curious person)," hang your nose" (sad), "led by the nose" (deceive), "nose to nose" (very close), etc.

The Slavs believed that beards had protective functions and pulling someone's beard was considered a terrible insult. The Russians have a proverb: "the beard is dearer than the head." Muslims to this day believe that the beard is part a particularly serious vow, *I swear by the beard of the Prophet!*

The quasi-synonyms lips and mouth can have different meanings and usage. The mouth is a specifically human organ, while the lips can be the organs of animal, etc. Usage of the word "lips" became wide-spread only in the 16th-17th centuries. Therefore, the word "mouth" is more useful for researching phraseologies and other archaic forms: mouth to mouth, straight from the mouth, on everyone's lips[239], don't let it out of your mouth, "the mouth of a child speaks the truth", "from your mouth to God's ear." The word "mouth" often stands for "talking person": "for a beautiful mouth can lie."

It should be noted that "tongue" is a term used as a concept in many phraseologies and has various meanings: as

---

[239] The literal translation of the Russian "у всех на устах" is "on everyone's mouth."

the instrument for speaking, "cat's got my tongue"[240] (does not have the nerve to speak), "a slip of the tongue" (how could I have said that); To denote the process of speaking, "to bite your tongue" (to control speech), "to loosen your tongue" (to speak freely), "to wag your tongue" (to speak too much), etc.

Other parts of the human face and head do not offer as many useful metaphors and phraseologies but, nevertheless, offer some: ears didn't move, (did not bat an eye) up to my ears, ears perked up, ears wilt (listening to something that makes you sick). These metaphors denote behavior, feelings or attitudes. To have a tooth (to hold a grudge), gets stuck in your teeth (to be bored); good on the lips (tastes good); doesn't ruffle the mustache (to express indifference), etc.

The parts of the body used most frequently in semantical formation are: the hands, feet, back, navel. They form the most diverse phraseologies, many of which have a mythological basis.

There are several notable phraseological archetypes that use "hand" as a component. For example, the hand as a symbol of strength, right and power: "to have a hand in", "someone's right hand", etc.; The hand is a symbol of wealth, an instrument for the acquisition of material goods, often unfairly, "to warm your hands" (line your pockets), "to have your hand in somebody's pocket" (Russian); to splinter your hands[241], "a bird in the hand", "under your thumb"[242] "grease the palm" (Belarusian). In order to take possession of a thing, to appropriate it, you must grab someone's hand with your own hand and in this way, declare your rule. The Russian word for "litigation"[243] relates to the fact that court litigants pull themselves into controversy with the stronger acquiring power.[244]

---

[240] The literal translation of the Russian "язык не поворачивается" is "tongue won't turn."

[241] Hold hands, руку заскабіць Belarusian.

[242] Literaly, to put under your hand. Can also mean to seize property.

[243] The word "Тяжба" litigation is related to the word "тянуть" to pull.

[244] (стяжать силы, to gather strength, is an outdated phraseology with positive connotations, while the contemporary стяжательство includes more negative connotations).

This of phraseology includes the component "pocket" as a place for the hands, even though hands themselves are not mentioned: "lining pockets", "to get into someone else's pocket" (Russian); to put in your pocket (Belarusian)[245].

Most phraseologies having the component "hand" have a negative context or connotation: "to be under your hand" (under your thumb), i.e., be under the power of; "to be passed around"[246] (one definition "unofficial distribution" is neutral, and the second refers to prostitution and is more negative); "the dog's paw is raised" (lacks determination), "empty-handed" (without bringing anything), "itching for a fight"[247] (wanting to fight), a hot head[248] (not controlling oneself), etc. The negative context of these phraseologies could form an archetype; however, we have not been able to establish one.

The Rus performed many important rituals using hand gestures: for blessing, repenting, taking oaths. These rituals fixed themselves onto many phraseologies: placing your hand over your heart (honesty), shake hands (make a deal, agree). Even something as simple as joining hands is a symbol of communication, of accord. Accordingly, a handshake is a gesture of welcome, of friendship. He who "vouches"[249] for someone accepts responsibility for that person.

Many phraseologies and old expressions using the word finger are still used: "pointing a finger", "hand of fate"[250], "don't lay a finger", etc. And, although the phrases with the word "finger" are uncommon, there are fixed and persistent associations in the native speaker's mind, which are supported by culturally important texts: religious, poetic, philosophical.

The pagan Slavs believed that "feet"[251] had demonic qualities: "the devil himself would break his leg[252] (about a cluttered place), what the left foot wants[253] (whatever pops to

---

[245] To earn or amass wealth.
[246] ходить по рукам, literally, to walk on hands.
[247] руки чешутся, literally, hands itch.
[248] под горячую руку, literally, hot hand.
[249] In Russian, to vouch for is, "ручаться", and the root of the word is рука, "hand."
[250] перст судьбы is literally, the finger of fate.
[251] "Ноги" can mean legs or feet.
[252] The devil himself couldn't make heads or tails of it.

mind) to get up on the left foot (to start off on the wrong foot), here the lexeme "left" relates to the devil; The ground burns underfoot (about a dangerous place), the earth is shaking under your feet (about an uncertain, dangerous situation), to shake the dust of your feet (to break away from something decisively and forever, forget), etc. Almost all Russian and Belarusian phraseologies using "foot" as a component have a negative connotation.

Russians believed all devils and demons had limps. Goblins, imaginary creatures in Russian fairy tales, were shaped like bears and had peg-legs. All mythological characters born on the Earth had bad legs.

The phraseologies: "grab your feet"[254] (shake a leg), "throw yourself at their feet"[255] (humbly ask for something), "move your feet"[256] (to escape danger), "never set foot here again", the proverb (a warning to never come back), "take a load of your feet"[257] (an invitation to sit down) and other expressions all have a negative connotation related to the archetype "feet = belong to the devil."

Many expressions that do not directly use the word feet are associated with this archetype: "tracks", 'steps", "path", "road", etc. Therefore, a person who has broken the law has veered away from the right path. This expression may not just refer to a person who has broken the law, but to a slovenly, dissolute or mistaken person. The phraseology "block one's path" means to "harm someone, block the path to a goal." The phrase, "to cover up the tracks" (hide something) has certain connotations: a snowstorm sweeping away the tracks of travelers causes one to stray; sweeping away the path is to lose your way back. The word "steps" is used in many phrases: take steps, in the footsteps of, etc.

Despite the small number of phrases with the word "spine"[258], they are important in the Russian mentality because

---

[253] как левая нога хочет; whatever pops into smb.'s head (of absurd whims)

[254] брать ноги в руки

[255] в ногах валяться.

[256] унести ноги, take to your heels.

[257] ногах правды нет, literally, the legs have no rights, the legs aren't your master.

they are associated with the concept of heavy, unbearable work: to work your tail off[259], to break your back (spine). However, the back is also a reliable defense. Hence the phraseology "behind a broad back" and others.

There are few phraseologies that use the word component "navel." The best known is "navel of the universe." However, in mythology the navel had a special role, probably based on the fact that a child is connected to the mother and is nourished through the umbilical cord. It is the most important organ for the fetus. And there is another important reason; the navel is the center of the abdomen, and the center is an essential concept in all mythologies and religions.

Many words for clothing are also associated with the parts of the human body, forming phraseologies such as "born in a shirt"[260], (about a fortunate person), to be left shirtless (about an impoverished person). According to Alexander Potebnja, their semantics are based on myths; caps and shirts were protective amulets for the Slavs. In addition, to be born in a shirt means an unusual birth and, according to Vladimir Propp, a miraculous birth is the sign of a hero.

The sayings "go cap in hand" (to humble oneself) and "Trishka's coat"[261] (unsuitable clothes) are semantically associated with another characteristic of clothes, interfering with the free movement of the body. This creates a negative context in most phrases that use the names of clothing.

Accordingly, we see that phrases that allude to the body (except for the head) generally have negative connotations; they express disapproval, disdain and contempt. Probably, this is because in mythology all parts of the human body were associated with demons, devils and evil spirits.

---

[258] "Спина" can mean both spine and back.

[259] "Гнуть спину"; literally, to bend your spine.

[260] Born under a lucky star.

[261] From Ivan Krylov's "Trishka's Coat" ("Тришкин кафтан"), Trishka tries to patch his coat by cutting off the sleeves to cover the elbows and then having to cut off the flaps and tails to lengthen the sleeves. Robbing Peter to pay Paul.

The Soul and Heart as the "Spiritual Centers" of Man

Pavel Florensky wrote that in Indo-European languages, phraseologies that use "heart" have their very roots in the concept of centrality. In other cultures and languages, the localization of emotions (sensations) is different. In the Chinese naive picture of the world, emotions are localized in the kidneys, in Africa (West African Dogon languages) it's in the liver and nose; In French it's in in the spleen.

In the Russian and Belarusian picture of the world, the heart is the focus of emotion: *sadness tormented my heart.* Expressing various emotions, the lexeme "heart" unites with many different verbs, forming metaphors with different meanings: the *heart beats, sings, boils* (Pushkin), *shrinks* (Chekhov), *tears, trembles, flutters* (Fet), *lights up, skips, freezes* (Furmanov), *fades, grows tight* (Green), *trembles, tears, sinks, tightens, rolls up* (Zoshchenko), *flames* (Zabolotsky), *hardens, becomes stale, coarsens, grows cold, softens* (Sholokhov); *Heart trembled, fluttered, pinned, fell, rolled* (Kuprin), etc.

Why are these metaphors understandable to every Russian native speaker, every Russian language personality? Because at the heart of such exchanges lie archetypes and mythologems that regulate metaphorical uses. For example, the mythologem "feelings = fluid" is taken from biblical mythology, it gives rise to the image of a cup from which a person drinks, experiencing feelings: to drink to the bottom (about feelings), the depth of feelings, "love is a vessel, hence full love (Marina Tsvetaeva), inexhaustible love; love is an ocean, a sea, hence love can be quiet, stormy, calm, etc. Thus, the mythologem "feelings = fluid" transmits and fixes fluidity, variability, dynamics.

When speaking of feelings and emotions, one cannot help but notice that there is another "parameter" - "top-bottom." Emotions are associated with vertical and horizontal parameters; therefore, calmness would be immobile on this scale, the "zero" coordinate; positive emotions are associated with upward movement (jumping for joy), and negative ones with downward movement (sunk with grief).

The difficulty in studying the symbols, images, and mythologies of the heart is that the heart is not just a "receptacle of emotions." Boris Vysheslavtsev[262] rightly states that the heart is the center of a circle from which an infinite number of radii can emanate, or a center of light from which an infinite number of various rays can be emitted. Therefore, the heart is the center of life in general: physical, mental, religious and spiritual. The heart is credited with all the functions of consciousness. Thinking and will result in decisions: "When he turned forty, his heart was filled with the desire to visit his brethren, the children of Israel "(Acts 7:23). The same is true of conscience. Conscience, according to the apostle, is a law written in the heart.

Boris Vysheslavtsev emphasized the importance of the heart as a symbol of religion, writing that religion expresses the inner center of personality. The heart is something more incomprehensible, impenetrable, mysterious and hidden than the soul, spirit or consciousness. The Gospel says that the heart is the organ of religion, the organ by which we contemplate God: "Blessed are the pure in heart, for they will see God" (Matthew, 5: 8).

On the one hand, the heart is the point of contact with God, the organ that establishes an intimate connection with him. From here we get "living with God in their heart, the compassionate" (about the kind and tender). On the other hand, it is the source of sin, the dark force, "heartless" (callow man), "a stone instead of a heart", "an icy heart", "angry" (inclined to rage, irritation). The phraseology "hot under the collar"[263] (angered, temper flaring), "in the heart" (in a fit of pique), "to rip the heart out of someone" (vent your anger). In the Bible, "heart" and "soul" are usually different, but sometimes act as interchangeable synonyms.

Another important mythologems of the heart is as the receptacle of the soul, the essence of life's force: "the heart

---

[262] (1877 -1954) Russian philosopher, religious thinker.
[263] под сердитую руку, literally under an angry hand.

groans in an evil heart"[264] (proverb), the abduction of the heart is tantamount to death, "you have stolen my heart" (metaphor) and the phrases, "pierce the heart", "break the heart", etc.

Let's name a few other mythologems regulating the modern usage of phraseologies that use "heart" as a component: The receptacle of desires, "follow one's heart", "with a sinking heart"; a place where feelings and desires are born, "a spark of love and hope grew in her heart"; the center of intuition, "my heart feels", "the heart knows"[265], "your heart will tell you", "creep into the heart"[266]; the center of conscience and other moral qualities, "to give your heart", "heart of stone", "heart of gold"; a source of light and warmth, "the heart burns", "warmed by the heart" (*The Flaming Heart of Danko,* by Maxim Gorky); a treasure trove "the keys to my heart", "give your heart" (and the Gospel: "A good man brings good things out of the good stored in his heart . . ." (Luke 6:45); the guarantor of growing love, "to offer hand and heart; a place in which feelings are hidden from prying eyes, "no one knew what was happening in his heart", "look into a person's the heart", etc.

The same mythologeme-archetype of the heart can be the basis of phraseological units describing a person's external and internal qualities, as well as various objects and a person's relationships to those objects.

Practically the entire world can be described using phraseologies that have "heart" as a component: 1) the various feelings and conditions of a person: "a cat is scratching at the heart"[267], "a frozen heart", a rock fell from his heart[268], lifted my heart[269], take to heart, my heart bleeds for you, butter on my heart[270], broken heart, my heart is not in place[271], the heart is weary, etc. 2) a person's relationship towards world objects:

---

[264] в злобном сердце душа стонет.

[265] у сердца есть уши, literally, the heart has ears.

[266] A feeling begins to grow.

[267] кошки на сердце скребут - something is gnawing in my heart.

[268] камень с сердца свалился - A load off my mind.

[269] отлегло от сердца

[270] как маслом по сердцу - like music to my ears.

[271] сердце не на месте - worried sick.

"purely from the heart", "a sinking heart", "hand over your heart", "with all my heart", "my heart belongs to", "my heart is taken", "from the heart", win your heart[272], etc.; 3) to describe someone: "a heart covered with moss[273], a soft heart, a kind heart, a heart of stone, an indomitable heart, a heart of gold, a the heart of a warrior, a warm heart, a foolish heart; 4) to characterize a person in society: to look into his heart, work your way into her heart, do as your heart wishes, break your heart, win the heart, open heart, shatter your heart.

Language shows that the heart is not only the center of consciousness, but of the unconscious, not only the center of the soul, but of the body, the center of sinfulness and holiness, the center of all emotions and feelings, of thought and will. It is not only an "organ of feelings", an "organ of desires", but an "organ of apprehension." The heart is the absolute center of the whole human; in the words of Boris Vysheslavtsev, "the heart is both an intelligent vision and an intelligent activity."

The no less complex relationship between the modern world and the mythological one is seen in the word "soul." Nature, according to the ancients, also had a soul, but of a lesser quality than man's. Aristotle, for example, believed that even stars had souls. Plato divided the soul into "rational" (human) and considered the stars as animated, and Plato divided his soul into "rational" (human) and "sensual" (animal). The main difference between nature and man, created in the image and likeness of God, was that man had a nonmaterial divine soul. According to Karl Jung, "the complexity of the soul grew in proportion to the loss of spirituality in nature."

Since antiquity, the soul was understood as fire (Democritus), then as air (Anaximenes), then as a mixture of all four elements (Empedocles). These representations are still preserved in language ("the soul burns", "the soul soars", "the soul ignites").

Different people believed that the receptacle of the soul was located in different organs: the diaphragm, the heart,

---

[272] войти в сердце – literally, enter your heart.
[273] сердце обросло мхом, a cold heart.

the kidneys, the eyes and even the heels (for example, in Russian there is the phrase "my soul left its heels"[274]). Primitive peoples believed that the connection between the soul and body was so close that if the dead body was disfigured the soul would also be disfigured. Therefore, they guarded their dead and deliberately disfigured the enemy dead.

The Slavs attributed creative forces to the human soul, without which life on earth was impossible. The soul was a spark of heavenly fire, "that sparks in the eyes, burns in the blood and warms the entire body" (Boris Vysheslavtsev). According to these representations, bound by metaphors, the soul glows, burns, has warmth, sparkles, and thaws. The soul is also the opposite; it's like ice, like a raging hell, etc. This mythology is closely related to the idea of the soul as a transitional state of fire (Heraclitus).

The soul is the alter ego of the person, the inner "I": a lower soul, a higher soul, a shallow soul, a tender soul, a sensitive soul, a noble soul, a sinful soul, a faithful soul, a wicked soul, an idle soul. The soul (like man) is mortal: to give your soul to God; the weary soul, the tormented soul, etc.

From an ethical point of view, the soul is the bearer of many ideals: a pure soul, a stained soul; the purse is empty, but the soul is pure (proverb), etc.

From a religious point of view, the soul connects man with the highest spiritual origins, thereby increasing the value of the soul. It acquires a special significance in man's conscious efforts towards self-improvement: to save the soul, the soul is immortal, with God in soul, etc. The soul preserves itself during the person's entire life trajectory, but is not destroyed in death; therefore, the soul is alive (a constant in religious discourse).

The soul is a receptacle, empty or full, etc. Olga Freidenberg said that the "soul" could be metaphorically expressed as a double, part fate and any of these metaphors, which are in turn duplicated in other metaphors. Alexander Afanasyev and Alexander Potebnja showed that destiny in Russian folklore is a counterpart of man: it is drowned, it is

---

[274] душа в пятки ушла, my heart was in my throat (due to fear).

thrown into the water, it is burned, it is hanged, etc. We see this coupling and interaction of metaphors in actual speech activity.

Images of the soul as breath, air, wind, birds, and butterflies occur in all peoples, including the Slavs: "the soul flew away", "inspire the soul", "the soul is gone"[275], "the soul departed", "a new soul has arrived". Even etymologically, the soul is closely associated with the wind: the soul – breath – spirit – blow- breath – air[276]. In Slavic fairy tales, one frequently hears about a shirt of feathers, girls with wings of swans. According to Plato's famous myth, the soul seeks an "otherworldly" heavenly home and has wings that grow. Plato believed that the soul fell to the ground from the sky. It has been living on the earth for ten thousand years and will not return to heaven until receiving inspiration. According to Slavic pagan beliefs, if a person has lived righteously the soul turns into a dove, if in sin into a black crow or into a sad cuckoo. The mythologeme "soul = bird" is associated with the Slavic custom of leaving colored eggs on graves during Easter celebrations.

The soul is localized, hence the phrase, "the soul is not in the right place"[277]; the soul can be a solid object, "scratches the soul"[278]; like a surface, similar to a floor – "a stone weights heavy on my soul", "a scar on the soul"; the soul is like a book, "read the soul"; the soul is like a latrine — "defecate on the soul", "rot the soul"; the soul is like bread – "the soul grows stale"; the soul is like a flower — "blossom of the soul", "the soul blooms"; the soul is like musical instrument — "the strings of the soul"[279], etc.

Many metaphors and idioms are associated with the mythologeme "soul = small child." One hypothesis sets forth the idea that idioms are encoded with the birth process: in the depths of the soul, worry the soul, pry into the soul, to irritate

---

[275] To give up the ghost.

[276] душа—дыханье— дух—дуть—дуновение—воздух (In Russian, soul and breath are etymologically related.

[277] душа не на месте - to have a bad feeling about something.

[278] A feeling of loneliness.

[279] струны души – heartstrings.

the soul, open your soul, capture the soul, the soul weeps, strain the soul, etc. (The Russian icon "Dormition of the Mother of God" depicts the soul as a child).

The ancients believed that the soul is closely connected to the afterlife. This is why the ancient Slavs supplied the dead with various provisions. Men were buried with flint spears and arrows; women were given bronze bracelets. Pots of food were included.

The souls of the dead fly to heaven, where birds spent the winter. But the souls of the dead could also turn into birds and fly back. On the feast of "Dziady", Belarusians prepare to these dead souls by cleaning the house and preparing ritual meals.

The mythologeme "soul = smoke" is supported by the custom of burning the dead, a custom observed by many peoples, including the ancient Slavs. This was done to easily and immediately free the soul from the body for its heavenly flight. This myth is preserved in the idiom "the soul has flown to another world."

Thus, ideas about the heart and soul are complex, contradictory and inconsistent. This has found full expression in language, and these perceptions shape a person's picture of world.

An individual is the bearer of national mentality, and this can be explored through language, an important form of human identity.

Researchers have identified several levels within the structure of linguistic personality, each level having different characteristics. Personality is the totality of socially significant, spiritual and physical qualities reflected in language. Man appears in two forms—male and female; therefore, linguistic personality and verbal behavior differ between males and females.

At the core of culture should be the principle that the evolution of life and betterment of humanity must be done through the fusion of two opposites — male and female. We must have programs that account for the individual characteristics of the child, not ignore or hypertrophy them under the pressure of gender stereotypes.

The image of a man has been forever imprinted in idioms, proverbs and folkloric texts; this is why the study of these materials is of such interest for linguistic-cultural studies.

Questions and tasks

1. Consider how you might modify the experiment proposed by Yuri Sorokin? Can you name some of the advantages of experiment-based research?

2. What components can be identified in language personality?

3. What kind of research has been done about the gender differences in language?

4. Name several phraseologies that use the component "head", how many with the component "legs." What explains the sharply opposite connotations (positive and negative) of these phraseological units?

5. Which mythologems form the basis of phraseologies having the components "soul" and "heart"? Provide examples.

CHAPTER 6
Man in the Mirror of Comparison

Comparison: The Linguistic-Cultural Aspect

Comparison is the most ancient form of intellectual activity, older than mathematics (Edward Sapir). Comparison and culture cannot be separated from one another, and, in a broad sense, comparison is about similarities and differences. In "A conversation about Dante", Osip Mandelstam wrote: "I compare therefore, I live."

According to Michel Foucault, comparison (similarity) is "the most universal and visible process; however, it is also the most hidden, underlying but revealing. Comparison defines the shape of perception . . . and guarantees the richness of its content."[280]   Indeed, comparisons are sometimes incomprehensible, such as *drunk as the earth*[281]; such comparisons require some deciphering and additional knowledge. For example, one must remember that land is a symbol of fertility. It suggests fullness (like *Mat Zemlya*).[282] Comparisons often rely on the most unexpected characteristics: a tablecloth is white as snow. Here, it is not the color (white) of the table cloth, but purity; white as canvas, is the ability to change intensity.

---

[280] Michael Foucault. *The Order of Things: An Archaeology of the Human Sciences.* SPB, 1994, pg. 66, 144. (Author's citation.)

[281] This expression is found in Belarusian folklore. It refers to the fullness of Raw-Mother-Earth; Nikita Ilyich Tolstoy used this expression. It could be less literally translated as "drunk as a mother" or "drunk as dirt."

[282] Mat Zemlya (Mother Earth) is the personalized image of the earth in Slavic mythology. The earth gave life to all living creatures. She died in Fall and resurrected in Spring. Her counterpart was heaven, the god of thunder, who was believed to be her husband. Heaven The fertilized the Earth with rain, after which the Earth bore harvest.

In the Russian language picture of the world, people are constantly compared to one another. If they are similar in nature, behavior, social status or other personal characteristics, then it can be said that they are: *birds of a feather*[283], *they go like hand and glove*[284], *two boots in a pair, cut from the same cloth*[285], *carved from the same wood, same kind of wool, from the same watering hole, same suit, the same cut, smeared by the same myrrh, of the same type, both are good, one is worth the same as the other, husband and wife are one Satan, sparks from one flint*, etc. Belarusians also add: *both are just as bad.*

Lyudmila Lebedeva[286] noted 16 ideographic fields of personal characteristics: appearance *(hair soft as silk, black as pitch, a face as round as a pancake, eyes black as agates, a head as round as a watermelon, fingers thick as stumps, grimy as the devil)*, physical characteristics *(strong as an ox, solid as an oak; agile as a monkey, like a cat; a nose like a dog)*, physical condition *(hot as an oven; cool as a cucumber; frozen as a mutt, squeezed as a lemon)*, physical activities *(spins like an eel, jumps around like a ball, swallows like a shark)*, movement-immobility *(rush like a meteor; stand like a pillar, spin like a squirrel in a wheel, wander like the aimless)*, character traits, moral and professional qualities *(meek as a lamb; cowardly as a woman, sly as a fox, orderly as a German)*, skills and abilities *(swim like a fish, dive like a duck; write chicken scratch, sing like a nightingale)*, behavior (to die like a hero, behave like a beast, act like the boss, quiet as an owl), people and feelings *(to kill you like a dog, treated like a child, look like a freak, like a fish needs an umbrella)*, intelligence *(stupid as a child, stupid as a blockhead, clever as the devil; to look at like a sheep looking at a new gate)*, speech activity *(yell like a madman, talk like a book, chatter like a magpie, hiss like a snake)*, feelings and conditions *(walk as*

---

[283] Literally, одного поля ягода is berries from the same field.

[284] Literally, гусь (кулик) да гагара — пара, a goose, (sandpiper) and a loon are a pair.

[285] Literally, из одного теста сделаны, made from the same dough.

[286] Author of *Comparisons Used in the Russian Language: A Brief Thematic Dictionary*

though underwater; laugh like a madman, neigh like a horse),
lifestyle (*live like a gentleman, to live like a wolf, live like a
white man, to live like a savage*), work-idleness (*to work like
an ox, to work like a horse, work like an ant, sit like a guest*),
poverty-wealth (*as poor as a church mouse, a beggar, poor as
Job, rich as Croesus*), thoughts, feelings and ideas (*pierce like
a sword, stuck in my head like a nail, foggy memory, thoughts
flash like lightning*).

It is through comparison of similarities that metaphors
and symbols arise, and mythological consciousness is
expressed. Many riddles and jokes (Armenian radio jokes), are
based on comparison. In 1918, while studying Japanese
puzzles, Evgeny Polivanov identified "comparison-puzzles"
such as: "What's like a slacker?" - Answer: "a paper lantern -
both hang around uselessly."

The general topic of this section is cultural-national
language study. It focuses on the national features revealed
through the selection of images (comparison) that describe
human characteristics.

It is known that conceptual understandings of cultural
categories are embodied in natural language. National
mentality and spiritual culture are primarily embodied in the
figurative content of language units, and one of the most
obvious methods for obtaining clues about the secrets of
national consciousness is sustained comparison.

Like Lyudmila Lebedeva, we believe that sustained
comparison is not just an understanding, a figure of speech or
a stylistic device. It is a linguistic phenomenon, a particular
language unit having meaning and a particular way of
expressing it. In the Russian language, their forms are quite
diverse: it is the comparison of the instrumental case (heart
lips)[287], the comparative degree of adjectives with nouns in
the instrumental case (a face gloomier than clouds)[288],
comparisons with lexical elements "like", "similar to" (a
specialist is like a dental abscess)[289], compound adjectives,

---

[287] (*губы сердечком*) The instrumental case is used for making this
comparison, i.e. heart like lips.
[288] *лицо мрачнее тучи.*
[289] (*специалист подобен флюсу*) Greeks regarded specialized professional as

containing elements of "similar to", "shaped like" (arch shaped brows)[290], adverbs formed from the possessive adjectives using the formant "as" (sly as a fox)[291] and others.

In Russian linguistics, a theoretical understanding of sustained comparisons began in the 1960s. Victor Vinogradov was one of the first to focus attention on sustained comparison as a special type of idiomatic construction in which the internal convention of a phrase is defined by traditional national characteristics, proven accuracy, everyday reality and striking expressions.

The psychological basis of comparison was noted by Ivan Sechenov: "Everything that people perceive through the senses and all that results from their mental activity (from a complete picture of the world to individual characteristics and properties, abstracts of reality and dismembered concrete impressions) can be connected in our minds by association."[292] He uses comparisons as a method of perceiving the world and its features. A similar use of comparisons was made by Alexander Potebnja, who argued that the very process of knowledge is the process of comparison.

A specific national vision of the world is reflected in the *semantics of comparison*. We conducted several experiments with native speakers of the Kyrgyz language that revealed several of their typical comparisons. These comparisons are related to: a) the geographic features of the area: as majestic as the Alatau; eyes as bright as the Issyk-Kul; a face as clear as a spring; a mouth as big as a cave; b) to the plant and animal world: a nose hooked like an eagle's beak; built like an oriental plane tree of the Archi[293]; built like a red deer c) the Kyrgyz make frequent comparisons to fairytale and national epic heroes: a head as clever as Kanykeya's[294]; brave as Cholponbai[295], as Duishenkul Shopokov[296]; strong as

---

incomplete men, meant to be slaves, and treated them with contempt.
[290] *дугообразные брови*
[291] "по" *(по-лисьи хитер).*
[292] Ivan Sechenov. For Whom and How to Develop Psychology: Psychological Studies. - St. Petersburg, 1873. - pp. 190. (Author's citation).
[293] *стройный, как чинара, арча.*
[294] The wife of Manas. Literally the name means married to the Khan.

Manas[297]; voice deep as Konurbaya's[298]; a face as fair as Akmoor's[299]; a hand a big as Bacai's;[300] d) the semantics of comparisons related to the specific economy and cultural life of a people: hair as long as a noose; head a large as a kazan[301]; a voice as pleasant as a komuz[302]; a face beautiful as the moon; a nose as straight as a komuz.

Poetic comparisons are an even simpler way to capture the national specifics of a particular object or phenomenon. Thus, the famous Kyrgyz poet Joomart Bokonbaev writes: "The Tian Shan is like a sleeping camel. Between its humped backed ring sparkles the Issyk-Kul - a living miracle - like a birthmark on the face of a maiden." It reflects a typical scene of a member of the Eastern culture, where a birthmark (considered a defect by the Slavs) is perceived as something beautiful, which can be compared to the most beautiful lake in the world - the Issyk-Kul.

Comparison in Turkic poetry has its own specifics, based on a unique national perception of the world - its mythological and mystical forms. For example, the famous Kyrgyz bard Boogachy (end of nineteenth - early twentieth century) makes the comparisons: you are as a flexible as a willow twig, heady as honey sweet, white as a body, you are as tender as meat fat kazy[303]. The last *gastronomic* comparison would be unacceptable in the Russian and

---

[295] Cholponbai Tuleberdiev. Red army hero of the Soviet Union. Used his body to cover an enemy bunker, allowing for the capture of a strategic base during the Voronezh offensive of WWII.

[296] A soldier in Panfilov's Division's Twenty-Eight Guardsmen. The Soviet newspaper *Red Star* initially reported that 28 Red Army soldiers held off a column of German tanks during the 1941 advance on Moscow. They destroyed 18 German tanks before being killed. The story was shown to be a fabrication by prosecutors in 1948.

[297] Hero of the epic Kyrgyz poem, *The Epic of Manas*.

[298] Character in the Kyrgyz poem, *The Epic of Manas*.

[299] *The White Seal* Kirgiz poem and film.

[300] Character in the Kyrgyz poem, *The Epic of Manas*.

[301] A type of large cooking pot used throughout Central Asia, Russia, and the Balkan Peninsula

[302] An ancient stringed instrument used in Central Asian music. It is a national symbol of the Kyrgyz.

[303] Traditional dish of the Turkic people. Similar to a sausage.

Belarusian culture, where food has never had special mystic functions (such as the eating of enemies in some cultures).

The Kazakh poet and educator of XIX century, Abay Kunanbayev, makes these comparisons: "The world is a huge lake, time is a gusty wind, the first wave is an elder brother, the rear wave a younger brother, one by one they die, let things go on as usual." There are no explicit criteria for the comparisons, but they can be reconstructed based on the background knowledge of the reader. Such reconstruction provides unique expressiveness to the poetic text. Traditional Sanskrit poetry uses such comparisons to persuade and impress the reader with the beauty, depth and uniqueness of poetic language. Oriental (Turkic-speaking) poets were convinced that if one did not use metaphors, similes, allegories, and other tropes, poetry would be no different from normal conversation and lose its poetic nature.

Ariadna Efron made some very Russian comparisons: "Spring, dull and unwelcoming, like the old woman's daughter in the Russian fairy tale" (from Letters to Boris Pasternak).

Thus, comparison can serve as a way of understanding the world and as a way of consolidating this knowledge in culture.

Comparison is not just a way of representing the emotions and values of the speaker (author); It is also a way for the reader to detect them. It creates a uniquely expressive subtext. This is because comparison's effect on perception is not just as an addition of "pieces" of the world being compared; it is a multiplication. This can probably be explained by the following: when different elements of the world are brought together, in addition to similarities, significant differences appear. For example, "What happens to the snow drifts, like swollen eyelids, pressing against the basement window" (Boris Shergin). Comparing snowdrifts and eyelids stimulates the psyche of the recipient (the reader and the listener). It creates emotional tension and an image within the text, resulting in a more expressive segment. Comparing objects from distant spheres creates a series of additional associations that not only add information but enhance the expressive effect: the more different the objects compared, the brighter their expression. The heuristic function of comparison is also evident; it allows for a deeper and wider understanding of the real world, an understanding from the most diverse and often unexpected directions.

In Philology, comparison is considered a type of path; in psychology it is one of the thought processes; in philosophy it is a powerful means of understanding the world, etc. There has been a particularly large amount of work devoted to the study of comparison within the structural-typological and semantic-functional fields, but almost none within cognitive, linguistic-cultural, or pragmatic aspects. The purpose of this work is to close this gap by studying the ethno-psycholinguistic aspects of comparisons.

Different cultural (literary) epochs used different comparisons. Vladimir Propp[304] wrote that comparison occupies a secondary position in the Russian epic, because the whole structure of poetic expression in the epic is directed . . . not towards the convergence of similarity but towards differentiation. According to Dimitry Likhachov, during the Middle ages there was a bias towards different types of comparisons: based on visual similarities, occasional comparisons emphasizing similarities in feel, smell and taste. In Old Russian Literature, comparisons dealt with the inner essence of the objects compared, explaining this nature and trying to view it from all sides. Thus, Sergius of Radonezh in *The Panegyric* wrote that God: "shone brightly, was a beautiful color, a fixed star, perfumed incense."

In comparing antiquity, one notes a desire to convey movement and rhythm (time is compared with the water current, life on the road, etc.). As pointed out by Olga Freidenberg, "even in a rock one feels flight, and in the tower - the fall."

Victor Vinogradov noted that modern comparisons (XI- XX centuries) focus on reality. They typically convey the internal similarities of the objects compared, making the

---

[304] Vladimir Propp was a Russian anthropologist and linguist. He analyzed the basic components of popular fairytales in order to identify their basic narrative elements. *The Morphology of the Folktale* was published in 1928 and translated into English in 1958.

subject clear and creating an illusion of reality: "Like a desert leopard, angry and wild" (Mikhail Lermontov), "The train went slowly, like a caterpillar" (Mikhail Bulgakov). In Lermontov's comparison, the boy was imbued with a quality that, from the human perspective, initially belonged to the leopard - anger and savagery; in other words, comparison with reality creates a new internal form (IF) which, when reinforced by the epithet "desert", makes the comparison more expressive. Such comparisons draw attention to distinguishing features, making them more visible. From these observations one may conclude that reality-based comparisons are a way to revive faded images and internal forms, resurrecting their expressiveness. These comparisons do not merely reconstruct the original imagery or create a new one - they provide a panoramic image: "Yegorushka was sitting in the driver's seat, bouncing like a kettle on the burner" (Chekhov). This is how the image is shaped, imbued with meaning and symbolic stratifications. According to Viktor Zhirmunsky's definition, this creates "dvoemirie"[305].

In the modern era, comparisons do more than just provide descriptive functions highlighting the features of the object compared. Many of them are also a way of creating new meaning. This feature of comparisons was noted by Alexander Potebnja and then by Osip Mandelshtam who wrote in "A Conversation About Dante", "Dante's comparisons are never descriptive, i.e., pure imagery. They always pursue a specific task - to provide the internal structure of the image."[306] Such comparisons are an effective heuristic tool.

Comparison also performs text-forming functions: "Autumn rain on the street. It doesn't pour, drip or freeze—it's just in the air. As if it decided to stay in our city forever, in our life" (Alexander Volodin). The image underlying a comparison might reappear throughout fairly large portions of a text, becoming in this way a symbol-image. An example of this can be found in the parable novel *Father-forest* by Anatoli

---

[305] Literally, "two worlds." In Russian literature of the twentieth century, it the conflict between this world and the other world.
[306] Osyp Mandelstam Word and Culture. - M., 1987. - S. 121. (Author's citation).

Kim, where the image of the forest acts as a kind of plot support based on one of the novel's central concepts. Here, the comparison does not simply grow from the text, it germinates into the text, cementing it, and thus ensuring the text's cohesion into a single structural unit. This comparison has a special role in organizing the text, serving as a means of implementing an important textual element: cohesion.

In a literary text, comparison builds *image*. Particularly vivid images are created by impressionistic (in the terminology of Eugene Zamyatin) comparisons. One example is the comparison used by Chekhov in, *The Seagull*, where Trigorin compares a cloud to a piano. Here, one can draw parallels with the art impressionists who saw the world in a uniquely new way and then revealed it to the public. For example, they did not use flesh tones to depict human skin: they saw reddishness when it was under the sun (Kuzma Petrov-Vodkin), and greenish when it was under the moon, sometimes blue (Edgar Degas), pink (Renoir), etc.

Impressionistic comparisons are widely used in poetic speech. An example is the poem by Semyon Lipkin "Notes on Prose":

Like youth the moon is two-horned,
Like the Steeps' golden sunset
Bunin shines brightly on me
A verbal splendor
Like the day's unremitting thirst,
Like a fusion of fire and fog
Platonov's words go up
Into the Divine light out of the pit...

These comparisons enliven the faded, indistinct images that exist in the consciousness of the linguistic personality, forming the unified image of contemporary prose perceived by the author. Here, along with others, comparison performs a structurally-composite function; as in scaffolding, system images are built within a framework of comparisons.

The emotional impact on the recipient is the foundation of these of comparison. Reason does not allow large semantic distances between the objects compared, but there should be some distance. Accordingly, Lev Tolstoy compares eyes not with coal or soot, but with wet currants, lips not with blood but with ripe cherries, cheeks with rose petals. Another example from Tolstoy: "A lake as blue as burning sulfur."

Contrasting unexpected and distant objects is particularly expressive; however, the recipient must be prepared for it. For example, these comparisons would seem absurd at first glance: "like a horse on baked ice, like the slim man[307], the movement's Apostle" (Boris Grebenschikov). An image appears: a horse is an animal of another era, a saved relic. The verbal form "baked" superimposes on the recipient an image different from first: a horse violently sacrificed to nature.

What is the pragmatic function of such comparisons? To help explain complex ideas. Bright and unexpected images assist understanding and memorization, making them highly persuasive. The old and familiar in such comparisons seems transformed and recreated. But, these comparisons are not just ornamented speech. Their textual essence provides a broader worldview. And, in revealing this world, such comparisons seem to create a distinct mood in the reader.

Undoubtedly, comparisons are similar to metaphors. The identifying characteristic of the metaphor is the omission of comparative conjunctions (like, as, as though, etc.) and predicatives (is similar to, resembles). By discarding the comparative marker (whether conjunction or predicative), metaphor directly casts off the basis of the comparison. Thus, a comparison is tripartite (A is similar to B on the basis of C), while a metaphor is bipartite (A is B). Metaphor is laconic, fitting easily into the "cramped lines of verse" (Yuri Tynianov), and is not generally used to indicated random similarities.

---

[307] The Slender Man is a legend about a strange, supernatural being who abducts and kills people. According to the legend, he can stretch or shorten his arms to any length. His appearance can cause memory loss, insomnia, paranoia, nosebleeds and coughing.

A modern type of comparison is the **comparison-metaphor**, which is difficult to distinguish from **comparison-images**, and particularly difficult to distinguish from impressionist style images. Comparison-metaphors are a challenge to the linguistic consciousness. There is a non-trivial relationship between the concepts of comparison and metaphor. These comparisons somehow undermine the logical and rational. As a rule, comparison-metaphors are divorced from reality: "the heart weeps like an apple tree" (Alexander Blok). A special artistic reality is created here, probably even a symbol of reality. This comparison keeps the reader under the power of the author, but still leaves freedom for creation.

With the help of similes, metaphors create a special world, the "word made manifest", resulting in semantic and expressive enhancement. An example is the poem of Osip Mandelstam "Century" where an age is compared to a beast whose back has been broken. And though life continues, the outcome is a foregone conclusion:

And with a meaningless smile you
look back, cruel but weak,
like a beast, once supple and lithe,
at the tracks left by your paws.

According to a survey of student-philologists, the most frequent comparison by the recipient was the relationship: an age — an unfortunate victim.

This grouping of comparisons is relative and does not purport to be a complete classification. However, it indicates the functional-semantic features of most comparisons and combines them into groups. The most detailed and coherent classification of comparison types in the language of poetry was done by Ekaterina Alekseeva Nekrasova.

The comparisons described here primarily belong to the language of fiction. But how do comparisons function in a modern living language? What are their national-cultural characteristics? How do lasting comparisons function in language? The experimental research we conducted answers some of these questions and will be further developed. Any linguistic-cultural manifestation can be similarly researched (using the system proposed by us).

Pilot Study of Comparisons (Practical Work)

The objective of this psycholinguistic experiment is to investigate the cultural-national characteristics of the comparisons used by Russians and Belarusians to describe a person's appearance and inner qualities. Why do we fix so much attention on the person? The fact is that it is impossible to know language without going beyond its confines, without referring to its creator, the speaker, the user— to a specific linguistic identity.

This objective requires a resolution of the following challenges:
1) determine how language is categorized by standards and stereotypes through the national vision of the person;
2) establish the cultural-ideographic fields used by the person for effective self-evaluation:
3) explain how the individual understands the experience of linguistic personality.

To achieve these goals and solve the above-mentioned problems, a working hypothesis about the universality of basic categories, characteristics and functions was used to describe the ethnic and cultural specificity of the person. We fully share Edward Sapir's idea that the inner content of all languages is the same: an intuitive awareness of experience. It is only their external forms that are infinitely varied (Sapir, 1993, p. 193). The external form is indeed infinitely varied in different cultures, but at the same time, it is fairly stereotypical for each specific culture.

To test this hypothesis, we modified the method used in associative experiments. We believe that associative experiments are correctly considered to be methods applicable to various types of research, because the associative reaction is focused, and the test subjects indicate how they understand the given word and its representation. It is known that the meaning of words used in the experiments are derived from their direct and indirect understanding as well as from the potential information from the text, stimulus words and their opportunities for choice.

It's as if the entire complex of word meaning was penetrated by associative rays, uniting parts of individual meanings and parts of different meanings associated with the word-stimulus. Every movement of human thought involves associative links, and Pavlov for good reason wrote that the mind is nothing but associations. The modified experiment we conducted limited associations by using frameworks of comparison: we propose conducting the associative experiment by using words that come to mind first. For example, "he's tall as . . ."

We concluded that similar associative reactions were not only typical of particular subject groups, but of entire linguistic communities. If there was answer entirely unique from the rest, it was discarded. We conducted the experiment in two stages. In the first stage, we established comparisons to describe a person's external appearances and in the second stage to internal qualities.

In the first stage, the test subjects included 149 students from Vitebsk University Department of Russian Philology and 100 students from the Department of Belarusian Philology. Their ages ranged from 19 to 22 years and were of both sexes.

The first stage of the experiment

For the study of outward personal appearances, the following thematic word-stimulus groups were used:
1) the anatomical characteristics of the person: height, shape, features of the body and its parts (chest, arms, knees), face (eyes, eyebrows, nose, lips, cheekbones, mouth, teeth, chin, hair);
2) the aesthetic quality of certain parts: dirty (hair), pleasant (voice), expressive (eyes), handsome (face), etc.;
3) dynamic physical features: quick, agile, playful, clumsy, strong;

4) physical condition and social status: voice, weary, majestic, awkward, talkative, hungry, poor, rich, sociable, etc.

QUESTIONAIRE 1

eyebrows as thick as ... teeth as sharp as ... voice as coarse as ... eyes as intelligent as ... eyebrows as thin as ... as few teeth as ... voice rings like a ... eyes as clear as ... eyebrows as black as ... teeth as even as ... voice as gentle as ... knees as round as ... hair as dirty as ... he is as short as ... voice as pleasant as ... knees as sharp as ... hair as long as ... he is as sociable as ... voice as sharp as ... face as pale as ... hair as curly as ... he is as quick as ... breasts as big as ... face as beautiful as ... hair as soft as ... he is as strong as an ... chest as sunken as ... face as round as ... hair as straight as ... he is slender as ... lips as scarlet as ... face as pretty as ... eyes as sparkly as ... he is fat as ... lips as beautiful as ... face as oval as ... eyes as expressive as ... he is tired as an ... lips as red as ... nose as big as ... eyes as blue as ... he is poor as ... lips as ... plump as ... nose as straight as ... eyes as hazel as ... he is rich as ... lips as thin as ... nose as snub as ... eyes as beautiful as ... he is chatty as an ... nose as crooked as ... mouth as big as ... he is as fast as ... body as muscular as ... chin as determined as ... mouth as little as ... he is as tall as ... body as strong as ... chin as sharp as ... hands as big as ... he is hungry like ... figure as majestic as
chin as sharp as ... hands as gentle as ... he is agile like ... figure as angular as ... chin dimpled like ... cheekbones as broad as ... as clumsy a ...

QUESTIONAIRE 2

The same stimulus words were used for the Belarusian language.

The test subjects were asked to write down the first comparison that came to mind. The time allowed was 10-12 minutes.

Results and analysis of the experiment.

EYES

Native Russian speakers use the following comparisons to describe eyes (the answers of those tested are given in groups and in descending order):

1) comparisons to nature: *eyes blue as the sky, like lakes, like the sea, like a cornflower field; brown like the earth, as a maelstrom, like sand, like the darkening sky, like dark water; expressive as a clear sky; beautiful as the sky, as the sea; shiny, as a drop of water, as the stars, as the sun, as water, as lakes, as a river in a summer day, as the surface of a lake in a moonlit night, like the surface of a lake in the sun; clear as the sky, as the sun, as stars, as water, as a spring, as a lake;*
2) to natural phenomena: *eyes beautiful as the sunset; sparkling like dew, like rain; clear as a morning sunrise, like dewdrops;*
3) to the eyes of animals: *eyes as brown as the eyes of a horse; smart as a dog, as a dolphin, as a horse, as an owl, as a cow, as an elephant; expressive as a cow, as a doe, as d dog, as a horse, as a cat, as a snake; beautiful as a gazelle; shiny as the coat of a cow, as the fur of a cat;*
4) to plants: *eyes as blue as cornflowers, as forget-me-nots; hazel as cherries, as oak bark, as chestnuts; as beautiful as a flower;*
5) to the time of day: *eyes brown as night; expressive as day; beautiful as the night; clear as the day, like a sunny day, like the Lord's day;*
6) to cultural phenomena, cultural figures, literary characters: *eyes expressive as the eyes of Philipp Kirkorov, as a painting, as the eyes of Madonna; eyes as beautiful as Madonna's, as a picture, as beautiful as Malvina[308];*

---

[308] Character in *The Golden Key, or the Adventures of Buratino* by Alexey Tolstoy. Based on *The Adventures of Pinocchio* by Carlo Collodi.

7) to biblical, folkloric or mythological characters: *eyes as intelligent as those of Vasilisa the Wise[309]; blue as an elf; beautiful as Aphrodite, as a siren, as a goddess;*

8) to the eyes of certain professionals: *eyes as smart as those of a scientist, like those of a psychologist; expressive as an actor, like an actress, like a model, like a teacher; as beautiful as an actor's, like model's;*

9) to the eyes of people of other nationalities: *eyes as hazel as those of a gypsy, like those of a black man; expressive as those of a Hindu woman, like an oriental beauty;*

10) to different age groups: *eyes as intelligent as those of an old man; expressive as those of a child, like those of a girl; beautiful as a child's, clear as a child's, like an old woman's eyes;*

11) to the eyes of people in different emotional states: *eyes as intelligent as those of a wise man; as expressive as an intelligent man's; sparkling like a crybaby's; shiny like those of a drunk, like a sick person's; as beautiful as mine, as my mother's;*

12) to man-made objects (artifacts as defined by Aristotle): *eyes brown like chocolate, like tea, like coffee, like buttons; expressive like a mirror; shiny as a mirror, as crystal, as a lantern, as glass, as beads, like the steel of a blade, as a button; clear like glass;*

13) to jewels: *eyes as beautiful as diamonds; shiny as gold, like diamonds, like pearls, like agates, like emeralds; clear as diamonds.*

Native speakers of Belarusian use similar groups of objects to describe eyes:

1) objects in nature: *eyes as blue as the skies, as lakes, as the sea; brown like the soil, like the earth; expressive as the sun, as dawn; beautiful as dawn, as the sun; shiny as dawn, as the sun, like water, as a creek; clear as the sun, as the sky, as lakes, as a spring, as seas, like a sheet lightning;*

2) natural phenomena: *eyes that flash like lightning, like the dew;*

---

[309] Character from Russian fairy tales such as The Frog Tsarevna and Vasilisa the Beautiful.

3) animals: *eyes as intelligent as a dog's; brown as a dog's; expressive as a cow's, as a cat's, as an owl's; as shiny as a cat's;*

4) plants: *eyes blue like cornflower, like flax flowers; hazel like cherries, like plums, like chestnuts, like old leaves; beautiful as flowers;*

5) the time of day: *eyes as clear as daylight;*

6) cultural phenomena, literary characters, biblical, folkloric and mythological characters: *eyes as smart as Pushkin's; as expressive as a painting, as a poem, as Bagheera; as beautiful as those of Venus, as those of a princess;*

7) members of other professions: *eyes as smart as those of a mathematician, like a scientist's; as beautiful as those an actress;*

8) other nationalities: *eyes as hazel as those of a gypsy, like an Arab's;*

9) appearances, body conditions: *eyes as expressive as beauty; beautiful as a model's; shiny like a drunk's;*

10) to self and those near: *eyes as intelligent as a human's, as mine; hazel like my girlfriend's; beautiful as those of my beloved, like mine;*

11) man-made objects: *eyes hazel like chocolate, like coffee, like tar, like tea; expressive as a painting, like a mirror; beautiful as a painting, as a picture; shiny like a lamp, like a mirror, like beads, like beads.*

We reach the following conclusions when comparing the answers: Native Russian speakers have more groups and the groups are more diverse. Belarusians have no comparisons to age, to jewelry, to the time of day (daylight only), but Belarusians have more poetic comparisons: *eyes expressive as a poem, eyes blue as flax flowers,* comparisons associated with materials - *eyes hazel like tar; beautiful as dye.*

Both Russians and Belarusians usually compare eyes to nature: air, sun, sea, water, spring. Belarusians, most likely subconsciously, believe that their people have blue eyes, whereas hazel eyes are compared to the eyes of other nationalities – such as Gypsy, African, Arab, etc.

EYEBROWS

For ease of comparison, we combined Russian and Belarusian answers. To describe eyebrows, the native speakers used the following groups:

1) objects in nature: (Russian) *eyebrows black as a whirlpool before the storm; thin like a brook; thick like a forest, like a thicket, like a spruce forest; arched like a rainbow;* (Belarusian) *eyebrows thick as a forest;*

2) animals:(Russian) *eyebrows black as a raven's wing; thick as stubble; eyebrows black like swallow's wings;* (Belarusian) *eyebrows black like a raven's wing, like a swallow's wing;*

3) plants: (Russian) *eyebrows thick as bushes, like grass;* (Belarusian) *eyebrows thick as grass, as moss, as bushes, like branches;*

4) time of day: (Russian) *eyebrows as black as night;* (Belarusian) *eyebrows as black as night;*

5) literary characters, biblical figures, folkloric characters and mythological creatures: (Russian) *eyebrows bushy as those of Viy[310]; eyebrows thin as those of Barbra the fair[311]';* (Belarusian) *brows as thick as a goblin's browns.*

6) members of other nationalities (Russian) *eyebrows black as a Gypsy's, as an Indian's; eyebrows as thick as those of an Arab;* (Belarusian) *eyebrows as black as those of a Ukrainian, like those of an African, as those of a Gypsy;*

7) historical figures: (Russian) *eyebrows black as Brezhnev's; eyebrows thick as Brezhnev's;* (Belarusian) *eyebrows as thick as Brezhnev's, eyebrows as black as those of the general secretary;*

8) man-made objects: (Russian) *eyebrows black as tar, like soot; thin as thread, like arcs, like an arrow, like ropes, like shoelaces; thick as a brush; eyebrows as black as coal;* (Belarusian) eyebrows as black as tar, like soot, like coal, thin as a thread, like an arch, like shoelaces, like an arrow, as a trail, like a ribbon, as smoke; thick as a brush.

Native Belarusian speakers do not use comparisons to literature, folkloric characters or mythological creatures.

---

[310] In East Slavic mythology, this was a character of the netherworld whose glances could kill. His eyes are usually covered with huge eyelids and eyelashes which he can't lift without help.

[311] Barbara the Fair with the Silken Hair (fairytale, The Tale of Tsar Berendey)

However, the section includes more poetic comparisons, for example, eyebrows as black as the wings of a swallow.

For both Russians and Belarusians, the most common comparison to eyebrows are man-made objects.

HAIR

The following groups were formed based on the Russian and Belarusian answers:

1) to natural objects: (Russian) *hair as long as a river, like a waterfall, like a stream; dirty as a swamp;* (Belarusian) *hair as long as* a river, as *a forest;*

2) to natural phenomena: (Russian) *hair as dirty as icicles; straight as rain; curly like the clouds;* (Belarusian) hair as dirty as icicles;

3) to animals: (Russian) *hair as long as a horse's mane, like a horse's tail; soft as fur, as down; dirty as a pig, like a stray dog, like fur; curly as a ram, like a sheep, like a lamb;* (Belarusian) *hair as long as a horse's mane, dirty as a boar's snout, as an animal, like fleece; curly like a lamb, as astrakhan, as a poodle;*

4) to plants: (Russian) *as soft as flax, as seaweed; dirty as straw; curly as a birch; as straight as straw;* (Belarusian) *hair as long as flax, as a tree; soft as flax; dirty as straw, curly as a ram; straight as straw;*

5) to the time of day: (Russian) *hair as long as the night;*

6) to the time of year: hair as long as winter;

7) to cultural phenomena; literary heroes, biblical, folkloric and mythological characters: (Russian) *hair as curly as Pushkin's, like Minaev's[312] hair, like Víctor Carreno's[313] hair, like Buratino's hair; long as Snow White's hair, like a mermaid's hair, like Eve's hair, like Ariadne's thread, like a witch's hair; dirty as Baba Yaga's,* (Belarusian) *hair as curly as the hair of Biadul[314]; like Víctor Carreno's hair; dirty as hell;*

---

[312] Sergey Minaev. Soviet and Russian singer, musician, TV host.

[313] Character in the Mexican soap opera, *Simplemente María*.

[314] (April 23, 1886 – November 3, 1941), Żmitrok Biadula. Jewish Belarusian poet, prose writer, cultural worker, and political activist in the Belarusian independence movement.

8) to people of other nations: (Russian) *hair as dirty as a Chukchi's; curly as the hair of an African; straight as the hair of a Finn, like a Swede's, like an Indian's;* (Belarusian) *curly as the hair of an African;*

9) to people of different ages, social strata: (Russian*) hair as dirty as a tramp's, like a bum's, like a beggar's; soft like a child's;* (Belarusian) *hair as soft as a child's, curly as my girlfriend's;*

10) to man-made objects: (Russian) *hair as long as a road, like a rope, like a thread, like linen, like twigs; soft as silk, as cotton; dirty as hemp, as a floor rag, as a road, as shoelaces; curly like a spiral, like wood shavings; straight as sticks, like hemp, as threads, as a line, like a string, like twigs, like a whip; (Belarusian) hair as long as ropes, as long as threads, soft as silk; dirty as soot; straight as sticks, as an arrow, as a line.*

Unlike Russians, Belarusians do not make comparisons to the time of day, time of year, or literary characters. The most frequent comparisons made by Russians was to man-made objects, for Belarusians it was to animals.

VOICE

Russians and Belarusians use the following comparisons to describe the voice:

1) to natural objects: *(*Russian) *a voice as pleasant as a murmuring stream, as a creek, like the sound of the tides; as course as a rock; ringing like a brook, like the murmur of a brook; gentle as a murmuring brook; (*Belarusian) *voice gentle like a brook* (Belarusian) *like a stream, ringing like a brook, as soft as a stream, like a river spring;*

2) to natural phenomena: (Russian) a *voice as pleasant as a drop; harsh as thunder; gentle like a summer breeze; sharp like the north wind, as a blizzard, as a winter wind, sharp as lightning;* (Belarusian) a *voice as pleasant as a breeze, harsh as thunder, like the wind; sharp as lightning, like the wind, like a tornado;*

3) to animals: (Russian) a *voice as pleasant as a nightingale's, like honey, like an oriole's; harsh like barking, like a the voice of a bear, like the trunk of an elephant; ringing like a nightingale, like the song of a lark; gentle as a bird, as a*

kitten; sharp as a crow, like the squeal of a piglet, like a woodpecker, like a peacock, like a parrot; (Belarusian) *a voice as course as a bear, as barking, as a howl, like an elephant, like honey, like a bird's; sharp as a crow, as a rooster*

4) to plants: (Russian) *a voice as pleasant as the smell of mint; gentle as the rustle of leaves, like a flower, like a violet;*

5) *to cultural phenomena, literary heroes, folkloric characters and mythological beings: a voice as harsh as Vysotsky's; like Shavrina's[315], like a melody; pleasant as a song, as music, like a melody; gentle like a melody, like a lullaby; rude as Azazello; gentle as a fairy;* (Belarusian) *voice as gentle as Lyudmila Senchina's; pleasant like a melody, like a song, like Leonid Utyosov's; ringing like a song, like music;*

6) to members of certain professions, organizations: (Russian) *voice pleasant as a newscaster's, the voice of a singer, a voice like the host of the "Good night, kids" TV show, like the voice of a psychiatrist; course as a sales-assistant, like a sailor, like a bus driver; sharp as a Gunnery Sargent's, as a military alarm; as a boy scout's;* (Belarusian) *a voice as welcoming as an orator's; a voice as sharp as a supervisor's;*

7) to people of different ages: (Russian) *a voice as pleasant as a girl's; ringing as a child's; gentle as a child's, like a girl's, like a child's breath;* (Belarusian) *a voice as ringing as a child's,*

8) to people of different social strata, possessing different internal qualities, to other people: (Russian) *a voice as course as a drunk, like an alcoholic's, like a smoker's, like someone with a cold, like a man's; a voice as pleasant as mother's; gentle as mother's, as gentle as a lover's;* (Belarusian) *a voice as pleasant as a bootlicker's, like a villain's; course as a man's, pleasant as the voice of mother, of grandmother;*

9) to man-made objects (Russian)*: a voice as coarse as a trumpet; ringing like a bell, like a musical cord, like a trumpet, like a horn, like the horn of a locomotive; gentle as velvet; as shrill as a creaking door, like the sound of a saw, like a knife, like a siren, like a razor, like lemonade;* (Belarusian) *a voice as coarse as a trumpet, as a bass, as a*

---

[315] Ekaterina Shavrina. Soviet/Russian singer.

drum, as a tambourine; ringing like a bell; sharp as a trumpet, as a bell.

The experimental data indicates that most of the subject groups to which voice is compared are the same for both Belarusians and Russians. Unlike Russians, Belarusians do not use comparisons to plants, folklore, mythological or literary characters. A distinctive feature of all the comparisons is an abundance of poetic comparisons (a voice pleasant as a drop; gentle as a summer breeze, etc.). Russians tend to make comparisons to cultural events, while Belarusians to man-made objects.

CHEST/BREAST

To describe chest/breast, native speakers of Russian and Belarusian make comparisons to the following:
1) to natural objects: (Russian) *breasts as big as mountains; chest as sunken as a gully;* (Belarusian) *breast as big as mountains;*
2) to animals: (Russian) *breasts as big as a cow", as udders, like those of a gorilla;* (Belarusian) *breasts as big as those of a cow;*
3) to plants: ((Belarusian) *breasts as big as water-melons, like melons, like apples;*
4) to cultural phenomena, literary, folkloric characters and mythological creatures: *breasts as big as Sarbina's, like Sophia Loren's, like Samantha Fox's, like Madonna's, like a Polish porn star's, a chest as big as Schwarzenegger's, like Hercules', like an athlete's; sunken like the chest of a Belarusian man, like the chest of Koschei;* (Belarusian) *breasts as big as a movie star's, like Sarbina's, like Samantha Fox's;*
5) to members of certain professions, ages, nationalities: (Russian) *a chest as sunken as a miner's chest, like an old woman's chest, like a decrepit old man's chest, like a German's chest; chest like a sailor's, chest, like an athlete's, like a sportsman's, like a fighter's, like a weightlifter's, like a bodybuilder's, a chest as big as a Cossack's, like a Ukrainian's;* (Belarusian) *a chest as big as an athlete's, as my neighbor's; sunken as an old man's;*

6) to people of certain social strata: (Russian) *a chest like that of someone with consumption, like the hungry*; (Belarusian) *a chest sunken like the sick, like someone with tuberculosis, like the hungry, like after tuberculosis*;

7) to man-made objects: (Russian) *chest sunken like a pit, like a dent, like a board; breasts big as footballs, like spheres, like wheels, as if made from silicone*; (Belarusian) breasts as flat as a board, chest like a pit, as big as footballs, as jugs, like balloons;

Most of the comparison groups are the same for Russians and Belarusians. However, unlike Russians, Belarusians do not use comparisons to the following objects: literary heroes, folkloric characters, mythological creatures, members of other nationalities. However, Belarusians have comparisons to plants, to themselves and other loved ones. Native speakers of both languages most often compare the human breast/chest to man-made objects.

LIPS

Lips are most often compared to the following object groups:

1) to natural objects: (Russian) *lips as beautiful as the sea, like a river*;

2) to natural phenomena: (Russian) *lips scarlet like the dawn, like the sunset; red like dawn, like sunset; beautiful like dawn*, (Belarusian) *lips red as the sunset*;

3) to animals: (Russian) *lips scarlet like corals, like blood; red like blood, like corals, like as a crab; plump like a camel's hump; thin as a snake*;

4) to plants: (Russian) *lips scarlet like poppy flowers, like rose petals, like raspberry, like a tomato, like berries, like cherries, like pomegranate juice, like a rowan berry; red like poppy flowers, like raspberries, like cherries, like a rose, like wild strawberries, like a tomato, as a beetroot, as a kalina berry, as a wild strawberry, as a berry; thin as flower petals; plump as a plum, beautiful as a rose, as a flower, as a ripe plum* (Belarusian) *lips red like raspberries, like poppies, like roses, like berries, as flowers, like cherries, like wild strawberries, as a kalina berry, like a rowan berry; scarlet like roses, as poppies, as strawberries, like raspberries, like tomatoes, like*

wild strawberries, like cherries, like a rowan berry; plump as a cherry, like a rose button; beautiful as flowers, as poppies, as roses, as berries, as a tomato;

5) to cultural events, literary heroes, folkloric characters and mythological creatures: (Russian) *lips as beautiful as a picture, as beautiful as Madonna's, like La Gioconda's, like Marilyn Monroe's, like Julia Robert's, as statue's, as a movie star's, like Anna Karenina's, like Margarita's, like a goddess's, lips of a Greek god, like Apollo's, like Venus', like angel's; red like vampire's lips; lips as beautiful as Madonna's;*
(Belarusian) *lips as beautiful as Madonna's, as the lips of Venus, as a fairy's, as those of a goddess.*

6) to seasons: (Belarusian) *lips as beautiful as spring;*

7) to members of different nationalities, people of different ages, to other people and to themselves: (Russian) *lips as full as an African's, like a child's; thin like an old woman's lips, like mine, beautiful as a girl's lips, as mine; as red as a young girl's lips;* (Belarusian) *lips as full as an African's, as a child's, as beautiful as a girl's, as those of a beautiful woman; lips as red as those of a beautiful woman;*

8) to the inner qualities of people: (Russian) *lips as thin as the lips of a witch, like a criminal, tight lipped as a Puritan, like a greedy man's lips, like cunning person's lips, like a miser's lips; plump like a sensual woman's lips, like the lips of an old pervert, lips of a glutton; lips as red as a sick person's lips;*
(Belarusian) *lips as thin as those of a witch, as a miser's, like a criminal's.*

9) to man-made objects:(Russian) *lips scarlet like a flag, like a president's tablecloth; red like a flag, like expensive wine, like bright lipstick; thin as a thread, as a strip, like a crack, as a line, as an arrow, as a blade, as a sheet of paper; plump like a pillow, like buns, like a donut, like a featherbed, like cotton, like cheesecake; beautiful as a drawing, as a ribbon;*
(Belarusian) *lips red as a flag; thin as a thread, as a scratch, as leaves; plump like buns, like a pillow, like dumplings, like sausages, like pancakes.*

Unlike native Russian speakers, Belarusian speakers do not compare lips to natural objects, animals, literary characters, members of certain professions, the inner qualities of people, to themselves or to other people. Russian speakers do not compare lips to seasons. Most Russian comparisons are: to plants and man-made objects. Most Belarusian comparisons are to plants.

TEETH

Teeth are compared to:

1) animals: (Russian) *teeth as straight as the teeth of a horse, like squirrel's; sharp as a wolf's, like the teeth of a shark, like fangs, as a pike's, like a squirrel's, like cat's, like the teeth of a mouse, like ferret's teeth, like a predator's teeth, like the teeth of a fox, like a tiger's teeth, like a rat's, like an beast's, like a dog's, like a crocodile's, like the teeth of a fish, like boar's teeth, like a river rat's; teeth as rare as an old animal's teeth*; (Belarusian) *teeth as even as a beaver's; sharp like a wolf's, like pike's, like a fox's, like a hyena's, like a hare's, like a beaver's, like a tiger's, like a squirrel's; sharp as a wolf's*;

2) to plants: (Russian) *teeth rare as lumber*; (Belarusian) *teeth even as a forest, as smooth as garlic; as few as a felled forest, like a forest, like trees in a field*;

3) cultural phenomena, folkloric characters and mythological creatures: (Russian) *teeth as even as Brigitte Bardot's, like in a toothpaste commercial, as a movie star's teeth; rare as Pugacheva's, like Baba Yaga's; sharp like a vampire's*;

4) to tools: (Belarusian) *teeth as sharp as a knife, like a needle, like a saw, like a rake, like a hayfork*;

5) members of certain professions, people of certain age and character: *teeth as even as a dentist's, teeth like those of an actress, like a model's; teeth as rare as an old woman's teeth, like a bum's, like mother's*; (Belarusian) *rare as an old man's teeth*;

6) man-made objects:(Russian) *teeth as even as a fence, as railings, as if drawn by a ruler, like a wall, like railing, like false teeth, like threads, as if they were filed, like a hedge; sharp like a dagger, like spikes, like a razor, like a spear, like a blade; gapped like a fence, like a railing, as a comb, like a broken fence, as a hedge, like a sieve, as a picket fence, flattened thin, like they've been kicked in, like railings, like a weaving, like a fence* (Belarus) teeth even as a fence, as

railing, as a comb, as smoke, as pillars; sharp as a blade, as a razor, like stakes; gapped as fence, as railing, like a picket fence;

7) jewelry: (Russian) *teeth even as pearls*; (Belarusian) *like beads*.

Native speakers of both languages compare teeth to: animals, plants, people of a certain age, man-made objects. Belarusians do not use comparisons to cultural phenomena, mythological and folkloric characters or to members of certain professions. Russian do not compare teeth to tools.

KNEES

Native speakers of these languages use the following comparisons to describe knees:

1) to natural objects: (Russian) *knees sharp as stones*;

2) to animals: (Russian) *knees as round as the knees of elephant*;

3) to plants: (Russian) *knees sharp like knots on wood; round like apples, like a watermelon, like an orange*; (Belarusian) *knees round like apples, like watermelons, like oranges*;

4) to tools: (Russian) *knees sharp like needles, like knives, like nails,* (Belarus) *sharp like needles, like a knife, like an awl*;

5) to literary characters: (Russian) *knees sharp as the knees of Buratino*;

6) to people of different ages: (Russian) *knees sharp as the knees of a teenage girl, as a teenager's knees; round like a girl's knees, like a little girl's knees*;

7) to other people:(Belarusian*) knees round as a fat woman's knees, like my girl-friend's knees*;

8) to man-made objects: (Russian) *knees sharp like stakes, like arrows, like spears, as an angle, like pikes, like sticks, like hairpins, like a razor, like bayonets; round like balls, like pillows, like cups, like beach balls*; (Belarusian) knees sharp as an angle, like a stick, like arrows, like a sword; round like a ball, like wheels, like a balloon.

Native speakers of both languages have only three comparison groups in common: plants, tools and man-made objects. Belarusians do not use comparisons to natural objects, to animals, to literary characters or to people of different ages.

FACE

The following comparison groups can be noted:
1) to natural objects: (Russian*)* *a face oval as the moon; round like the moon, like the sun; beautiful as a star, like a morning star; ruddy as the sun; pale as the moon;* (Belarusian) *a face as round as the moon, as the sun, beautiful as the moon; ruddy as the sun, pale as the moon*;
2) to natural phenomena: (Russian) a *face beautiful as dawn; ruddy like a frozen face, like dawn, like a sunset, like a sunrise; pale like snow*; (Belarusian) *blushing like dawn, pale as snow*;
3) to animals: (Russian) *a face as round as a flounder; oval like an egg*; (Belarusian) *a face oval like an egg;*
4) to plants: (Russian) *face oval like a melon, like a cucumber, like a plum, like a pineapple; round like an apple, like a watermelon, like a turnip, like a sunflower, like a tomato; pretty as a flower; beautiful as a flower, as a rose; ruddy like an apple, like a beet, as a ripe apple, as a peach, like ripe strawberries; pale as a toadstool*; (Belarusian*) a face oval like a melon, a plum, like a cucumber; round as a pumpkin, like an apple; beautiful like a rose, like a flower, like a lily; as darling as a flower; as ruddy as an apple, as a beet; pale as a toadstool*;
5) to the time of day: (Russian) *a face as pretty as a sunny day, as morning; beautiful as the day*;
6) to seasons: (Russian) *a face pretty like spring; beautiful like spring*;
7) to cultural phenomena, literary, folklore characters and mythological creatures: (Russian) *face oval like an icon; round like Larisa Dolina's; beautiful like Madonna's, as beautiful as a magazine cover, as beautiful as Marilyn Monroe's, as Kelly's, as a statue, as Venus, as Aphrodite, as the face of Vasilisa the Beautiful, as an enchantress; pretty as a fairy tale, as a painting, as Cinderella, as Thumbelina, as an angel, as the Snow Maiden, as Alyonushka[316]; as pale as Piero's, as death*; (Belarusian) a face as beautiful as Marilyn

---

[316] This refers to a painting by Víktor Vasnetsov (1848 – 1926). He specialized in mythological and historical themes, illustrating Russian fairy tales and epic poems.

Monroe's, as beautiful as a painting, as beautiful as Malvina's, a face as round as Kolobok[317]; pale as Death;

8) to members of certain professions: (Russian) *a face as beautiful as a model's, like a fashion model's, like an actress'*;

9) to people of different ages, possessing certain internal and external qualities: (Russian) *a face as pretty as the face of a child, as a girl's face, as a small girl's face, like the face of a beautiful woman; the round face of a kind person, as round as a fool's face*; (Belarusian) *as pretty as a child's*;

10) to people of a certain status, to themselves and to other people: (Russian) *the ruddy face of a healthy person; pale like the face of the deadly ill, pale as the sick, like someone who's been sick, like the face of consumption; pretty as a sweetheart's, as mom's, as a lover's; beautiful as a lover's, as mine, as my sweetheart's*; (Belarusian) *a face as beautiful as a princess's, as sweet as my beloved's; as beautiful as my lover's, as mom's, as mine.*

11) to man-made objects: (Russian) *a face oval like a pancake, like a mirror, like an inflatable balloon, like as a dish; round like a ball, like a pancake, like a plate, like a saucer; beautiful as a doll, as if drawn; ruddy like a matryoshka, like a pie, like a pancake, like a donut, like bread from the oven; pale as chalk, like canvas, like a sheet, like a sheet of paper, like flour*; (Belarusian) *a face oval like a pancake, an oval face, like a mirror; round like a bowl, like a globe, like a ball, like a pancake; beautiful like in a picture, sweet like a candy; ruddy like a pie, like a bun, like a matryoshka; pale as a canvas*;

One notes that a large variety of comparison groups are used by the native speakers of both languages and that many of the groups coincide: natural objects, natural phenomena, animals, plants, etc. Belarusians do not use comparisons to the time of day, time of year, to people of certain professions, or to persons with certain inner qualities and others. For both Russians and Belarusians, comparisons to plants are the most typical.

NOSE

---

[317] Kolobok is the main character of a Slavic fairy tale. He is analogous to the gingerbread man.

Russians and Belarusians use the following comparisons to describe noses:

1) to natural objects: (Russian) *a nose straight as a cliff; crooked as a mountain, like a hill, like a mound, like a chute, like a mountain slope, like a mountain range; flat as a trampoline;* (Belarusian) *a nose straight like a mountain, as big as a mountain; crooked as a mountain*;

2) to animals: (Russian) *a nose straight like a woodpecker's, like a stork's beak, like a vulture's, like the nose of a bird of prey; crooked as an eagle's, like a bird's beak; flat as a kitten's nose, flat like a duck's bill, pug nosed, like a puppy's nose, like a piglet's nose, like the nose of a hedgehog; as big as the trunk of an elephant, big as a woodpecker's nose, as a stork's nose;* (Belarusian) *a nose as crooked as a piglet's nose, as an eagle's beak, like a vulture's beak; hocked like an eagle's beak, like a bird's, as big as a heron's beak; a nose as crooked as an eagles beak, like a bird's beak, like a beak, big as a heron's beak, like a woodpecker's beak, like a log*;

3) to plants: (Russian) *nose snub as a potato, like a pear, like a cucumber, like a tomato, like a plum, like a melon, like a pumpkin;* (Belarusian) *nose like a spud, as big as a potato, like a plum, like an eggplant, like a watermelon, like a cucumber*;

4) to cultural events, literature, folkloric and mythological characters: (Russian) *a nose as straight as a Greek statue, as Apollo's nose; as hooked as Akhmatova's nose, like Gogol's nose, like Baba Yaga's nose; snub like Belmondo's nose, like Sirano's note, like Alyonushka's nose;* (Belarusian) *big as a giant's nose*;

5) to people of various professions, different ages and nationalities: (Russian) *a nose crooked as a boxer's, like a Georgian's, like a Greek's, like a Roman's, like someone from the Caucuses, like a Frenchman's; nose, snub like a Belarusian's nose, like a child's nose, like a clown's nose; a nose as straight as an aristocrat's nose;* (Belarusian) *a nose as straight as a Greek's, like a Roman's nose; a nose as hooked as a Jew's nose, like a Greek's nose, like someone from the Caucuses, like an Armenian's nose; a nose as snub as a child's nose*;

6) to people possessing certain qualities, to themselves and other people: (Russian) *a nose as turned up as a stuck up's nose, a nose as snub as a bully's nose, like mine, like my mother's nose;*

7) to man-made objects: (Russian) a nose straight like a ruler, like a stick, like an arrow, like a road, like a string, like a line, like a pillar, like a board, like a drainpipe; as big as a light switch; a nose crooked as a staircase, like an even road with barricades; snub like a nozzle, like a button, I like a hook, like a knob, like a doorbell, like an overshoe, like a samovar, like the Eiffel Tower, like the water tap; (Belarusian) a nose straight as a stick, like a crowbar, like an arrow, like a ruler, like a road, like a street, like a pillar, like a bridge, like a log, like string; bent like a button, like a hook, crooked like an arc; big as a shaft.

Unlike Russians, Belarusians do not use comparisons to cultural phenomena, folkloric and mythological characters, members of certain professions, members of particular social classes (aristocrats), to internal human qualities, to themselves or other people. For Russians, the most typical comparisons are to plants, animals and man-made objects. For Belarusians, it is to plants.

CHIN

Both nations use the following comparison groups to describe chins:

1) to natural objects: *a chin as sharp as a cliff, like a rock; square as a rock;*

2) to animals: (Russian*) a chin as determined as a bulldog; sharp like a fox, as sharp as a robin's beak*; (Belarusian*) as sharp as a stork's beak; as determined as a bulldog, as square as a bulldog;*

3) to plants: (Russian) *a chin dimpled like an apple, like a peach, like a berry*; (Belarusian) *chin dimpled like a knot, as an apple;*

4) to tools: (Russian) *a chin sharp as a knife, like a needle, like an awl, like a spatula; square like a shovel*; (Belarusian) *sharp as a knife, like shovel, like an awl, like an ax, like a trigger, like a square, like a sheave;*

5) to cultural phenomena, literary, folkloric and mythological characters: (Russian); *a chin determined like in the movies, as Superman's chin, like Mayakovsky's chin, like Schwarzenegger's chin, like a movie hero's, like Sharapova's, like Van Damme's, like Stallone's, like Joseph Kobzon's, like Valentina Serova's, like Placido's, like Stierlitz's, like Pavel Korchagin's[318], like Hercules'; dimpled like Valentina Serova's, like Samantha Fox's, like Eugene Martynov [319], like Valery Leontiev like Philipp Kirkorov, like Sofia Rotaru square like Schwarzenegger's, like Superman's, like Stallone's; sharp like Khlestakov's, like the chin of Koshchei the Deathless, like Baba Yaga's chin, like the chin of a witch;* (Belarusian) *a chin as determined as the chin of Schwarzenegger, like Serov's chin, like Samoilov's chin; a chin as dimpled Serov's chin, as Samoilov's chin; square like Arnold's chin, like the Nutcracker's chin;*
6) to members of certain professions: (Russian) *a chin as determined as a boxer's chin, as an athlete's chin, like a stuntman's chin, like a soldier's chin, like a fighter's, like a detective's, like a sailor's; square like a boxer's chin, like a fighter's, like a dock worker's chin, like an athlete's;*
7) to members of other nationalities: (Russian) *a chin as determined as an American's chin, like a Roman's chin; square like an American's chin;*
8) to people of a certain age group, physical condition, historical figures: (Russian) *a chin as dimpled as a child's chin, like a flirt's chin; determined as a strong man's chin, like Lenin's, like Napoleon's;* (Belarusian) *dimpled like a handsome man's chin;*
9) to themselves and other people: (Russian) *a chin as determined as my father's chin, as a man's chin; dimpled like mine;* (Belarusian) *determined as my friend's chin; dimpled like my friend's, like my sister's;*
10) to man-made objects: (Russian) *a chin as sharp as an angle, like a wedge, like a spear, like a triangle, like a sword,*

---

[318] Central character of the novel *How the Steel Was Tempered*, by Nikolai Ostrovsky.
[319] Eugene Martynov (1948-1990) - Soviet singer and composer.

like a dagger, like the corner of a table, like a razor, like an arrow; as determined as a wall; square like a table, like a box, as a brick, like a square, like a closet, like a cube, like a box, like a nightstand, like a TV set; (Belarusian) *determined as a wall, like a robot; sharp as an angle, like a razor, like a spike, like a triangle, like a blade; dimpled like a drain, like a button; chin like a square, like a cube, like a brick, like a table, like a robot's, like a nightstand, like a boot.*

Unlike Russian native speakers, Belarusians do not use comparisons to natural objects, to folkloric and mythological characters, to members of certain professions, to people of other nationalities and ages, or to historical figures. Comparisons to man-made objects are most typical for native speakers of both languages.

MOUTH

The test data revealed the following comparison groups:

1) to natural objects: (Russian) *a mouth as big as a cave, like an abyss*; (Belarusian) *as big as the ocean; like a cave*;

2) to animals: *a mouth as big as a hippo's, like a frog's, like a monkey's, like the mouth of a beast, like a duck's, like a whale's, like a pelican's; small like a mouse's, like a bird's, like a nestling's, like a beak, like a cat's, like a chicken's, like a sparrow's, like a hare's, like a kitten's*; (Belarusian) *big as a toad's, like a monkey's, like a horse's, like a crocodile's, like a hippo's; little as a mouse's, as a kitten's, as a bird's*;

3) to plants: (Russian) *mouth small like a cherry, like a bud, like a berry*; (Belarusian) *big as an apple; small like a pea, like a berry*;

4) to the time of day: (Russian) *a mouth as big as the day*;

5) to cultural phenomena, literary characters: (Russian) *a mouth as big as Leonid Agutin's, like Larisa Dolina's, like Sophia Loren's, like Buratino's, like the Nutcracker's; small like Thumbelina's, like a gnome's*; (Belarusian) *a mouth as big as Buratino's*;

6) to members of certain professions, having a certain age: (Russian) *a mouth as big as a clown's; small as a child's, like a baby's*; (Belarusian) *as small as a child's*;

7) to man-made objects: *a mouth big as a pit, as big as a garden, like a suitcase; small as a crack, like a button, like a dot, like a puncture, like a doll's mouth, like a whistle, like a pinhead, like a knob*; (Belarusian) *big as a pit, as a gate, as a tub, like a bucket, like a well, like a barn; small like a button, like a puncture, like a crack, like the head of a needle, like a string.*

Most of these groups are common to native speakers of both languages: natural objects, animals, plants and others. Belarusians do not use comparisons to the time of day, cultural phenomena, folkloric and mythological characters or members of certain professions. The most typical comparison for Russians is to animals. Belarusians mostly used comparisons to animals and man-made objects.

HANDS

The test data revealed the following comparison groups:

1) to natural phenomena: *hands as gentle as a southern wind, as a breeze*; (Belarusian) *like a summer breeze*;

2) to animals: *hands as big as paws, as bear paws, as a monkey's, as a lion's paws; as gentle as a cat's paws, as a kitten's*; (Belarusian) *as big as paws, like a monkey, like a bear; as gentle as wings*;

3) to tools: (Russian*) hands as big as shovels, as rakes*;

4) to literary, folkloric and mythological characters: (Russian) *hands as big like Gulliver's, like Bazarov's[320], like giant's*, (Belarusian) *as big as Bazarov's, like Asilka's[321]*;

5) to members of certain professions, classes: (Russian) *hands as big as boxer's, as peasant's; as tender as an aristocrat's*;

6) to a person's age: (Russian) *hands as gentle as child's; paws as little as a child's*

7) to inner qualities of people: (Russian) *hands as big as a tightwad's, soft like the hands of a shirker*;

---

[320] Character from *Fathers and Sons* by Turgenev.
[321] Can also be translated as "Strongman", the hero of many traditional Belarusian fairy tales.

8) to relatives: (Russian) *hands as gentle as mother's, as my sweetheart's;* (Belarusian) *as big as father's; as gentle as mother's; like my beloved's, like a woman's*;

9) to man-made objects: (Russian) *hands as big as buckets; as soft as silk, as velvet, as satin, as cotton;* (Belarusian) *as big as sticks, as poles, as a pit.*

Most of the comparison groups are the same for native speakers of both languages, but only Russians use comparisons to members of certain professions, classes or to the inner qualities of people. Comparisons to tools are very typical for both Russians and Belarusians.

CHEEKBONES

The following comparison groups can be distinguished here:

1) to natural objects: (Russian) *cheekbones as broad as a field, as the sea*; (Belarusian) *broad as a field*;

2) to animals: (Russian) *cheekbones as broad as bulldog's;*

3) to tools: (Russian) *cheekbones as broad as a shovel*; (Belarusian) *as broad as a shovel*;

4) to members of certain professions: (Russian) *cheekbones as broad as boxer's*;

5) to cultural phenomena: (Russian) *cheekbones as broad as Schwarzenegger's*;

6) to members of other nationalities: (Russian) *cheekbones as broad as a Mongol's, as a Tartar's, as an African's, like those of a Chukchi, like those of a Chinese, like an Asian's, like those of a Kalmyk, like a Kirghiz's*; (Belarusian) *like those of a Mongol's, like a Tatar's, like an Eskimo's*;

7) to man-made objects: (Russian) *cheekbones as broad as a plaza, as a road*; (Belarusian) *broad as a road, as a plate, as a circle, as a square.*

Four of these groups are the same for native speakers of both languages: comparisons to natural objects, to tools, to members of other nationalities and to man-made objects. Belarusians do not use comparisons to cultural phenomena, to members of certain professions or to animals. Comparisons to members of other nationalities is the most typical for both languages.

BODY

The following descriptions were used to characterize body types:

1) to natural objects: (Russian) *a body as strong as a rock*;

2) to animals: (Russian) *a body strong like an elephant's, like a lion's, life a horse's, as a tiger's, as a boa constrictor's, as an eagle's; muscular like a tiger's, like a lion's, like a snake's, like a cheetah's, like a gorilla's, like a whale's*; (Belarusian) *a body as strong as a bear's, as a lion's, as a bull's, as an elephant's, as a tiger's; as muscular as a tiger's, as a lion's, as a whale's*;

3) *to plants: (Russian) a body strong like an oak, like a tree, like the trunk of an oak; (Belarusian) as strong as a tree, like an oak*;

4) to cultural phenomena, literary, folkloric and mythological characters: (Russian) *a body strong like Schwarzenegger's, like Van Damme's, like the body of a Hollywood movie star's, like the body of Hercules, like an athlete's; muscular like Schwarzenegger's, like Stallone's, like Van Damme's, like Tarzan's, like Hercules'*; (Belarusian) *a body as strong as Schwarzenegger's, like Stallone's, like a giant's, Like the body of Hercules, like Asilka's; a body muscular like Schwarzenegger's, like Stallone's, like the body of Hercules*;

5) to members of certain professions: (Russian) *a body strong like an athlete's, like a sportsman's; muscular like a fireman's, like a sportsman's, like a bodybuilder's, like a fighter's, like an athlete's, like a weightlifter's, of a heavyweight*; (Belarusian) *a body as strong as an athlete's, as sportsman's, like a boxer's; muscular as an athlete's, as a sportsman's, a dockworker's, like a wrestler's*;

6) to people of other nationalities: (Russian) *a body as muscular as an African's*;

7) to man-made objects:(Russian*) a body as strong as a steel machine, like a coil; muscular like a tightrope, like a coil.*

The first five comparison groups are common in both Russian and Belarusian. Belarusians do not use comparisons to natural objects, to literary characters, to members of other nationalities or to man-made objects. Russians mostly make comparisons to members of certain professions. Belarusians primarily make comparisons to animals.

FIGURE

The test data revealed the following comparison groups:

1) to natural objects: (Russian) *a figure as magnificent as a mountain*;

2) to animals: a (Russian) *figure as angular as a bear's; as magnificent as a lion's, as a peacock, like a buck's*; (Belarusian) *a figure clumsy as a bear's, like a monkey's, like a rhino's, like an elephant's, like a turtle's, like a hippo's; majestic as a peacock, as a lion's, as a bison's, as a deer's*;

3) to plants: (Russian) *a figure as angular as a stub, as a spruce*; (Belarusian) *majestic like an oak, like a tree*;

4) to cultural phenomena, literary, folkloric and mythological characters: *a figure as majestic as a monument, like a statue, like a pedestal, like a palace, like the statue of Zeus, like the figure of a goddess, a figure like Apollo's; angular like Quasimodo's, like Baba Yaga's, like a hunchback's*; (Belarusian) *a figure as majestic a monument, as a statue, as a giant, as Apollo, clumsy as Baba Yaga.*

5) to a person's social position: (Russian) *a figure as majestic as a king's, like a queen's, like a czar's, like a czarina's, like an emperor's*; (Belarusian) *like a tsar's, like a princess', like a lord's, like an earl's*;

6) to historical figures: (Russian) *a figure majestic like Peter the Great's, like Napoleon's*;

7) to man-made objects: *a figure as angular as a wardrobe, as a table, as a box, as a brick, as dividers; majestic as the Ostankino Tower*; (Belarusian) a figure as ugly as a stick.

8) to geometric shapes: (Russian) *a figure as angular as a wardrobe, as a square, as a triangle, as a polygon, as a table, as an octahedron.*

Most of the comparison groups are the same for native speakers of both languages. Native Russian speakers have additional groups, such as comparisons to natural objects, tools, geometric shapes, literary characters and historic figures. Both Russians and Belarusians most often use comparisons to a person's social position.

SOCIAL STATUS

The following comparison groups were used to characterize the poor and the rich:

1) to natural objects: (Russian) *as rich as soil*;

2) to animals: *as poor as a church mouse, as a hare, as a mouse, as a falcon, as a dog, as a cockroach; rich as an elephant*; (Belarusian) *poor as a church mouse, as a hare, as a falcon*;

3) to cultural phenomena, literary characters, biblical characters: (Russian) *poor like Wild Rose[322], like Father Carlo[323], like Ostap Bender, like Lazarus*; (Belarusian) *as poor as Saint Damian[324], as Job; rich like in a fairy tale, as Luis Alberto, as Buratino; rich as a Hollywood star, as God*;

4) to members of certain professions, nationalities: (Russian) *as poor as a tailor, as a teacher, as a Romanian, as a Belarusian, as an Indian; rich as a businessman, as a merchant, as a banker, as a trader, as a Jew, as an American, as a Georgian* (Belarusian) *as poor as a villager, as a beggar, as a slave; as rich as a businessman, as a merchant, as a Jew, as a Georgian*;

5) *to social position: (Russian) as poor as a student, as a farmer, as a beggar, as a slave, as a bum, as a poor man, as a laborer, as a pensioner; as rich as a czar, as a king, as a bourgeois, as a Sultan, as a landlord, as a Shah, as a tycoon, as the President, as a Sultan, as a lord, as a Chief, as Rockefeller;* (Belarusian) *rich as a lord, as the czar, as a Sultan, as the President*;

6) to themselves and other people: (Russian) poor like everyone else, like us, like me;

7) to man-made objects: (Belarusian) poor as a bast shoe.

Most of the groups are common to native speakers of both languages. As in the other sections, Belarusian speakers use few comparisons to cultural phenomena, to literary characters, to themselves or to other people. For native speakers of both languages, comparisons to social standing are most common.

PHYSICAL CHARACTERISTICS

---

[322] Wild Rose, (Rosa salvaje) a Mexican telenovela.
[323] Papa Carlo was a character in Aleksey Tolstoy's *The Golden Key or the Adventures of Buratino* (1936).
[324] Saints Cosmas and Damian were Christian martyr's during the reign of Emperor Diocletian.

In this section, we used the following characteristics of a person: TALL, SHORT, SLENDER, FAT and STRONG. The following comparison groups were formed:

1) to natural objects: (Russian) *as tall as a mountain, as the sky, as a forest*; (Belarusian) *as tall as a forest, as the sky, as a mountain*;

2) to animals: (Russian) *as tall as a giraffe, as a kangaroo, as an ostrich; (Belarusian) tall as a giraffe*; (Russian) *as short as a pony*; (Belarusian) *short as a pony, as a mouse*; (Russian) as slender as a gazelle, like a doe; (Belarusian) *as slender as a doe*; (Russian) *as fat as an elephant, as a hippo, as a pig, as a piglet, as a bear, as a wild boar, as a cat, as a boar*; (Belarusian) *as fat as an elephant, as a pig, as a bear, as a hippo, as a wild boar, as a hamster*; (Russian) *strong as a lion, as a bear as an elephant, as a bull, as an ox as an ant*; (Belarusian) *strong as a bear, as a lion, like a bison, as an elk*;

3) to plants: (Russian) *as tall as a poplar, as a pine, as a tree, as an eucalyptus, as an oak*; (Belarusian) *as a tree*; (Russian) *as short as a shrub, as a tree stump, as a small birch, as a mushroom, as grass, as moss, as a cactus*; (Belarusian) *as a mushroom, as moss, as grass, as a bush, a tree knot, as a stump, as a small birch*; (Russian) *slender as a cypress, as a birch, as a poplar, as a reed, as an aspen, as a palm tree, as a pine tree*; (Belarusian) *as a blade of grass, as a birch, like a reed, as a branch, as an oak, as an aspen, as grass, as a twig, as straw*; (Russian) *fat as a baobab tree*; (Belarusian) *as a watermelon, as an oak tree; as strong as an oak*; (Russian) as an oak (Belarusian) as an oak;

4) to cultural, literary and mythological events: (Russian) *as tall as Uncle Styopa[325], as Gulliver, as a giant*; (Belarusian) *as Uncle Styopa, as a giant; as short as Thumbelina, as a gnome; slender as a poplar at Plyushchikha[326]; as fat as Sergei Krylov, as Winnie-the-Pooh, as Gargantua; strong as Stallone, as Schwarzenegger, as Hercules, as Ilya Muromets[327]*;

---

[325] A character from the five-volume series of poems written by Soviet writer Sergei Mikhalkov (February 1913 – 27 August 2009).
[326] Based on the 1967 Soviet film, *Three Poplars on Plyushchikha Street.*
[327] A folk hero of Kievan Rus.

(Belarusian) *as strong as Schwarzenegger, as Asilok*[328], as a giant, as Hercules, as Ilya Muromets, as Achilles;

5) to other people: (Russian) *as short as an Aborigine, as a Chinese person, as a dwarf, a Lilliputian; as slender as a fashion model; as fat as a glutton; as strong as an athlete, as a fighter*;

6) to man-made objects: (Russian) *as tall as a pillar, as a beanpole, as a house, as the Eiffel Tower, as a skyscraper, as a tower, as a telegraph pole, as a crane, as a TV tower*; (Belarusian) *as tall as a pillar, as a watchtower, a pole, a house like TV tower; slender as a mast, as a stick, as a needle, as a string*; (Russian) *fat as a barrel, as a donut, as a wineskin*; (Belarusian) *fat as a barrel, as a ball, like a sack.*

Relatively few object groups were used to describe a person's physical characteristics. For example, Belarusians used only two groups to describe a short person (animals and plants), three groups to describe a slim person (animals, plants and man-made objects), three groups to describe a fat person (animals, plants, man-made objects), and three groups to describe a strong person (animals, plants and cultural phenomena). Russians used six groups here. The most frequent comparisons were to animals, plants and man-made objects.

PHYSICAL CONDITIONS

Here we experimented with only two stimulus words: TIRED and HUNGRY. The test data revealed the following comparison groups:

1) animals: (Russian*) tired as a dog, as a horse, as an ox, as a stallion, as a beast, as a moth, as a beaten horse, as a camel*; (Belarusian) *tired as an ox, as a dog, as a horse, as a beast*; (Russian) *hungry as a wolf, as a dog, as a beast, as a crocodile, like a sperm whale, as twenty hippos*; (Belarusian) *hungry as a wolf, as a dog, as an beast, as baby cuckoos*;

2) plants: (Russian) *tired as a squeezed lemon*;

3) literary characters and mythological figures: (Russian) *tired like Papa Carlo, as the devil*; (Belarusian) *as the devil*;

---

[328] Belarusian giant.

4) other people: (Russian) *tired as a miner, as a long-haul trucker, as a traveler*; (Belarusian) *tired as a collective farmer, as a villager*; (Russian) *hungry like a student*; (Belarusian) *hungry like a student*.

There were groups of 3-4 (for Belarusians three) to describe a tired person. There were two groups to describe a hungry man. Comparisons to animals were the most typical.

CHARACTER TRAITS

This section applies to two personal characteristics: SOCIABLE and CHATTY. The test data revealed the following comparison groups:

1) to animals: (Russian) *sociable as a monkey, like a sparrow, like a magpie, as a parrot, as a little bird, as a dragonfly*; (Belarusian) *sociable as a dog, as a cat, as a fox*; (Russian) *chatty as a magpie, as a parrot, as a crow*; (Belarusian) chatty as a magpie, as a crow;

2) to cultural phenomena and mythological characters: (Russian) *sociable as Xenia Strizh*[329], *as Ostap Bender, like Winnie-the-Pooh*; (Belarusian) *sociable as Helen; chatty as the devil*;

3) to members of certain professions, nationalities: (Russian) *sociable as a television host, as a journalist, as an entertainer, as an actor, as a psychologist, as a Frenchman, as an Italian*;

4) to age: (Russian*) sociable as a child; chatty as an old woman*; (Belarusian) *chatty as an old woman, as a child*;

5) to themselves and other people: (Russian) *sociable as a student, as a congressman, as I am*; (Belarusian) *sociable as I am, as a friend, as a neighbor; chatty as a chatterbox, as a fool, like a girl, like a fishwife; chatty like a fool, a woman, a neighbor*.

For both Russians and Belarusians, the most typical comparisons were to animals; the group number is relatively small: Belarusians have three groups, Russians four to five.

DYNAMIC CHARACTERISTICS

Here, the following stimulus words were included: FAST, LIVELY, AGILE and CLUMSY. The test data revealed the following comparison groups:

---

[329] Russian actress and television host.

1) natural objects: (Russian) *fast like a river, like the wind, like a hurricane, like lightning*; (Belarusian) *fast like a river, like lightning; lively as the wind*;

2) animals: (Russian) *fast like a deer, like a hare, like a doe, like a leopard, like an ostrich, like an antelope, like a kangaroo, like a lynx, like a gazelle, like a bird, like a young race horse*; (Belarusian) *fast like a rabbit, like a deer, like a bird, like a horse, like an ostrich, like a lion*; (Russian) *lively as a colt, as a hare, as a kitten, as a deer, as a baby goat, as a doe, as a stallion, as a puppy, like a mouse, like a horse, like a pony, like a she-goat; like a panther, like a gazelle, like a flea*; (Belarusian) lively like a horse, like a rabbit, like a colt, like a kitten, like a dog, like a deer, like a monkey, like a goat, like a sparrow, like a deer; (Russian) *agile as a monkey, like a hare, like a tiger, like a cat, like a lynx, like a mouse, like a fox, like a squirrel, like a beast*; (Belarusian) agile like a monkey, like a fox, like a squirrel, like a rabbit, like a panther, like a lynx, like an elephant, like a doe, like a tiger, like a deer, like a mouse; (Russian) *clumsy like a bear, like an elephant, like a hippo, like a penguin, like a camel, like a turtle, like a puppy, like a goose, like a bull in a china shop, like a duck*; (Belarusian) *clumsy as a bear, as an elephant, like a pig, like a seal, like a cow; as a duck*;

3) to people: (Russian) *lively as a child*; (Belarusian) *lively as a child, as a gymnast*; (Russian) *agile as a circus performer, as an athlete, as a magician; like a juggler, like a gymnast, like an acrobat, like a shop assistant, like Mowgli, like the devil*; (Belarusian) agile like Bruce Lee, like the devil, like a stuntman; (Russian) *clumsy like a fat person*;

4) to man-made objects: (Russian) *fast as an airplane, as an arrow*; (Belarusian) *fast as an airplane, as a train*; (Russian) *lively as an arrow*; (Belarusian) *clumsy as gates, as a shaft, as a wardrobe.*

Here one notes an almost complete coincidence between the Russian and Belarusian groups. There is a total coincidence of words used to describe a fast, lively or agile person. In addition to comparisons shared with Belarusians, Russians use the comparison "clumsy like a fat person" to characterize a clumsy person, while Belarusians use comparisons to man-made objects, "clumsy like gates, like a shaft, like a wardrobe." The most commonly used comparisons are to animals.

CONCLUSION

The test subjects were asked to use 31 stimulus words to characterize human appearance. The results included 4619 responses from Russians and 3100 from Belarusians. A total of 7719 responses were analyzed in this section of the experiment.

The experiment found that Russians and Belarusians compare human appearance to 13-14 object groups: to natural objects (sky, sea, earth, field, etc.), to natural phenomena (rain, sunset, storm, etc.), to animals (dog, horse, cow), to plants (cherry, cornflowers, birch), to the time of year and time of day (winter, night, etc.), to cultural phenomena; literary, folkloric characters and mythological creatures; to members of certain professions, nationalities, ages, to themselves and other important people (mother, beloved, friend), to man-made objects and jewelry.

Native Russian speakers use more varied comparisons than Belarusians. For example, Belarusians have almost no comparisons to seasons or the time of day (hair as long as the night, as long as winter) and they have few comparisons to folkloric characters or mythological creatures. Nor do they use comparisons to textual references. By textual references, we mean not only direct quotations, but also the names of characters, book titles, and separate words referring to specific situations in the text.

Belarusian native speakers, unlike Russians, make frequent comparisons to themselves and those close to them (snub nosed like me). This data can be explained by the fact that the social experience of the native speaker influences language. This becomes even more apparent when analyzing the comparisons used to characterize a poor man. Both Russians and Belarusians made comparisons such as: like a teacher, like a student, like a pensioner, like everyone else, like me, etc.

This point is further proven by the numerous comparisons to cultural phenomena found in mass media and tabloid culture, such as 'like Schwarzenegger', 'like Madonna', and other celebrities. Because the subjects were young adults (from 19 to 22 years), the deep penetration of mass culture into the environment of the young is noticeable.

The experiment revealed certain stimulus words (in this case, physical features) that had a variety of associations (eyes, hair) and some with rather standard responses (mouth, teeth, cheekbones). This can be explained by the various communicative roles that facial features play when one person perceives another, i.e. as paralinguistic signs.

The world of comparisons is multifaceted and diverse. They may be comparisons to mundane realities (*hair as straight as a hem, as a stick, hands as big as shovels, as rakes*), as well as poetic comparisons (*hands as gentle as a southern breeze; hair as straight as rain; a voice as pleasant as a murmuring brook; hair long like night, long like winter*). The Belarusian responses had a greater number of poetic comparisons, striking due to being unexpected and picturesque: *eyes expressive as a poem; eyebrows black like the wings of a swallow; hands delicate like wings; as hungry as a baby cuckoo*, etc.

There are stimulus words that evoke association to a particular reality, and these comparisons occur more frequently than others. For example, both nationalities most often compare EYES to natural objects and natural phenomena: to the sky, sea, lake, cornflower fields, whirlpools, stars, sun, springs, sunset, rain, morning dawn; however, HAIR and TEETH are mostly compared to animals: to a horse's mane, to the fur of various animals, their fluff; to the teeth of horses, squirrels, wolves, sharks, mice, dogs, crocodiles, and others.

Probably, this can be explained by how humans perceive the teeth and fur of animals (teeth are a threat to a human being, hair allows for better identification of animals), a perception which is then made directly analogous to humans and fixed in speech and language.

The inner state of the person is reflected by the physical world, "the world of things can be a symbol of the world of the mind . . .. We all know that our bodies express our minds." (Fromm). The eyes, the voice, the lips evoke a large number of poetic comparisons (*eyes shining like a star, like a drop of water, like a river in summer day, as the surface of the lake in the moonlight; a voice as gentle as a summer breeze, like a wafting breeze; pleasant as drops; lips red as the dawn, as the sunset, like rose petals, like cherries, like as poppies* and others). These facial features help express a person's emotional state, and lead to the emergence of emotional associations to natural phenomena that cause similar emotions (night, breeze).

In many cases, the comparisons suggested by the test subjects could constitute an entire treatise about how one can determine a person's emotional state, character and other personality traits based on the person's external appearance: lips thin like an evil man's lips, like a greedy person's, like a wise person's; lips thick like those of a sensual woman, like those of the debauched, like those of a glutton; hands big like a tightwad's; hands gentle like those of a shirker; the square chin of a strong-willed person's; a chin dimpled like a coquette's, and so on.

On notes a rather large amount of comparison groups where all that is good, gentle and affectionate for the native speakers of both languages is associated with child, mother and girl: a voice gentle as a girl, eyes clear as a child's, hands as gentle as a mother's; a face as pretty as a girl's, etc.

Most of the comparisons in the experiment are simple and consist of one word, but more extensive types are also found: a nose hooked like a smooth road with obstacles, clumsy like a bull in a china shop, tired as a driven horse, hungry as 20 hippos. Such comparisons are more imaginative, expressive, poetic.

As evidenced by the experimental data, comparisons are a complex mechanism with many structural and semantic features.

Most of the comparison experiment results (see the listed groups) are based on similarities between the human body and various objects in the real or imaginary world (which is as it should be), for example, a nose aquiline like a hill. There are associative comparisons that are evoked by standard forms of expression: as pale as a toadstool, as poor as Damián[330]. There are also comparisons based on contrast: a face as beautiful as a witch's; a nose as straight as a vulture's; nimble like an elephant (these comparisons are usually used in an ironic context).

More will be said about the national specifics of the comparisons after studying the inner qualities of the person. Here it may be noted that, as the experiment shows, Russians and Belarusians have similar outlooks, values and vocabulary that includes regular semantic links between words and concepts. For example, both nationalities evaluate and perceive the dynamic characteristics of a person (FAST, LIVELY, NIMBLE and CLUMSY) in almost the same way. Both Russians and Belarusians compared a fast person to the wind, to lightning, to a river, to a deer, to a hare, to a doe; lively was compared to baby animals (a foal, a kitten, a goat, a puppy); nimble was compared to a monkey, a hare, typhus, a cat, a lynx, a squirrel. The choice of comparisons to characterize a clumsy person was more interesting. Belarusian native speakers, in addition to comparisons to animals (which was the same for both nationalities), used comparisons to man-made objects: a fence, a shaft, which is not typical for the Russian perception of the world. The comparison of a fat person to a pumpkin is specifically Belarusian (see the characteristics of physical qualities). A short person was compared to a stump; a hungry person was compared to a baby cuckoo, etc. Here, cultural peculiarities have been included in figurative language schemes (i.e. comparisons) through cognitive-cultural interpretation made by an ethnic subject.

THE SECOND PART OF THE EXPERIMENT

This section of the psycholinguistic experiment analyzed the person's inner world and personality. Word stimuli were separated into different groups based on psychological classification: a) expressing the attitude of the individuals themselves (e.g. sleepy); b) to other people and

---

[330] Damian the Poor was the pen name of Yefim Prodvorov, a Russian and Soviet writer, poet, publisher.

society (e.g. a patriot); c) to work and its results (e.g. lazy); d) character traits that reflect the characteristics of the mental processes of the personality: emotional (e.g. cheerful), willful (e.g. brave), intellectual (e.g. inquisitive). In this section, the following questionnaire was provided to the test subjects:

QUESTIONAIRE 3

as careful as ... as determined as, as active as, as shy as ... as licentious as ... as vain as ..., as hot-tempered as ... as independent as ... as stupid as ... as sentimental as, as sad as, as modest as ... as kind as ... as stingy as, as greedy as ... as brave as, as violent as ... as sleepy as... as jealous as ... as calm as, as evil as, as hardworking as ... as critical as ... as cowardly as, as frivolous as ... as clever as ... as lazy as .. as stubborn as ... as deceitful as, as boastful as ... as inquisitive as ... as courageous as ... as observant as, as purposeful as, as persistent as, as honest as ...as intrepid as ... as cheerful as ... as patriotic as ... as generous as ...

QUESTIONAIRE 4

We translated the same stimulus words for Belarusians. The test subjects included: 93 Russian native speakers, students of philology at the University of Vitebsk and 80 Belarusian native speakers, also students. The procedure used for the experiment was the same as in the previous series.

EXPERIMENT RESULTS AND ANALYSIS
CAREFUL

The following comparison groups can be distinguished here:

1) to animals: (Russian) *as a cat, as a raccoon*; (Belarusian) *as a cat, as a hamster, as a pig, as a squirrel, as a chipmunk*;

2) to members of certain professions, nationality, age: (Russian) *as an accountant, as an Englishman, as a German, as a girl*; (Belarusian) *as a German, as a girl;*

3) to other people: (Russian*) as a pedant, as an A student, as a first grader, as an excellent student, as a hostess*; (Belarusian) *like mother, as someone who's just had a bath, like a goody-goody.*

Russians used comparisons to other nationalities most frequently; Belarusians used comparisons to animals most frequently.

ACTIVE

1) to members of certain professions: (Russian) *as a cultural activities organizer*; (Belarusian) *like a member of Congress, like an athlete, like an organizer, as a disc jockey*;

2) to membership in a political party: (Russian) *like a member of the Komsomol, like a pioneer[331], like a communist*; (Belarusian) *like a communist, like a pioneer, like a member of the Komsomol, like a member of a youth organization, like a trade union leader*;

3) *to other people*: (Russian*) like a child, like a student;* (Belarusian) *like a smart-aleck, like me, like a woman, like a girlfriend*;

4) to animals: (Russian) *like a bee*; (Belarusian) *like an ant*.

Native speakers of both languages most often compare an active person to members of political parties.

LASCIVIOUS

1) to animals*: like a cat, like a she-cat, like a pup, like a tomcat, like a goat, like a fox, like a bear awakened from hibernation, like a dog,* (Belarusian) *like a cat, like a dog, like a monkey, like a fox*;

2) to literary heroes: (Russian) *like Don Juan*; (Belarusian) *like Don Juan, like a Casanova*;

3) to other people: (Belarusian) *like a prostitute, like a tart, like a womanizer, like a libertine, like a geisha.*

Russian native speakers do not make comparisons to other people, most often they compare a lascivious person to animals, while Belarusians compare them to literary heroes and other people.

CHEERFUL

1) to natural objects and natural phenomena: (Russian) *like a brook, like a summer rain*; (Belarusian) *like a rainbow, like a sunny day, like a patch of sunlight, like the sun*;

---

[331] Boy scout / Girl scout

2) to animals: (Russian) *as a kitten, as a puppy, as a bird*; (Belarusian) *as a lark, as a puppy, as a bird, as an elephant, as a mosquito, as a penguin*;

3) to the time of year: (Russian) *as spring*;

4) to cultural, literary and folkloric events: (Russian) *like a song, like Pinocchio, like Petrushka*; (Belarusian) like *Charlie Chaplin*;

5) to members of different professions and other people: (Russian) *like a clown*; (Belarusian) *like a clown, like a comedian, like an actor, like me, like a drunkard.*

Both Russians and Belarusians use similar comparison groups here, although there are some response variations within the groups: Russians compare a cheerful person to a brook, summer rain, spring; Belarusians compare them to a rainbow, a patch of sunlight, the sun.

HOT-TEMPERED

1) to natural objects, natural phenomena: (Russian) *like a volcano, like a fire, like dry grass*; (Belarusian*) like fire*;

2) to members of other nationalities, historical figures, other people: (Russian*) like a person from Caucasus, like an Italian, like a choleric, like a crazy person, like Peter the Great*; (Belarusian) *like a friend, like a bully, like father*;

3) to man-made objects: (Russian) *as gunpowder, as matches, as a fire*; (Belarusian) *as fireworks, as fire, as gunpowder, flammable as a haystack*;

Native speakers of both languages most often compare a hot-tempered person to man-made objects like fire, gunpowder, matches.

STUPID

1) to animals: (Russian) *as sheep, as a donkey, as a chicken, as a monkey, as a turkey, as a bear, as a puppy, as a duck, as a sparrow, as a cow, as a penguin*; (Belarusian*) as sheep, as a puppy, as a chicken, as a donkey, as a mouse, as a sparrow, as a fly*;

2) to plants: (Russian) *like a tree*, (Belarusian) *like a stump*;

3) to people: (Belarusian) *as a baby, as a new born, as Ivanushka[332], as a fool, as a first grader*;

---

[332] Ivan the Fool.

4) to man-made objects: (Russian*) as a cork, as a felt boot, as a boot, as a Siberian felt boot*. (Belarusian) *as a boot*.

Russian native speakers in this experiment did not compare a stupid person to other people, the other comparison groups are the same for both Russians and Belarusians. Russians mostly compare a stupid person to man-made objects, Belarusians made comparisons to other people and animals.

SAD

1) to natural phenomena: (Russian) *as a rain, as a sunset, as an autumn rain, as autumn*; (Belarusian) *as autumn, as the day, as a cloud, as the moon, as rain, as the fall*;
2) to animals: (Russian) *as a horse, as an elephant, as a donkey, as a sick animal*; (Belarusian) *as a horse, as an elk, as a canary in a cage*;
3) to plants: (Russian) *as a willow*; (Belarusian) *as a cactus*;
4) to literary heroes, folkloric characters: like Pierrot, like the Unsmiling Tsarevna, like sister Alyonushka[333]; (Belarusian) Like Pierrot;
5) to people: (Russian) *as a melancholic;* (Belarusian) *as a sick person, as a bride, as Alexander Blok*.

Russians mostly compare sad persons to literary heroes and folkloric characters; Belarusians compare them to animals.

KIND

1) to animals: (Russian) *like an elephant, like a bear, like a seal, like a dog;* (Belarusian) *like an elephant after a bath*;
2) to literary heroes, folklore characters: (Russian) *like Sonia Marmeladova, like Papa Carlo, like Cinderella, like Santa Claus*; (Belarusian) *like Leopold the Cat[334], like Cinderella, like Dr. Aybolit[335], like God*;
3) to themselves and other people: (Russian) *like mother, like grandmother, like my own mother*; (Belarusian) *like mother, like me, like a sister of mercy*.

---

[333] "Sister Alyonushka and brother Ivanushka" is a Soviet cartoon, created in 1953.
[334] "Leopold the Cat" was a Soviet cartoon series about a kind cat named Leopold. Filmed from 1975 to 1987.
[335] Literally, Aybolit means "Ouch, it hurts."

The third group has the largest number of comparisons. A kind person is compared to other people. Russians and Belarusians most often attribute this quality to mother.

GREEDY

1) to natural objects: (Belarusian) *as a swamp, as a bog, as a crater*;
2) to animals: (Russian) *as a hamster, as a wolf;* (Belarusian) *as a wolf, as a bull, as a wild boar, as a beetle, as a hyena*;
3) to literary heroes, folkloric characters: (Russian) greedy like Gobsek, like Stepan Plyushkin, like Koschei;(Belarusian) like Gobseck, like Barmaley[336], like the Miserly Knight[337];
4) to members of certain professions: (Russian) *as a usurer, as a merchant, as a priest*; (Belarusian) *as a priest*;
5) to other people: *like a Jew, as a cheapskate, as a miser, as a landowner, as a rich man, as a neighbor*; (Belarusian) *as a millionaire, as a capitalist, as a briber, as a hungry person.*

Russian native speakers do not make comparisons to natural objects, while for Belarusians, who live in swampy areas, comparison to a bog is naturally relevant. Russians mostly compare a greedy person to literary heroes, Belarusians compare them to other people.

CRUEL

1) to animals: (Russian) *like a beast, like a wolf, like a wild boar*; (Belarusian) *like a wolf, like a dog*;
2) to folkloric and mythological characters: (Russian) *as the devil, as Zeus;* (Belarusian) *as Genghis Khan*;
3) to historical figures, members of certain nationalities, members of certain parties: (Russian) *like a German, like a fascist*; (Belarusian) *like Ivan IV, like Nero, like a fascist*;
4) to other people: (Russian) *like a sadist, like an executioner, as a murderer, as a barbarian, as an enemy, as a tyrant, as a despot*; (Belarusian) *as a rapist, like a sadist, as an executioner, as an emperor.*

---

[336] A pirate and an ogre. A character in the poetic tales "Barmaley" (1925) and "Stronger than Barmaley!" (1942), as well as in the novel "Doctor Aybolit" (1936).
[337] "The Miserly Knight", written by Pushkin.

Native speakers of both languages most often compare a cruel person to other people having the same evil qualities.

ENVIOUS

1) to animals: (Russian) *like a fox, like a jackal, like a magpie, like a dog*; (Belarusian) *like a wolf, like a magpie, like a fox, like a hamster*;

2) to cultural, literary, folklore phenomena: *like Iago; like the crow in the fable, like the stepmother in the fairytale, like Esther, like Jagiełło*[338];

3) to other people: (Russian) *as a neighbor, as the girl next door, as a rich man, as a looser, as a stepmother, as an old maid, as a girlfriend, as an enemy, as a woman*; (Belarusian) *as a student, as a hungry student, as a small child, as a man.*

Comparisons to animals are few here. A jealous person is mostly compared to other people.

ANGRY[339]

1) to animals: (Russian) *angry as a wolf, as a dog, evil as a snake*; (Belarusian) *angry as a wolf, as a dog*;

2) to folkloric and mythological characters: *like the devil, like Koschei, like Baba Yaga*; (Belarusian) *like the devil, like Koschei, like Baba Yaga, like a villain, like a witch*;

3) to other people: (Belarusian) *evil as an enemy, evil as a German.*

Russian native speakers do not compare an angry or evil person to other people; native speakers of both languages usually compare them to animals.

CRITICAL

1) to members of different professions: (Russian) *like a critic, as a superior, like a teacher, like an examiner*;

(Belarusian) *like a critic, like a censor, like a superior, like a correspondent, like a politician*;

---

[338] Became Grand Duke in 1377 and King of Poland in 1386. In September, 1380 Jogailla tried to join Mamai, commander of the Golden Horde, to fight against the Prince of Moscow Dmitry Donskov and his allies. However, before reaching the Don, he learned that the Golden Horde had been defeated in the Battle of Kulikovo and he retreated. Jagiełło is credited for having Christianized Lithuania.

[339] In Russian and Belarusian, ЗЛОЙ can mean both wicked and angry.

2) to cultural figures, literary heroes: (Russian) *like Vissarion Belinsky, like Pisarev*[340], *like Chatsky*[341]; (Belarusian) *like Vissarion Belinsky, like Nikolay Dobrolyubov, like Homer*;

3) to other people: (Russian) *like a member of the Komsomol, like an old maid*; (Belarusian) *like a woman, like a teenager, like a friend*;

4) to abstract notions: (Belarusian) as realism, like the mind.

Belarusians, unlike Russian native speakers, made some comparisons that we included in the "abstract notions" group. The second group has the biggest number of comparisons by native speakers of both languages.

THOUGHTLESS

1) to natural phenomena: (Russian) *like the wind*; (Belarusian) *like the wind*;

2) to animals: (Russian) *as a dragonfly, as a moth, as a cuckoo*; (Belarusian) *as a moth, as a monkey, as a crow*;

3) to people: (Russian) *as a girl, as a child, as a young lady, as a little boy, like a flirt, as a fool, as a lady, as a woman;* (Belarusian) *as an idiot, as a fool, as a dreamer.*

Native speakers of both languages most often compare thoughtless people to animals and women.

LAZY

1) to natural phenomena: (Russian) *as an autumn rain*; (Belarusian) *as a hot day*;

2) to animals: (Russian) *as a bear, as a cat, as a seal, as a drone bee, as a she-cat, as a piglet, as a fat cat, as a penguin, as a bear cub, as a badger, as a hippopotamus*; (Belarusian) *as a cat, as a bear, as a hippopotamus, as a sloth, as a drone bee, as a seal*;

3) to literary heroes, folkloric characters: (Russian) *like Oblomov*, (Belarusian) *as Emelya on the stove*[342];

4) to people: (Russian) *like me*; (Belarusian) *like my friend, like a dormouse.*

---

[340] 14 July 1803 — 15 March 1828, Moscow— Russian dramatist, vaudeville writer, theater critic.

[341] Alexander Chatsky, the main character in "Woe from Wit" by Alexander Griboyedova.

[342] Russian folk tale, published in "Russian Fairy Tales" by Alexander Afanasyev.

Native speakers of both languages most often made comparisons to animals.

DECEITFUL

1) to animals: (Russian) *as a fox, as a jackal, as a dog, as a grey gelding, as a snake*; (Belarusian) *as a fox, as a jackal, as a cat*;

2) to cultural and literary phenomena: (Russian) *like the Pravda newspaper, like Khlestakov[343], like Tartuffe*; (Belarusian) *like Khlestakov*.

3) to people: (Russian) *like Gorbachev, like a president, like a woman, like an unfaithful wife*; (Belarusian) *like a president, like a villain*.

Native speakers of both languages most often compare deceitful people to animals.

CURIOUS

1) to animals: (Russian) *as a crow, as a magpie, as a monkey, as a fox, as a turkey, as a cat*; (Belarusian) *as a small bird, as a hedgehog, as a magpie, as a rat*;

2) to literary heroes: (Russian) *like Pinocchio*; (Belarusian) *like Pinocchio*;

3) to events of folklore: (Russian) *like Varvara*; (Belarusian) *like Varvara*;

4) to people: (Russian) *like a journalist, like a child, like an old woman, like a woman*; (Belarusian) *like a small child, like a student, like a teacher, like a fool, like an intellectual*.

Native speakers of both languages most often compare a curious person to other people.

OBSERVANT

1) to animals: (Russian) *like an eagle, like a falcon*; (Belarusian) *like a falcon, like an eagle*;

2) to literary heroes: (Russian) *as Sherlock Holmes, as Hercules, Poirot*; (Belarusian) *as Sherlock Holmes, as Tarzan*;

3) to representatives of different professions: (Russian) *as a scout, as a spy, as a scientist, as a detective, as a lookout, as a pathfinder, as a researcher, as an investigator, as a policeman, as an artist*; (Belarusian) *as a path finder, as a*

---

[343] Character from Gogol's *Inspector General*.

244

tutor, as a spy, as an artist, as a detective, as a psychologist, as a scientist;

4) to other people: (Russian) *like a child*; (Belarusian) *like a friend, like a child, like an old woman, like Lomonosov*;

5) to man-made objects: (Belarusian) *like a telescope, like glasses, like Post DA1[344], like a barometer*.

In addition to common groups, Belarusian native speakers compare an observant person to man-made objects. Native speakers of both languages most often make comparisons to people of certain professions.

PERSISTENT

1) to animals: (Russian) *like a ram, like a woodpecker, like a mosquito*; (Belarusian) *like a donkey, like an ant, like a ram, like a cuckoo*;

2) to members of certain professions: (Russian) *as a ticket collector*; (Belarusian) *as a teacher, as a ticket collector on the bus*;

3) to other people: (Russian) *as a person in love, as a fool in love, as a lover, like a man, as a creditor*; (Belarusian) *as a child, as a pioneer, as Amundsen[345], as a someone being interrogated, as a student, as Napoleon, like a man*;

4) to man-made objects (Russian) *like a tank;* (Belarusian) *like a pillar, like a map, like a tank.*

Native speakers of both languages most often compared a persistent person to other people.

COURAGEOUS

1) to animals: (Russian) *like a lion, like a tiger, like a beast, like an eagle*; (Belarusian) *like a lion, like a tiger, like a bull, like a panther*;

2) to people of different professions: (Russian) *like a captain, like a pilot, like a sailor, like a seaman, like a pirate*; (Belarusian) *like a warrior, as a wrestler*;

3) to other people: (Russian) *like a knight, like a soldier, like a hero, like a warrior*; (Belarusian) *like a knight, like Zoya*

---

[344] Honor guard at the Eternal Flame for the tomb of the unknown soldier in Moscow.

[345] Roald Engelbregt Gravning Amundsen.

Kosmodemyanskaya, like Napoleon, like Matrosov[346], like Anthony, like Spartacus.

The number of groups and their contents are similar for native speakers of both languages. Most often, they compare a courageous person to people of certain professions.

PATRIOTIC

1) to specific historical figures: (Russian*)* *like Marat Kazei, like Pavel Morozov, like Maresyev[347], like Kutuzov, like Ivan Susanin, like Korchagin, like Matrosov, like a heroic Youth Guard*; (Belarusian) *like Marat Kazei, like a member of the Komsomol, like Zinaida Portnova, like Alexander Lukashenko, like Konstanty Kalinowski, like Ivan Susanin, like Nikolai Gastello, like Lenin, like the defenders of the Brest Fortress, like Ivan Kupala, like the Youth Guard*;

2) to members of other nationalities: (Russian) *like a Georgian, like an American*; (Belarusian) *like an American.*

Native speakers of both languages most often describe patriotism by referencing specific historical figures.

DECISIVE

1) to natural phenomena: (Russian*)* *as lightning*; (Belarusian) *as lightning, as an iceberg, as the wind*;

2) to animals: (Russian) *like a tiger*; (Belarusian) *like a lynx, like a rooster, like a falcon, like an eagle*;

3) to historical figures: (Russian*)* *like Caesar*; (Belarusian) *like Alexander the Great, like Napoleon, like Timur, like Caesar*;

4) to representatives of different professions: (Russian) *like a soldier, like a war leader, like a military leader, a commander, like a general officer commanding, like a businessman, like a police officer*; (Belarusian) *like a student at an exam, like a commander, like a soldier*;

5) to literary heroes: (Russian) *like Danko[348], like Don Quixote*; (Belarusian) *like Loverboy[349]*;

6) to other people: (Russian) *like me, like a lover, like a leader*; (Belarusian) *as a drunk, as a lover, as a hero*;

---

[346] Alexander Matveyevich Matrosov
[347] Alexey Petrovich Maresyev
[348] Character in *Old Isergil*, by Maxim Gorky
[349] 1989 American film.

7) to man-made objects: (Russian) *like an arrow*; (Belarusian) *like a wall*.

Native speakers of both languages most often compare a decisive person to members of various professions.

SHY

1) to seasons: (Russian) *like an early spring*; (Belarusian) *like spring*;

2) to animals: (Russian) *like a hare, like a mouse, like a chicken, like a lamb, like a doe, like a rabbit, like a gopher, like a jerboa, like a deer, like a penguin*; (Belarusian) *like a hare, like a cockroach, like a lamb, like a hedgehog, like a squirrel, like a bird*;

3) to plants: (Russian) *like a flower*; (Belarusian) *like a flower; as a branch*;

4) to people: (Russian) *as a girl, as a little girl, as a child*; (Belarusian) *as a child, as a young girl, as a youth, as a humble person, as a fugitive, as a fool*.

Native speakers of both languages most frequently compare a shy person to animals.

VAIN

1) to animals:(Russian) *as vain as a peacock, as a lion, as a turkey, as a camel, as a goose, as a cockerel, as a ram, as a donkey, as a deer*; (Belarusian) *as a turkey, as a donkey, as a peacock, as a magpie, as a Siamese cat, as a ram, as a chameleon, as a rooster*;

2) to plants: (Russian) *as a rose*; (Belarusian) *as a maple tree*;

3) to cultural, literary, mythological phenomena: (Russian) *as vain as Chatsky, as Narcissus*; (Belarusian) *like Narcissus, like Irene, as a god*;

4) to people: (Russian) *as a Pole, as Napoleon, as a beauty, as an egoist*; (Belarusian) *as me, as a proud person, like an egoist*.

Native speakers of both languages most frequently compare a vain person to animals.

INDEPENDENT

1) to natural phenomena: (Belarusian) *like the sun, like the wind*;

2) to animals: (Russian) *like a cat*; (Belarusian) *like a cat, like a rooster, like a shark*;

3) to literary heroes: (Russian) *like Mitrasha*[350]; (Belarusian) *like the Wildman of the Woods, like Pinocchio*;

4) to people: (Russian) *like an adult, like a grown-up, like a grown-up man, like an orphan, like a man*; (Belarusian) *like an adult; like a poet, like a teacher, like a president, like a teenager, like a student, like an orphan*;

5) to different countries: (Belarusian) *like Ukraine, like America*.

Native speakers of Belarusian had a greater variety of answers, providing two additional comparison groups: to natural phenomena and to different countries. More than a half of the comparisons used by the Russians included the phrase "like an adult" or its modifications "like a grown-up man" and "like a grown-up."

SENTIMENTAL

1) to natural objects: (Belarusian) *like a cornflower field, like dawn, like a rain, like a cloud*;

2) to the seasons: (Russian) *like a late winter, like autumn*; (Belarusian) *like autumn*;

3) to cultural phenomena, fictional heroes: *like Poor Liza*[351], *like a romantic song, like Wild Rose*[352], *like Nikolay Karamzin, like a novel, like Rousseau, like Indian cinema, like an old book, like Julia*; (Belarusian) *like Werther*[353], *like a comedy, like Nikolay Karamzin, like a comedy, like a poet, like a journey, like Lensky*[354], *like a hero in an Indian movie, like Poor Liza, like a writer of the 19th century*;

4) to different people: *like lovers, like a romantic, like a girl, like an old man, like Brezhnev, like a lady, like a woman*; (Belarusian) *like a girl, like an old woman*.

Native speakers of both languages most frequently compare a sentimental person to cultural phenomena and literature.

MODEST

---

[350] Main character in the fairy tale *The Sun's Closet*, by Mikhail Prishvin.
[351] By Nikolay Karamzin.
[352] Character in Mexican telenovela *Rosa salvaje*.
[353] Protagonist in "The Sorrows of Young Werther" by Goethe.
[354] Romantic character from the novel, *Eugene Onegin*.

1) to animals: (Russian) *like a mouse*; (Belarusian) *like a hen, like a cat*;

2) to plants: (Russian) *like a flower*; (Belarusian) *like a blade of grass, like a chamomile, like grass, like an aspen leaf*;

3) to characters in works of literature: (Russian) *like Cinderella, like Snow White, like Natasha Rostova, like Devushkin*[355]; (Belarusian) *like the Snow Maiden*;

4) to people of a certain age: (Russian) *like a girl, like a maiden, like a child, like a little girl*; (Belarusian) *a little girl, like a child*;

5) to other people: (Russian) *like a monk, like a poor man*; (Belarusian) *like a monk, like a cowed person, like a first grader, like a student, as a collective farmer in the city.*

The most frequent comparison for Russians is to people of a certain age and for Belarusians it is to other people.

STINGY

1) to literary and folkloric characters: (Russian) *like Plyushkin*[356], *like Tartuffe, like Koschei*; (Belarusian) *like Gobseck, like Patriarch Tikhon of Moscow*;

2) to natural objects: (Belarusian) *like the sun in winter; like water in the desert*;

3) to animals: (Belarusian) *like a hamster, like a crow, like a stallion*;

4) to different people: (Russian) *like a money lender, like a Jew, like a rich man*; (Belarusian) *like a Jew, like a Polish landowner.*

5) to the products of human vital functions: ((Belarusian) *like a tear.*

Belarusians have two groups of comparisons which do not coincide with the Russian groups: to objects in nature and to products of human vital functions. These comparisons are poetic, imaginative and expressive. However, native speakers of both languages most frequently compare a stingy person to "literary characters."

BRAVE

---

[355] Character in Poor Folk by Dostoevsky.
[356] Character in *Dead Souls* by Nikolai Gogol.

1) to animals: (Russian) *like a lion, like a tiger, like an eagle, like a falcon, like a lynx*; (Belarusian) *like a lion, like a bear, like a dog, like a wolf*;

2) to literary and mythological characters: (Russian) *like Malchish-Kibalchish*[357], *like Achilles*; (Belarusian) *like Artemon, like Gavroche, like Dick Sand, A Captain at Fifteen*;

3) to people: (Russian) *like a knight, like a warrior, like a hero*; (Belarusian) *like an Afghan, like a warrior*.

Native speakers of both languages most frequently identify brave people to "animals."

SLEEPY

1) to animals: (Russian) *like a fly, like an owl, like a bear, like a grouse, like a cat*; (Belarusian) *like a fly, like a bear, like a groundhog, like an owl, like a sloth, like a hamster, like a seal*;

2) to themselves and other people: (Russian) *like me*; (Belarusian) *like a student at a lecture, like me, like someone dragged out of bed*.

Native speakers of both languages most frequently compare a sleepy person to animals that represent sleepiness in that nation.

CALM

1) to natural objects:(Russian) *as a lake, as a stone*, (Belarusian) *as a pin, as a stone, as the sea, as a stream, as water*;

2) to animals:(Russian) *as a boa constrictor, as an elephant, as a dead lion*; (Belarusian) *as a boa constrictor, like a lion, hedgehog, like an elephant, like a pig, like a mammoth, like a cow, like a fish*;

3) to cultural phenomena, literary heroes: (Russian) *like a statue, as Kaa*; (Belarusian) *like a cradle*;

4) (Russian) *to man-made objects: like a tank*; (Belarusian) *like a tank*.

5) to people: (Belarusian) *like me, like a baby, like the dead, like a pilot*.

Native speakers of both languages most frequently compare a calm person to an animal.

HARDWORKING

---

[357] *Tale of Malchish-Kibalchish* by Arkady Gaidar.

1) to animals: (Russian*)* *like a bee, like an ant, like an ox, like a horse, like a squirrel, like a beaver*; (Belarusian) *like a bee, like an ant, like an ox, like a stallion, like a bison, like a bull*;
2) to literary characters: (Russian) *like Cinderella*; (Belarusian) *like Cinderella*;
3) to real people: (Belarusian) *like a villager, like a Belarusian man.*

In addition to two common groups, Belarusian native speakers made comparisons to real people. The most common comparison for native speakers of both languages is to animals (to bees).

COWARDLY

1) to animals: (Russian*)* *like a hare, like a jackal, like a mouse, like a rabbit*; (Belarusian) *like a hare, like a mouse, like a bird, like a cockroach, as a wild animal, like a deer*;
2) to people: (Belarusian) *like a first grader, like a girl.*

The main group of comparisons here is to animals. Comparisons to people are few and are made only by Belarusians.

CLEVER

1) to animals: (Russian*)* *like an owl, like a dog, like a mouse, like a duck, like a raven*; (Belarusian) *like a fox, like an owl, like a cat, like a stallion, like a dog*;
2) to literary heroes: (Russian) *like Znayka[358], like Bazarov; like Basilio the Cat[359]*;
3) to specific people: (Russian) *like Einstein, like Socrates, like Lenin, like Solomon*; (Belarusian) *like Lenin, like Socrates*;
4) to other people: (Russian) *like a professor, like an academic, like a scientist, like a diplomat;* (Belarusian) like a professor, like a scientist, like grandmother, like a teacher;
5) to man-made objects: (Russian) *like an encyclopedia*; (Belarusian) *like a bookcase.*

---

[358] Character from *Dunno on the Moon* by Nikolay Nosov.
[359] Character from *The Adventures of Buratino or The Golden Key* by Alexey Tolstoy.

These comparison groups are the same for native speakers of both languages. Most frequently, they compare a clever person to other people.

OBSTINATE

1) to animals: *like a donkey, like a ram, like a goat, like a bull*; (Belarusian) *as an ass; like a goat, like a ram, like a donkey, like a bull*;

2) to people: (Russian) *like a friend, like an elder, like Napoleon, as a competitor.*

The only comparison group that native Russian speakers identified here was to animals. Belarusian native speakers made some comparisons to people, but they were few.

BOASTFUL

1) to animals: (Russian) *like a hare, like a magpie, like a fox, like a peacock, like a parrot, like a rooster, like a monkey*; (Belarusian) *like a turkey, like a parrot, like a monkey, like a fox, like a rooster*;

2) to literary heroes: (Russian) *like Shvonder[360], like Shchukar[361], like Khlestakov[362]; (Belarusian) Khlestakov*;

3) to people: (Russian*) like a Tatar, like a child*; (Belarusian) *like a graduate, like a neighbor, like a fool, like a proud person, like a graduate, like Lenin.*

The most frequent comparison made by Russians was to animals; Belarusians most frequently made comparisons to people.

BRAVE

1) to animals:(Russian) *like a lion, like a tiger, like a rooster, like a wounded animal, like a drunken hare*; (Belarusian) *like a lion, like a lynx, like an elk, like a bison, as a Caucasian goat, like a wolf, like a tiger, like a bear*;

2) to literary and folkloric characters: (Russian) *like Don Quixote, like Ilya Muromets, like a bogatyr, like a knight*; (Belarus) *like Hercules, like Stierlitz*;

---

[360] Character from A Dog's Heart by Mikhaíl Bulgakov.
[361] Character from *Virgin Soil Upturned* by Mikhail Sholokhov.
[362] Character from *The Government Inspector* by Nikolai Gogol.

3) to various people: (Russian) *like a soldier; like Chapaev*[363], (Belarusian) *like a partisan, like Kutuzov, like Suvorov, like a warrior, like a man.*

Native speakers of both languages most frequently compare an intrepid person to animals.

PURPOSEFUL

1) to natural objects: (Russian) *like a river*; (Belarusian) *like a river, like a road*;

2) to literary characters, historical figures:(Russian) *like Pavel Korchagin, like Bazarov*; (Belarusian) *like Prince Vladimir, like Faust, like Lukashenko, like Stalin, like Caesar*;

3) to people: (Russian) *like a scientist, like an athlete, like a pioneer, like a member of the Komsomol*; (Belarusian) *like me, like a man, as a graduate student, like a student, like a ruler, like a pathfinder*;

4) to man-made objects: (Russian) *like an arrow, like a rocket, like a train, like a bullet, like a nuclear bomb in flight*; (Belarusian) *like a train, like a plane, like a vector, like an arrow.*

Native speakers of both languages most frequently compare a purposeful person to man-made objects (an arrow).

HONEST

1) to natural phenomena: (Belarusian) *as nature*;

2) to animals: (Russian) *like a fox, like a dog*; (Belarusian) *like a bee, like an ant*;

3) to members of certain political parties and movements: (Russian) *like a communist, like a pioneer, like a member of the Komsomol*; (Belarusian) *like a pioneer, like a Komsomol*;

4) to other people: (Russian) *like Lenin, like Pavel Morozov, like a fool, like a judge, like a poor man, like a knight*; (Belarusian) *like a graduate, like a first grader, like mother, like me, like a professional, like a student, like a peasant woman, like a naked girl, as a priest at confession*;

5) to abstract concepts: (Russian) *like conscience; as a superman*;

6) to man-made objects: (Russian) *like glass*; (Belarusian) *like a transparent mirror.*

---

[363] Vasily Ivanovich Chapayev.

Native speakers of Russian most frequently compare an honest person to political parties, while native speakers of Belarusian most frequently compare honest people to other people.

GENEROUS

1) to natural objects: (Russian) *as the earth, as the nature, as the sun*; (Belarusian) *as the earth, as the sun, as nature, as a cloud before the rain*;

2) to seasons: (Russian) *like autumn*; (Belarusian) *like autumn, as snow in winter*;

3) to literary heroes, folkloric characters: (Russian) *like Buratino, like a magician, like Santa Claus; like God*; (Belarusian) *like Santa Clause, like Ivan Kalita, like the horn of plenty*;

4) to members of other nations: (Russian) *like an Armenian, like a Georgian*; (Belarusian) *like a Russian, like a Georgian*;

5) to other people: (Russian) *like a spendthrift, like a king, like a rich man, like a sultan, like a millionaire, like a tsar; like a small child, like a friend, like grandmother*; (Belarusian) *like a sponsor, like me, like grandmother*;

6) to organizations: (Belarusian) *like the Soras Foundation, like a country*.

Belarusian native speakers had a comparison group that Russians did not: to organizations. Native speakers of both languages most frequently compared a generous person to the earth and other natural objects.

FINDINGS

In the second part of the experiment, 6920 test responses were received and then separated into several groups. The number of groups is somewhat smaller than in the first series. For example, there are no comparisons to jewelry and only a few to plants. But compared with the first series, where the test subjects characterized a person's appearance, the second series describing a person's inner world and character had comparisons of less varied characterizations. The number of groups made for each stimulus words was much smaller, from 2 (sleepy, cowardly) and up to 6 -7 (decisive, honest, generous). Most of the stimulus words had 3 – 4 groups.

These facts can be explained as follows. Material objects, such as a person's appearance and real-world objects such as natural and man-made objects, are outwardly perceived physical entities reflected by the same perceptual mechanisms. Under these conditions, there are unlimited opportunities for the emergence of various associations on which to base the comparisons. As for the character traits studied in the second part, they are not physical, but mental, ideal objects having a different nature and ontology. They are not directly reflected in the consciousness of the native speaker through relevant sense organs, but indirectly and repeatedly through that person's observation of a complex set of movements, actions, behavior and speech.

They are reflected in the consciousness of a native speaker not through direct impact on the relevant sense organs, but through the person's indirect and repeated observation of a complex set of the movement, action, behavior and speech. Under such circumstances, the objective conditions for the emergence of associations underlying the comparison of character traits to real-world objects (natural phenomena, plants, animals, etc.) are extremely narrowed. These word classes result in a rather high probability of a specific reaction and variations will be much smaller.

The following pattern stands out: words indicating positive social character traits had a greater variety of responses than those having negative social connotations. The latter where more uniform and stereotyped. At first glance, this contradicts the commonly known fact that everything negative in language is recorded with greater detail, care and variety. However, closer examination reveals that words having a negative connotation (in this case character traits) are more frequent and divide the continuum of the picture of the world into smaller segments, i.e. more accurately. Therefore, comparisons to negative stimulus words must be fewer than comparisons to the more semantically blurred positive stimulus words

The results of the comparison tests are structurally different. Most are simple one-word responses. However, there are also more complex results: *sad as a sick animal; sad as a canary in a cage; sad as a rainy day; calm as an aspen in a lull; kind as an elephant after a bath; purposeful as a nuclear bomb in flight; determined as a student at exams*, etc.

The most frequent results of the comparisons experiment are distributed as follows: for both Russians and Belarusians, the most frequent thematic group for 26 stimulus words out of 40 are the same. For example, native speakers of both languages compare an active person to members of various political parties and organizations: *active as a pioneer, as a member of the Komsomol, like a communist, like a* Timurite, *like a trade union leader*. A cruel and envious person is compared to others: *like an executioner, like a sadist, like a murderer, like an enemy, like a tyrant*, etc. Jeal*ous as a neighbor, as a friend, as a stepmother*, etc.; a lazy person is most often compared to animals: *like a cat, like a seal, like a drone bee, like a hippopotamus*, etc.

A comparative table of the most frequent responses of the subjects according to the language they speak would look like this:
Native Russian speakers, native Belarusian speakers:
comparisons to animals - 16, comparisons to animals - 16
comparisons to people - 9, comparisons to people - 13
to a certain profession - 4, to a certain profession - 2
to a nationality - 1, to a nationality - 0
to members of a certain party - 2, to members of a certain party - 1
to cultural phenomena - 4, to cultural phenomena - 3
to natural phenomena - 1, to natural phenomena - 3
to man-made objects - 3, to man-made objects – 2

In general, Belarusian native speakers use comparisons to different people and natural phenomena more often than Russian native speakers. Russians are more inclined to make comparisons to cultural phenomena, to literary characters, to people of certain nationalities and to man-made objects. Overall, the registry of comparisons of both languages correlates perfectly. Therefore, this work's hypothesis about the universality of principle categories, characteristics and properties to describe a person and the ethno-cultural specifics of their contents was confirmed by our experiment.

The hypothesis is also confirmed by the following data: native speakers of both languages do not apply negative character traits to themselves (greedy, lazy, lascivious, stupid, etc.), although they actively use them in comparisons to other people (greedy like a neighbor, but not greedy like me). In this respect the characteristic of a boastful person speaks for itself; the most frequent answers are *like a fool, like a scoundrel, like a proud person, like a man with a guilty conscience* (about 50% of the responses).

Ethno-cultural influences are clearly seen in several of the comparisons made by Belarusians: *as greedy as a bog, like the marshes*. This is explained by the geographical features of their habitat, most of which is occupied by swamps. Belarusians compare a sentimental person to a field of cornflowers and, as is known, the cornflower is the symbol of Belarus. Belarusians compare a fat person to a bag and a clumsy one to a fence (a 36-37% response rate; these comparisons are not found in the responses provided by Russian native speakers.

Accordingly, the choice of comparisons naming the character traits of a person requires a selection of objects from the real and fictional world that is characteristic for this nation and its world view. Proof of this can also be seen when analyzing the comparisons used for the stimulus word "patriot." Russians make comparisons to real people (Marat Kazei, Maresiev, Matrosov). Belarusians consider their president Alexandere.Lukashenko to be a patriot (8% of the responses) and make comparisons to the defenders of the Brest Fortress (8% of the responses), to their national poet Yanka Kupala (7% of the responses) and, in spite of the Soviet propaganda, to Konstanty Kalinowski (11% of the responses), who led the struggle against the tsarist oppressors. In this regard, a number of other stimulus words also prove the point, such as "independent": the Russian native speakers compared an independent person to an adult: *like an adult, like a grown-up man, like a grown-up* (52% of the responses), and the

Belarusian native speakers made comparisons to Ukraine and America (26% of the responses).

The similar responses provided by native speakers of both languages can be explained by various factors. For example, native speakers of both languages compare a deceitful person to a fox or a jackal, etc. These responses can be explained by the influence of fairy tales in forming the consciousness of the test subject. It is precisely in fairy tales where a fox appears as a cunning and deceitful animal. Other responses reveal the obvious influence of economic activity, lifestyle, history and national culture. For example, native speakers of Belarusian compare a generous to the Soros Foundation or to a patron and the word majestic to a bison.

The results obtained from the comparison experiments allow us to identify some implicit aspects about the semantics of figurative language units. If we analyze the responses to synonyms and antonyms denoting individual character traits (for example, brave, courageous, intrepid; kind - evil, sad - cheerful, generous - stingy), we get an interesting picture: both nationalities gave similar answers to all the three stimulus words (brave, courageous, intrepid). They also compared them to the same animals - lion, tiger, beast, eagle; and they compared them to the same literary heroes - Hercules, Gavroche, etc. However, the native speakers of both languages most frequently responded to the stimulus word "brave" by using comparisons to the professions: *courageous like a captain, like a pilot, like a sailor, like a seaman.* This suggests that this word has social connotations that distinguish it from the others. Academic dictionaries, unfortunately, do not note this distinction, although actual native speakers sense it very well.

Our experiment is a valuable source of information. It helps reveal connections and interactions between words and realities that exist in the mind of the native speaker. With objective data about typical or stereotypical comparisons, we can understand the ontology and the mechanism of their function in language and text.

It is this experimental data that provides the basis for identifying the stereotypical comparisons that have become clichés and are specific to the culture and to the native speakers of a language. For instance, Russians associate all that is beautiful with the sea, sky, sunset, flower, night, rose. For Belarusians, the associations are to the stars, sun, flowers, colors, poppies and spring. Stereotypical comparisons are also different: for Russians it is *beautiful as a doll, like a painting*, for Belarusians it's *like a berry*.

Russians associate all that is cheerful with brooks, summer rain and spring; Belarusians make these associations to rainbows, a patch of sunlight, and a smile. Russians associated soft things with fluff, wool, silk, cotton; Belarusians make these associations to fluff and linen. Russians compared a pleasant voice to the murmur of a brook, the sound of the tide, drippings, honey; Belarusians associate it to a brook, nightingales, the smell of mint. Russians associate thin with: a thread, string, an arrow; Belarusians compare it to a stitch or a ribbon; Russians compare round to: an apple, a ball; Belarusians make comparisons to: a pumpkin, a dish, a pancake. Therefore, Russian and Belarusian experimental data shows that although many of the stimulus words evoke similar reactions, their "profile" is quite different. Even though Russians and Belarusians have similar cultures and languages of national-linguistic consciousness, there are a few differences in aesthetic ideals. The psycholinguistic experiments help define the national language picture of the world through their objective reality.

These results, along with other experimental data, confirm the validity of Veronica Teliya's findings: national cultural connotations are a special macro-component of meaning. Essentially, it is a correlation of associative and imaginative connotations with cultural signs from other worldview systems (folklore, mythology, popular culture). Our experiment reveals the specifics of cultural-national comparisons and confirms the validity of national-cultural connotations.

The experiment shows that connotations affect the pragmatic potential of the original stimulus words, connotations well understood by the native speaker. This means that comparisons in general are a way of evaluating the world based on the internal decisions of native speakers of a language.

The experiments we conducted make it possible, at least hypothetically, to answer the questions of how cultural content gives meaning to linguistic signs. It is known that culture has no relation to biological inheritance and, in a broad sense, is passed on from generation to generation through tradition (language, customs, beliefs, myths, folklore, etc.). As Yuri Lotman noted, "culture is a form of communication between people," (Lotman, 1994, p. 6). However, culture is more than communication, it has a symbolic function as well, i.e. bread, sword, knife, etc. For instance, in Central Asia knives, salt, pepper are put away after a meal, because all sharp things cut the prayer and prevent it from reaching Allah.

Thus, symbols are given meaning, and the cultural sphere "is always a symbolic sphere" (Yuri Lotman).

As the experimental data shows, national linguistic personality perceives objects (including other humans) not only through the dimensions of space and time, but through meaning, which includes cultural stereotypes and standards. We live in a world of stereotypes. Linguistic stereotypes are not the same as psychological stereotypes; they are generalized representations of objects, phenomena of the social and natural environment. The presence of linguistic stereotypes is a prerequisite for the formation of a national picture of the world.

Members of a particular national community look at and see the world through these stereotypes, which are reflected and enshrined in language with the help of linguistic stereotypes and norms. These norms are a type of idealized stereotype. At a socio-psychological level, these norms act as an expression of ideas about a person, the world, society; for example, *as healthy as an ox, as hungry as a wolf*, etc.

Comparisons of this kind are quite a frequent in our experiment and the various understandings of personality, including moral and ethical understandings, are fixed within these comparisons: *kind like mother; hardworking as a bee; cowardly like a hare; generous as the earth; stubborn as a donkey; stupid as a ram*, etc. Such comparisons are not very complex. They live in each language as a separate image, often very specific to each nation: *greedy as a bog*; *beautiful as a field of flax; eyes like cornflowers* (Belarusian); *as thin as a rake* (Russian); *as thin as a closure* (Belarusian), *as thin as a ladder* (Kirghiz), *as thin as a mosquito's skeleton* (Japanese). These observations show a similarity in the norms and stereotypes of a number of people. For instance, the expression "angry like a dog" exists in Russian, Belarusian and Kyrgyz. However, it does not exist in England, where dogs are valued, and does not exist in Vietnam, where dogs are a symbol of filth.

Many of these comparisons are supported in language parallel to relevant metaphors: *a mitten* is used to characterize *the mouth*; *a booth or a signboard* characterizes *a face*, *a pot* characterizes *a head*. Native Russian speakers look at the world and perceive it through these stereotypes and standards.

These and other observations allow us to understand how culture penetrates and attaches itself onto language. Firstly, through encyclopedic knowledge about the individual attributes and physical appearance of a person; secondly, through national-cultural connotations and creative content; thirdly, through symbols, stereotypes and standards, stored in the language and consciousness of each national linguistic personality.

Even a simple quantitative analysis of the stereotypes in the experiment shows that compared to Russians, the linguistic consciousness of Belarusians has much fewer stereotyped expressions. It seems that this fact can be explained as follows: the more ancient the culture, the more stereotyped it is. Indirect confirmation of this is found in the works of Russian psycholinguists who researched the linguistic consciousness of Russians in comparison to the linguistic consciousness of Americans, French, Germans and the British. It was found that the Russian linguistic consciousness was the least stereotyped of all (Ufimtseva, 1995, p. 151). Belarusian culture, being younger and weaker than the Russian one, is even less stereotyped. The well know story about Alexander Pushkin supports this thesis. Pushkin was seen talking to a lady. Afterwards, he was asked if she was intelligent. Pushkin said: "How would I know, she spoke French." This joke reveals Pushkin as a prophet. He anticipated the latest advances in cultural studies. Because French culture is more ancient, it has more stereotypes, clichés and standards, which hide the identity of the speaker (the lady, in this case). Thus, stereotypes facilitate social contact.

We found that the amount of comparisons made to a particular stimulus word was directly dependent on the number of associations to that word. The greater the associative potential of a word, the greater the variety of comparisons. At first glance it would seem that you can compare anything to anything, as long as there is at least one common feature (similarity, proximity, association). But, there are limitations. For instance, the experiment revealed no examples where abstract entities were used to describe a person's appearance or physical features. Eugene Zamyatin wrote: "If in describing the head of a fisherman one compares it to, let's say, a globe or the head of a hippo, it would be a mistake. The image itself may be good, just not on a fisherman. This image interferes with the reader's sense of the environment depicted."

It seems that the subjects always have a choice in making comparisons. For example, a thin person can be compared to a Caspian roach, a pole, a stick, a board, a skeleton, Koshchei, etc. But different images appear in the minds of the recipients. Koschei is also an old man; a board is a flat-chested woman; a pole can certainly be tall man standing straight, etc. Such comparisons are genetically shaped since they are motivated by an emerging image (a picture). But there were also bad comparisons among the responses provided by the test subjects: deceitful as a grey gelding, good as a pickle. The basis for the comparison is unclear in these cases, so the comparisons have somehow lost their relevance.

Most likely, the choice of comparison is supported by the framework of the surrounding world, culture, communicative situations and specific characteristics of the communicants.

A person's social experience leaves a distinct mark on language. Even when describing the same objects, the test subjects compared them to different realities, ones closely related to the living conditions of the native speakers of a particular language, to their culture, customs and traditions. These comparisons embody the national mentality and spiritual culture of the Russian and Belarusian nation. Accordingly, our experimental data is the source of linguistic and psychological information.

Questions and tasks
1. What is the role of comparison in language and though?
2. Why are fixed comparisons important to Linguistic-culturology?
3. What differences in how Russians and Belarusians perceive the word "eyes" are noted in the experiment.

Conclusion

This book is dedicated to the development of a new branch of knowledge – linguistic-culturology, which arose at the intersection of linguistic and cultural studies. Linguistic-culturology explores cultural manifestations reflected and fixed in language.

Questions about the relationship between language and culture are interdisciplinary. Therefore, answers are possible only through the application of several sciences - from philosophy and sociology to ethnolinguistic and linguistic-culturology. Linguistic-culturology itself is an interdisciplinary science.

This six-part textbook tries to establish theoretical foundations and principles for the analysis of language through linguistic-culturology. The work shows that culture shapes and organizes linguistic personality, forming language categories and concepts that help us understand the fundamental function of language: an instrument of creation, development, storage and transmission of culture.

Sections 4 and 5 examine specific language data from the perspective of linguistic-culturology, allowing allows students to see language afresh, explaining aspects such as dialects, idiolects and other linguistic phenomena.

The need for this kind of work is long overdue. University students must become familiar with contemporary concepts of linguistics; they must learn to analyze language not only from the perspective of system-structural linguistics, but through the culture the native speaker of another language. This special course has already been approved for students: in 1999 a special course was held at Vitebsk State University, at Tauride State University (Crimea) in 2000, and the course will be held at the University of Gdansk (Poland) in 2001.

It is hoped that the textbook, "Linguistic-culturology" will better prepare humanities students.

Bibliography

Abaev Vasily, *Language and Thought.* — Moscow, 1948 (Published in Russian).

Averinzev Sergei Sergeyevich, *Attempts to Explain: Conversations about Culture.* Moscow, 1988 (Published in Russian).

Averinzev Sergei Sergeyevich *Symbols // A Literary Encyclopedic Dictionary.* Moscow, 1987 (Published in Russian).

Avoyan, Roland Grigorevich, *Meaning in Language // A Philosophical Analysis.* — Moscow, 1985 (Published in Russian).

Agapkina, Tatyana Alexeena. *South Slavic Faith and Rituals Associated with Fruit Trees, A General Slavic Perspective // Slavic and Balkan Folklore.* Moscow, 1994 (Published in Russian).

Aksenchuk G. J. *The Human Soul in Russian Phraseology //* Belarusian State University Journal. Series 4 - 1996. - № 1 (Published in Russian).

Antipov Georgi, Donskikh Oleg, Markovina Irina, Sorokin Yuri. *Text as a Cultural Event.* Novosibirsk, 1989 (Published in Russian).

Apresyan Yuri. *An Integral Description of Language and Dictionary // Linguistic Issues.* 1986 № 2 (Published in Russian).

Apresyan Yuri. *The Image of Man Through Language: A Systematic Approach. Linguistic Issues.* 1995 № 1 (Published in Russian).

Arzakanyan, Armon Georgievich. Culture and Civilization: Problems of Theory and History // Journal of World History and Culture. 1961. — № 3 (Published in Russian).

Aristotle. *Poetry.* Leningrad, 1927 (Published in Russian).

Arnoldov Arnold Isaevich. *An Introduction to Cultural Studies.* Moscow, 1994 (Published in Russian).

Arutyunov Sergei, Bagdasarov, Artur, and others. *Language — Culture — Ethnos.* Moscow, 1994 (Published in Russian).

Arutynova Nina. Image; (Experience of Conceptual Analysis) // References and Problems of Text Formation. Moscow, 1988 (Published in Russian).

Arutynova Nina. *Types of Linguistic Meaning. Evaluation. Events. Facts*. Moscow, 1988 (Published in Russian).

Arutynova Nina. *Metaphors and Discussion // Theory and Metaphors*. Moscow, 1990 (Published in Russian).

Arutynova Nina. *Language and the World of Man*. Moscow, 1998 (Published in Russian).

Afanasyev Alexander. *The Origins of Myth*. Moscow, 1996 (Published in Russian).

Babushkin Anatoly. *Concept Types in Lexical-Phraseological Semantics of Language*. Voronezh, 1996 (Published in Russian).

Bakusheva Elena. *Sociolinguistics and the Analysis of Speech Conduct of Men and Women in Modern Society*. Ryazan, 1992 (Published in Russian).

Baiburin Albert. *Ritual in Traditional Culture*. Saint Petersburg, 1993 (Published in Russian).

Bally Charles. *French Stylistics*. Moscow, 1961 (Published in Russian).

Alexei Baranov, Karaulov Yuri. *Russian Political Metaphors (A Dictionary Supplement)* Moscow, 1991 (Published in Russian).

Barthes Roland. *Myth Today // Collected Works. Semiotics. Poetics*. Moscow, 1989 (Published in Russian).

Bartmiński Jerzy. *Ethnocentric Stereotypes: Investigation Results of German (Bochum) and Polish (Warsaw) Students in 1993—1994 // Speech and Mental Stereotypes in Synchrony and Diachrony. Conference Abstract*. Moscow, 1995 (Published in Russian).

Bakhtin Mikhail. *Aesthetics of Verbal Creativity*. Moscow, 1979 (Published in Russian).

Bely Andrei. *At the Crossroad. Culture in Crisis*. Moscow, 1910 (Published in Russian).

Belyanin Victor, Butenko Irina. *Explanatory Dictionary of Modern Colloquial Phraseology and Terms*. Moscow, 1993 (Published in Russian).

Benveniste Émile. General Linguistics. Moscow, 1974 (Published in Russian).

Benveniste Émile. *Dictionary of Indo-European Social Terms.* Moscow, 1995 (Published in Russian).

Nikolai Berdyaev. Sources and Meanings of Russian Communism. Moscow, 1990 (Published in Russian).

Bizheva Zara. *Cultural Concepts of the Kabardian Language.* Nalchik, 1997 (Published in Russian).

Bogin Georgi. *A Model of Linguistic Personality in Text.* L., 1984 (Published in Russian).

Boguslavsky Mikhail. *Dictionary of Human Appearance.* Moscow, 1994 (Published in Russian).

Baudouin de Courtenay Jan. *Selected Works.* Moscow, 1963 (Published in Russian).

Bromley Yulian. *Ethnos and Ethnography.* Moscow, 1973 (Published in Russian).

Bryusov Valery. Far and Near. Female-Poets. Moscow, 1912.

Buber Martin *The Problem of Man.* Kiev, 1998.

Buslaev Fedor. *Russian Proverbs and Saying Collected and Explained.* Moscow, 1954.

Buslaev Fedor. *Historical Sketches of Russian Folk Literature and Art.* Moscow, 1961. Vol. 1.

Waldenfels Bernhard. *My Culture and the Other Culture. A Paradox of Science "The Other"* // Logos. 1994. — № 6.

Introduction to Ethnic Psychology. SPb., 1995

Weber Max. *Selected Works.* Moscow, 1990.

Wierzbicka Anna. *Language. Culture. Cognition.* Moscow, 1996.

Wierzbicka Anna. *Universal Semantics and Linguistic Descriptions.* Moscow, 1999.

Weisgerber Leo. *Native Language and the Formation of the Soul.* Moscow, 1993.

Weisgerber Leo. *Language and Philosophy* // Linguistic Issues. 1993. — №2.

Vereshchagin Evgeny, Kostomarov Vitally. *A Linguistic-Area Study of Word Theory.* Moscow, 1980.

Vernadsky Vladimir. *Human Autotrophy* // Russian Cosmis. Moscow, 1993.

Vernadsky Vladimir. *The Philosophical Thoughts of a Naturalist*. Moscow, 1988.

Vinogradov Viktor. *The Language of Pushkin*. Mo scow; Leningrad., 1935.

Vinogradov Viktor. History of the Word "Personality" in the Russian Language of the Mid-19th Century //From the Documents and Reports of the Philology Department, Volume 1. Moscow, 1946.

Vinogradov Viktor. *On the Relationship between the Lexical-Semantic and Grammar in the Structure of Language // Thoughts About the Modern Russian Language*. Moscow, 1969.

Vinogradov Viktor. *From the History of the Word*. Moscow, 1994.

Vinokur Grigori. Selected Works on the Russian Language. Moscow, 1959.

Voloshinov Valentin. *Marxism and the Philosophy of Language*. Moscow, 1929.

Wolf Elena. *Functional Semantics of Value*. Moscow, 1985.

Vorobyov Vladimir. *Culturological Paradigm of the Russian Language*. Moscow, 1994.

Vorobyov Vladimir. *Linguistic-culturology*. Moscow, 1997.

Vygotsky Lev. *Thought and Speech // Collected Works*: Volume 6. Moscow, 1982. — T. 2.

Vysochina E. *Metamorphosis of Mythologization (survey) // Culture in the Modern World: Experience, Problems, Solutions*. Issue 2. — Moscow, 1990.

Vysheslavtsev Boris. The Heart in Christian and Indian Mysticism // Questions on Philosophy. 1990. № 4.

Hans-Georg Gadamer *The Relevance of the Beautiful*. Moscow, 1991.

Gak Vladimir. *Comparative Lexicology*. Moscow, 1977.

Gamkrelidze Tamaz., Ivanov Vyacheslav. *The Indo-European language and the Indo-Europeans*. - Tbilisi, 1984. — Vol. 1-2.

Golovanivskaya Maria. *The French Mentality From the Perspective of a Russian Native Speaker*. Moscow, 1997.

Gol'din Valentin, Sirotinina Olga. *Speech Culture // Russian Language. Encyclopedia*. Moscow, 1997.

Wilhelm von Humboldt. *On the Diversity of Human Language Construction and its Influence on the Mental Development of the Human Species* // Selected Works on Linguistics. Moscow, 1984.

Wilhelm von Humboldt. Language and the Philosophy of Culture. Moscow, 1985.

Gurevich Aron. *Categories of Medieval Culture.* — Moscow, 1984.

Gurevich Aron. *Man and Culture: Individuality in the History of Culture*. Moscow, 1990.

Gurevich Paul. *Philosophy of Culture*. Moscow, 1994.

Gulumian, Kira. *Folk Elements in the Phraseology of Modern Slavic Languages.* Minsk, *1978.*

Dobrovolsky Dimitry. *On National-Cultural Specificity in Phraseology* // Linguistic Issues. 1997. — № 6.

Dridze Tamara. Language and Social Psychology. Moscow, 1980.

Yemelyanov Yuri. *Introduction to Cultural Studies. SPb.,* 1992.

Yerasov Boris. *Social Cultural Studies. M., 1994. - Part 1, 2. Woman, Gender, Culture. - Moscow, 1999.*

Zhinkin Nicolai. *Speech as the Conduit of Information.*

Zhinkin Nicolai. *Language. Speech. Creativity.* Moscow, 1998.

Zavalova Natalia, Lomov Boris, Ponomarenko Vladimir. *The Role of Image in Regulating Mental Activity.* Moscow, 1986.

Zamyatin Yevgeny. *Technique of Literary Fiction* // *Literary Studies. 1988. - No.*1.

Zelenin Dimitry. *East Slavic Ethnography. Moscow, 1991.*

Zelenin Dimitry. *Selected Works: Essays on Spiritual Culture. Moscow, 1994.*

Zolotova Galina, Onipenko Nadejda, Sidorova Marina. *Communicative Grammar of the Russian Language.* Moscow, 1999.

Kagan Mosey. Philosophy of Culture. SPb. 1996.

Canons, Standards and Stereotypes In Linguistic Consciousness and Discourse: Scientific Discussion at the Institute of Linguistics RAS // Language, Consciousness, Communication. Vol. 9. Moscow, 1999.

Kant Immanuel. *Works*. Moscow, 1966. Vol. 6.

Yuri Karaulov. *Russian Language and Linguistic Personality*. Moscow, 1987.

Karamin Anatoly. *The Basics of Cultural Studies. Morphology of Culture*. Moscow, 1997.

Kasatkin Leonid. *Russian Dialects and Linguistic Politics // Russian Speech. 1993. - No. 4.*

Kasevich Vadim. *Buddhism. A World Picture. Language. SPb. 1996.*

Kasevich Vadim. *Culturally Conditioned Differences in Language and Discourse Structures // XVI Congries international des Linguistes. - Paris, 1997.*

Kartsevskiy Sergey. *Comparisons // Readings in General Linguistics. Minsk, 1976.*

Kirilina Alla. *Gender: Linguistic Aspects. Moscow, 1999.*

Klizovskiy Alexandra. *Man and Woman. Minsk, 1996.*

Klobukova Lyubov. *The Phenomenon of Linguistic Personality in Light of Linguo-didactics // International Jubilee Conference Dedicated to the 100th Anniversary of Academician V. Vinogradov. Moscow, 1995.*

Kolominsky Yakov. *Social Standards as Stabilizing Factors, "Social Psyche" // Questions of Psychology. 1972. — No. 1. Canon V. People in the Coordinates of Culture / / Neman. - 1995. — No. 2.*

Kopylenko Mosey. *Fundamentals of Ethnolinguistics.* Almaty, 1995.

Kotenka Roman. *Question about Man in the Philosophy of Martin Buber // Man. 1997. — No. 4.*

Krysin Leonid. *Study of Modern Russian from a Social Perspective // Russian Language in School. 1991. —* No. 5.

Kubryakova Elena, Aleksandrova Olga. On the Contours of a New Paradigm of Knowledge in Linguistics // Structure and Semantics of Literary Text. Reports of the VII International Conference. Moscow, 1999.

Culture, Man and the Picture of the World. Moscow, 1987.

Culture and History. The Slavic world. Moscow, 1997.

Cirlot Juan. *A Dictionary of Symbols.* Moscow, 1994.

Lebedeva Ludmila. *Persistent Comparisons Found in Russian Language Phraseology and Phraseographs.* Krasnodar, 1999.

Levas Ilya. Culture and Language. Minsk, 1998.

Levi-Bruhl Lucien. *Primitive thinking.* Moscow, 1994.

Lem Stanisław, *A Model of Culture // Questions of Philosophy. 1969. — No. 8.*

Leontiev Alexey. *People and Culture. Moscow, 1961.*

Leontiev Alexey. *Thinking // Questions of Philosophy in 1964. — No. 4.*

Leontiev Alexey. *The Psychology of the Image // Moscow State University Journal. Series 14. Psychology. 1979. - No. 2.*

Leontiev Alexey. *Psychology of Communication. Tartu, 1976.*

Leontiev Alexey. *General Information About Associations and Associative Rules // Dictionary of Associative Norms of the Russian Language. - M., 1979.*

Likhachev Dimitry. *Poetics of old Russian literature // Selected works. works: in 3 t. - L., 1987.-Vol.1.*

Likhachev Dimitry. *Past-Future. Moscow, 1985.*

Likhachev Dimitry. *Culture as a Holistic Dynamic System // Journal of the Russian Academy of Science – 1994. - No. 8.*

Likhachev Dimitry. *Conceptosphere of the Russian language / / Russian literature: anthology //* edited by Neroznak Vladimir. Moscow, 1997.

Logical analysis of Language: Language and Time. Moscow, 1997.

Logical analysis of language: The Image of Man in Culture and Language. Moscow, 1999.

Lorenz Konra. *Aggression (The so-called evil). Moscow, 1994.*

Losev Aleksei. *Sign. Symbol. Myth. Works on Linguistics. Moscow, 1982.*

Losev Aleksei. *Symbol // Philosophical Encyclopedia. Moscow, 1970.*

Losev Aleksei. *Philosophy of Name. Moscow, 1990.*

Lotman Yuri. *Inside Worlds of Thought// Symbol in the Culture System. Moscow, 1996.*

Lotman Yuri. *On Two Communication Models in the System of Culture // Semiotics.* Tartu, 1971. — No. 6.

Lotman Yuri. *Some Thoughts on the Typology of Cultures // Languages of Culture and Translation Problems. Moscow, 1987.*

Lotman Yuri. *Conversations On Russian Culture: The Life and Traditions of Russian Nobility.* — SPb., 1994.

Luria Alexander. *On the Historical Development of Cognitive Processes.* Moscow, 1974.

Luria Alexander. *Language and Consciousness.* Moscow, 1979.

Lyutikova Galina. *Computer Civilization-Technotronic Dream in Reality // Culture in the Modern World.* - Moscow, 1995.

Lyutikova Vera. *Linguistic Personality and Idiolect.* Tyumen, 1999.

Makovsky Mark. *The Amazing World of Words and Meanings.* Moscow, 1989.

Makovsky Mark. *At the Origins of Human Language.* Moscow, 1995.

Makovsky Mark. *Comparative Dictionary of Mythological Symbols in Indo-European Languages: The Image of the World and The world of Images.* Moscow, 1996.

Malishevskaya D. *Basic Concepts in Light of Gender (Based on the Oppositions of "Man/Woman") // Phraseology in the Context of Culture.* Moscow, 1999.

Mamardashvili Merab. *The Devil Plays Us When We Don't Imagine Accurately... // Theatre.* 1989. - No. 3.

Mamardashvili Merab. *Science and culture // Methodological Problems of Historical and Scientific research.* Moscow, 1992.

Mandelstam Ossip. *Word and Culture.* - M., 1987.

Markaryan Eduard. *Essays on the Theory of Culture.* - Yerevan, 1969.

Markaryan Eduard. *Theory of Culture and Modern Science (A logical and methodological analysis).* Moscow, 1983.

Markov Boris. *Mind and Heart: History and Theory of Mentality.* SPb. 1993.

Markovina Irina, Sorokin Yuri. *The National-Specific of Intercultural Communications //* Antipov Georgi. et al. Text as a Cultural Phenomenon. Novosibirsk, 1989.

Maslova Valentina. *An Experimental Study of the National-Cultural Specificity of a Person's External and Internal Qualities (Based on data from the Kyrgyz language).* Ethno-psycholinguistics. Moscow, 1988.

Maslova Valentina. *Introduction to Linguistic-culturology.* Moscow, 1997.

Maslova Valentina. *The Connections Between Myth and Language // Phraseology in the Context of Culture. Moscow,* 1999.

Maslow Abraham. *Psychology of Being.* Moscow, 1997.

Mathieu Militsa. Myths of Ancient Egypt. — Moscow; Leningrad, 1956.

Metaphor in language and text. Moscow, 1988.

Mechkovskaya Nina. *Social linguistics.* Moscow , 1996.

Miller Orest. *Historical Review of Russian Literature.* SPb., 1866.-4.1.

Milyukov Pavel. Essays on the History of Russian Culture: in 3 vol., 1993. - T. 1.

Mirolyubiv Yuri. *Russian Pagan Folklore.* Moscow, 1995.

Mikhailova Tatyana. *On the Concept of "Right" and Linguistic Evolution. // Linguistic Issues.* 1993. — No. 1.

Mokienko Valerie. *Images of Russian Speech.* Leningrad, 1986.

Murzin Leonid. *On Linguistics, Contents and Methods //* COLLEGIUM. - 1997. - No. 1.

Mylnikov Alexander. *The Slavic Picture of the World: The View From Eastern Europe.* - SPb. 1996.

Nalimov Vasily. *In Search of Other Meanings.* Moscow, 1993.

Nekrasova Ekaterina. *The Unrealized Plan of 1920's to Create a Symbolarium (Dictionary of symbols) and the First Issue of "Tochka" // Monuments of Culture. New Discovery.* Leningrad, 1984.

Nikitina Serafima. *Oral Folk Culture and Linguistic Consciousness.* Moscow, 1993.

New in Foreign Linguistics. Vol. XVI. Moscow, 1985.

Ovchinnikov Vsevolod. *The Sakura Branch.* Moscow, 1971.

Olshansky G. *Linguistic-Culturology: Methodological Foundations and Basic Concepts // Language and Culture.* Vol. 2. - M., 1999.

Oparina Elena. *Lexicon, Phraseology, Text: Linguistic-Culturological Components // Language and Culture.* Vol. 2. Moscow, 1999.

Essays on the History of the Language of Russian Poetry of the XX century. Moscow, 1994.

On the Human in Man. Moscow, 1991.

Pavlov Ivan. *Selected works.* Moscow, 1949.

Parakhonsky Boris. *The Language of Culture and the Genesis of Knowledge: (Value-Communicative aspect).* Kiev, 1989.

Petrenko Olga. *Ethnic Mentality and the Language of Folklore.* Kursk, 1996.

Peshkovsky Alexander. *Objective and Normative Perspectives on Language // History of Linguistics in the XIX and XX Centuries Through Essays and Extracts, edited by Vladimir Zvegintsev.* Moscow, 1960. - Part 2.

Pimenova Marina. *Mentality: The Linguistic Aspect.* Kemerovo, 1996.

Piskoppel Anatoly. *The Category of the Individual From the Perspective of European Cultural Traditions // Questions of Methodology.* 1997. — No. 1, 2.

Padyukov Ivan. *Folk Phraseology in the Mirror of Popular Culture: A Textbook.* Perm, 1991.

Shapovalov Irina. *Language as Activity: An Effort to Interpret the Concepts of W. Humboldt.* Moscow, 1982.

Potebnja Alexander. *Aesthetics and Poetics.* Moscow, 1976.

Potebnja Alexander. *Theoretical Poetics.* - M., 1990.

Potebnja Alexander. *Lectures on the Theory of Literature. Lecture Eight // Russian Literature: Anthology.* Moscow, 1997.

Potebnja Alexander. *Symbol and Myth in Popular Culture.* Moscow, 2000.

Propp Vladimir. *Morphology of the Fairy Tale. Leningrad,* 1928.

Propp Vladimir. *Historical Roots of the Fairy Tale.* Moscow, 1946.

Propp Vladimir.. *Folklore and Reality.* Moscow, 1976.

Propp Vladimir. *The Russian Heroic Epic.* Moscow, 1958.

Prokhorov Yuri. *National Socio-Cultural Stereotypes of Speech Communication and their Role in Teaching Russian to Foreigners.* Moscow, 1996.

Radina Nadejda. *The Use of Gender Analysis in Psychological Studies // Questions of Psychology*. 1999. — No. 2.

Radchenko Oleg. *Language as a Worldview: Linguo-philosophical Concept of Neo-humanism*. Moscow, 1997. Voume. 1,2.

Speech and Mental Stereotypes in Synchrony and Diachrony: Conference Abstracts. Moscow, 1995.

The Human Factor in Language: Language and Thought. Moscow. 1989.

Rudenko Dimitry. *Linguo-philosophical Paradigm: The Limits of Language and the Boundaries of Vulture // Philosophy of Language: Within Borders and Beyond Borders*. Kharkov, 1993.

Russian Associative Dictionary. Books 1, 2. Moscow, 1994; Books 3, 4. Moscow, 1996.

Russian Cosmism. Moscow, 1993.

Savel'ev Victor. *Essays on Applied Cultural Studies: Genesis, Concept, Contemporary Practice*. Moscow, 1983. - Part 1.

Sagatovsky Valery. *The Russian Idea: Continuing Along the Same Path?* SPb., 1994.

Savitsky Boris. *The Origin and Development of Russian Proverbs*. Moscow, 1992.

Sakulin Pavel. *Philology and Cultural Studies*. Moscow, 1990.

Svasyan Karen. *The Problem of Symbols in Contemporary Philosophy*. Yerevan, 1980.

Semantics and Pragmatics in Cultural Dialogues. Samara, 1998.

Senderoff Savelie. *Revision of the Jungian Theory of Archetype // Logos*. 1994. — No. 6.

Sapir Edward. *Selected works on Linguistics and Cultural Studies*. Moscow, 1993.

Serebrennikov Boris. About materialistic approach to the phenomena of language. - M., 1983.

Sériot, Patrick. *In Search of the Fourth Paradigm // The Philosophy of Language Within our Borders and Outside*. Vol. 1. - Kharkov, 1993.

Sechenov Ivan. *For Whom and How to Develop Psychology: Psychological Studies*. — SPb., 1873.

Sirotinina Olga. *Speech Portrait of a Dog: Illusion or Reality* // *Questions of Stylistics*. Vol. 28. - Saratov, 1999.

Slavic and Balkan Folklore. Moscow, 1986.

Dictionary of Figurative Expressions of the Russian Language / edited by Veronica Teliya. Moscow, 1995.

Sokolov Eduard. *Concepts, Essence and Primary Functions of Culture*. Moscow, 1989.

Sokolov Eduard. *Cultural Studies*. - M., 1994.

Sologub Yuri. *National Specificity and Universal Properties of Phraseologies as a Subject of Linguistic Study* // *Philology. Scientific Documents of the Higher School*. 1990. - No. 6.

Sorokin Yuri. *The Speech Markers of Ethnic and Institutional Portraits and Self-Portraits* // Linguistic Issues. 1995. — No. 6.

Sorokin Yuri. *Stereotypes, Categories, Clichés: The Problem of Defining Concepts* // *Communication: Theoretical and Pragmatic Issues*. Moscow, 1978.

Sorokin Yuri, Markovina Irina. *The National-Cultural Specificity of Literary Text*. Moscow, 1989.

Sorokin Yuri. *Introduction to Ethno-psycholinguistics*. Ulyanovsk, 1998.

Saussure Ferdinand de. *Course of General Linguistics* // Linguistics. Moscow, 1977.

Stepanov Yuri. *Within the Three-Dimensional Space of Language: Semiotic Problems of Linguistics, Philosophy and Art*. Moscow, 1985.

Stepanov Yuri. *Constants: Dictionary of Russian Culture*. Moscow, 1997.

Sukolenko, Nonna. *Reflection of Everyday Consciousness in Figurative Language Picture of the World*. Kiev, 1992.

Sumtsov Niloai. *Symbolism of Slavic Rites*. Moscow, 1996.

Suprun Adam. Lectures on the Theory of Speech Activity. - Minsk, 1996.

Tylor, Edward. *Primitive Culture*. - Moscow, 1989.

Tarlanov Zamir. *Ethnic Language and Vision of the World* // *Language and Ethnic Mentality*. Petrozavodsk, 1995.

Teliya Veronica. *On the Methodological Foundations of Cultural Linguistics* // *XI International Conference "Logic,*

Methodology and Philosophy of science". Moscow; Obninsk, 1995.

Teliya Veronica. *Russian Phraseology*. - Moscow, 1996.

Toynbee Arnold. *Comprehension of History*. Moscow, 1996.

Tolstoy Nikita. *Relations of Binary Oppositions Such as Right—Left, Male—Female // Language of Culture and the Problem of Translation*. Moscow , 1987.

Tolstoy Nikita. *Language and Folk Culture: Essays on Slavic Mythology and Ethnolinguistics*. Moscow, 1995.

Tolstoy Nikita. and Tolstaya Svetlana. *On the Problems of Ethnolinguistic Study of Polesia // Polesian Ethnolinguistic Collection*. Moscow, 1983.

Toporov Vladimri. *A Study of Baltic-Slavic Spiritual Culture*. Moscow, 1994.

Toporov Vladimri. *Myth. Ritual. Symbol. Image: Research in the field of Mythology*. Moscow, 1995.

Toporov Vladimri. *On the Archetype of "water" in Ancient Greek Cosmogony // Linguistic Issues*. 1996. — No. 6.

Toffler Alvin. *Race, Power and Culture // New Technocratic Wave in the West*. Moscow, 1986.

Trubachev Oleg. *History of Slavic Terms of Kinship*. Moscow, 1959.

Trener Victor. *Symbol and Ritual*. Moscow, 1983.

Tulviste Peeter. *Cultural and Historical Development of Verbal Thinking*. Tallinn, 1988.

Ufimtseva Natalia. *Structure of Linguistic Consciousness of Russians: 70s-90s // Ethnic and Linguistic Self-Consciousness: Conference Proceedings*. Moscow, 1995.

Fedorov Alexander. *Siberian Dialect Phraseology*. Novosibirsk, 1980.

Feuerbach Ludwig. *The Main Provisions of Future Philosophy // Selected Philosophical Works*. Moscow, 1955. - P. 203.

Florensky Pavel. *The Pillar and Ground of Truth*. Moscow, 1914.

Formanovskaya Natalia. Speech Etiquette and Culture of Communication. Moscow, 1989.

Frank Semyon, Struve Peter. *Features of Philosophical Culture. Culture and Individuality // Culture in the Modern*

World: Experience, Problems, Solutions. Informational Compilation. Issue 1. — Moscow, 1990.

Freud Sigmund. *Totem and Taboo.* Moscow, 1992.

Freidenberg Olga. *The Origin of the Epic Comparison (Based on Material From the Iliad) // Proceedings of the Jubilee Scientific Session. 1819-1944.* Leningrad, 1946. Pages 111-113.

Fromm Erich. *The Heart of Man.* Moscow, 1992.

Fromm Erich. *Escape From Freedom.* Moscow, 1990.

Frumkina Rebecca. *"Middle-Level Theories" In Modern Linguistics //* Linguistic Issues. 1996. — No. 2.

Frumkina Rebecca. *Does Modern Linguistics Have Its Own Epistemology? //* Linguistic Issues. *1995. — No. 2.*

Frumkina Rebecca. *Linguistics In Search of Epistemology // Linguistics at the end of the XX Century: Results and Prospects: Theses of The International Conference.* Moscow, 1995. - Volume 11.

Frumkina Rebecca. *Cultural Semantics From the Perspective of Epistemology // Bulletin of the Academy of Sciences. Series: Literature and Language. Volume 58. - 1999. — No. 1.*

Fraser John. *Golden Bough.* Moscow, 1983.

Fraser John. *Folklore in the Old Testament. - Moscow, 1993.*

Foucault Michel. *Words and Things. The archeology of the Humanities. — SPb., 1994.*

Huntington Samuel. *Clash of Civilizations? // Polis. 1994. — No. 1.*

Huizinga Johan, *Homo Ludens. In the Shadow of Tomorrow.* Moscow, 1992.

Khrolenko Alexander. *Poetic Phraseology of the Russian Lyric Folk Song.* Voronezh, 1981.

Tsivyan Tatiana. *Linguistic bases of the Balkan model of the world.* Moscow, 1990.

Tsivyan Tatiana. *Movement and path in the Balkan model of the world. –* Moscow 1999.

Chavchavadze Nicholai. *3 Culture and values.* Tbilisi, 1984.

Cherdantseva T. Z. *Idiomatics and Culture (problem statement) //* Linguistic Issues. 1996. — No. 1.

Cheshko Sergey. Man and Ethnicity // Ethnographic Review. — 1994. - № 6.

Chikalova Irina. *Belarusian* Women between the "social" and the "personal" in the years of Soviet power. // A Different View. 2000. — May.

Chmykho, Nikolai. *Sources of Russian Paganism.* — Киев, 1990.

Shelestyuk Elena. *On the linguistic study of symbols* // Linguistic Issues. 1997. — № 4.

Spengler Oswald. *The Decline of the West.* — Moscow, 1993.

Shpet Gustav. Works. — Moscow,1989.

Shcherba Lev. *Linguistic Systems and Speech activity.* — Moscow, 1974.

Epstein Mikhail. *Nature, the World and the Hiding Place of the Universe.* — Moscow, 1990.

Ethnic and Linguistic Identity: Conference Material. — Moscow, 1995.

Ethnography of Eastern Slavs: The Features of Traditional Culture. — Moscow, 1987.

Ethnolinguistic Dictionary of Slavic Antiquity. — Moscow,1984.

Jung Carl. *Psychology of the Unconscious.* — Moscow, 1996,

Jung Carl. *Archetype and the Collective Unconscious.* — Moscow, 1991.

Ekaterina Yakovleva. *On understanding cultural memory as applied to the semantics of words.* // Linguistic Issues. — 1998. — № 3.

Bartmiński Jerzy Stereotyp jako przedmiot lingwistyki // Z problemow frazeologii polskiej i slowianskiej. Warsaw, 1985.

Bruckner Aleksander. Mitologia slowianska i polska. — Warsawa, 1980.

Kassirer Ernst. *The Philosophy of Symbolic Forms, Vol 2: Mythical Thought.* - New-Haven; London, 1970.

Kassirer Ernst. *Philosophie der symbolischen Formen.* — Berlin, 1923.

Kroeber A L. and Kluckhohn Clyde. *The Concept of culture.* Papers of the Peabody. — Museum, 1950.

Frye Northrop. *Symbol* // Encyclopedia of poetry and poetics. — Princeton, 1965.

Heiman John. Natural Syntax: Iconicity and Erosion. — Cambridge., 1985.

Lakoff George, Johnson Mark. *Metaphors We Live By.* —
Chicago, 1980.
Lerman Claire Lindegren *1991. "On metaphoric
communication as the original protolanguage"* // Studies in
language origins. V. 2. — Amsterdam; Philadelphia, 1991.
Lippmann Walter. *Public Opinion.* — NY, 1992.
Malinowski Bronislaw. *Myth in Primitive Psychology.* —
London, 1926.
Smuts Barbara. "The Evolutionary Origins of Patriarchy" //
Human Nature. — 1995.
Tannen Deborah. *That's Not I meant! How Conversational
Style Makes or Breaks Relationships.* Ballantine Books. —
NY, 1994.

Made in the USA
Monee, IL
29 January 2020